lonely planet

Singapore

Ria de Jong, Morgan Awyong, Jaclynn Seah

ANA FLASKER/SHUTTERSTOCK

Chinatown (p68)

CONTENTS

Plan Your Trip

The Guide

SPARTANPHOTO/SHUTTERSTOCK

Flamingo, Bird Paradise (p157), Mandai Wildlife Reserve

Toolkit

Storybook

MAISON PHOTOGRAPHY/SHUTTERSTOCK

Dragon dance performance, Buddha Tooth Relic Temple (p72), Chinatown

SINGAPORE

THE JOURNEY BEGINS HERE

The saying 'good things come in small packages' could have been coined to describe the tiny island nation of Singapore. Just two-thirds the size of New York City, the 'Little Red Dot' celebrated 60 years of independence in 2025, making now the perfect time to visit. This city is a realm of perpetual contrasts, hurtling into the future with out-of-this-world architecture, lightning-fast efficiency and an impeccable image. Yet just a stone's throw from the bustling thoroughfares lie buzzing village markets alive with chatter, pockets of lush jungle where hornbills swoop overhead, kaleidoscopic smoky temples and streets lined with pastel-hued heritage shophouses. One moment you're gazing up at a sky garden floating above the city; the next, you're wandering a quiet backstreet steeped in history. And then there's the food – from the creations of celebrity chefs to hawker delights, nothing can quite match the thrill of feasting your way across this island.

Ria de Jong

@ria_in_transit (Instagram)

Ria is a travel writer and has been based in Southeast Asia for 15 years, 10 of which have been spent in Singapore. This is her fifth Singapore update for Lonely Planet.

My favourite experience is a Singaporean breakfast set. I can't say no to one, even in the afternoon. I love the way the gooey eggs combine with the sweet *kaya* (coconut and egg jam), salty soy sauce and toasty grilled bread.

WHO GOES WHERE

Our writers choose the experiences that, for them, define Singapore.

STEPHEN DOREY/ALAMY

The revamped **Chinatown Heritage Centre** (pictured; p72) tugged at my heartstrings and is now one of my top visitor recommendations. With its realistic recreations of shophouse life, it was a vivid throwback to my childhood days at Boon Tat St. Trace the grit and hope that carried early Chinese immigrants through, and before you leave, be clued in to some nearby heritage businesses. Don't miss Amacha next door – it serve somes delicious bubble tea with a tonic twist.

Morgan Awyong

@morgaga (Instagram)

Morgan is a roving writer from Singapore who loves exploring places on foot.

WONG YU LIANG/SHUTTERSTOCK

I've found that the one thing most visitors to Singapore remember is the incredible hawker food they ate. I usually take visiting friends to a local-favourite hawker centre so they can indulge in a smorgasbord of dishes ranging from chilli crab to *char kway teow* (wok-fried rice noodles; pictured). **East Coast Lagoon Food Village** (p141), right by the sea, and Old Airport Road Food Centre in eastern Singapore, with its many famous hawker stalls, are my go-tos.

Jaclynn Seah

theoccasionaltraveller.com

Jaclynn is a Singaporean travel writer, tourist guide and occasional traveller perpetually juggling work and wanderlust.

HISTORICAL HAUNTS

The small but strategically located island of Singapore evolved over the centuries under the influence of various empires, from a fishing village and a centre for Malay, Thai, Javanese, Chinese, Indian and Arab traders, through to a British trading post, WWII Japanese occupation, a failed merger with Malaysia and gaining independence in 1965. Immerse yourself in this rich history by exploring heritage trails, museums, historic districts and preserved neighbourhoods that vividly tell the story of Singapore's evolution.

Free Tours

Many of Singapore's museums offer free guided tours in various languages. Check websites for details, and register early as most are first come, first served.

Trendy Gifting

Forget tacky T-shirts and garish magnets: Singapore's galleries and museums have elevated their souvenir game with design-focused curios that are gloriously local.

Onward, Singapore!

'Majulah Singapura' (Onward Singapore) is the national anthem. With lyrics in Bahasa Malay, the anthem was composed in 1958 by Indonesian-born Zubir Said.

FROM LEFT: JACK HONG/SHUTTERSTOCK, TUPUNGATO/SHUTTERSTOCK, PACCEKA/SHUTTERSTOCK

Indian Heritage Centre (p89), Little India

BEST HISTORY EXPERIENCES

Delve into Chinatown's gritty, chaotic and often scandalous past at the immersive ❶ **Chinatown Heritage Centre** (p72), where bygone tales come to life.

Learn about Singapore's rich and eventful history at the ❷ **National Museum of Singapore** (p61), the nation's oldest museum and an architectural landmark.

Travel through time at the evocative ❸ **Asian Civilisations Museum** (pictured far left; p52), an engrossing ode to Asia's cross-cultural connections.

Explore the vibrant world of Straits Chinese culture through historical artefacts and immersive displays at the ❹ **Peranakan Museum** (p67).

Immerse yourself in the state-of-the-art ❺ **Indian Heritage Centre** (p89), which spotlights the origins and heritage of Singapore's Indian community.

JUNGLE WALKS

Contrary to its urban reputation, Singapore proudly showcases a vast expanse of lush nature reserves and green spaces, offering myriad experiences for those seeking solace from the city's fast-paced lifestyle. Whether you prefer to explore jungle paths, coastal routes or reservoir trails, all are accessible to various fitness levels and beautifully maintained.

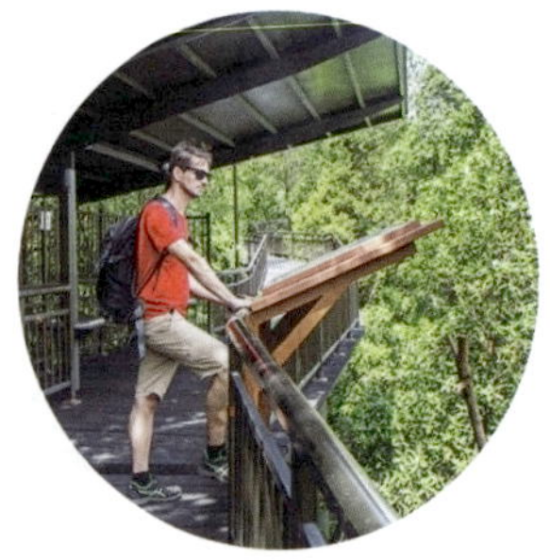

FROM LEFT: OLIVER FOERSTNER/SHUTTERSTOCK, MARTIN PELANEK/SHUTTERSTOCK, FLORIAN AUGUSTIN/SHUTTERSTOCK

Get Kitted Out

Dress in comfortable, breathable attire and wear a good pair of trainers or hiking boots. Apply sunscreen and mosquito repellent, and always carry water.

Wildlife

Maintain a safe distance from birds and animals, and never feed them – you'll face a fine of up to S$10,000 if you're caught.

Stay Safe

Always stay on the designated trails; in the event of bad weather, seek cover at the nearest shelter until the storm passes.

TreeTop Walk (p158), MacRitchie Reservoir

BEST HIKING EXPERIENCES

Tackle the 24km trans-island ❶ **Rail Corridor** (p148), which is divided into three sections – the central trail (4km) is the most popular.

Take your pick from the ❷ **Southern Ridges** (p176), where easy trails weave through forest canopies and across striking bridges.

Roam 200 hectares of coastal habitat at ❸ **Sungei Buloh Wetland Reserve** (p175), a paradise for birdwatchers.

Spot plenty of wildlife at ❹ **MacRitchie Reservoir** (p158) and don't miss TreeTop Walk, a 250m suspension bridge high above the forest canopy.

Explore the coastal boardwalks at ❺ **Chek Jawa Wetlands** (p194) on rustic island getaway Pulau Ubin.

SKYLINE VISTAS

Singapore has experienced astounding transformations, with gleaming skyscrapers and architectural masterpieces constantly reshaping its panorama. The iconic Marina Bay Sands is now accompanied by innovative landmarks such as the futuristic Gardens by the Bay and Esplanade – Theatres on the Bay. Embracing sustainability, Singapore has seamlessly integrated greenery into its urban landscape, adding a touch of nature to the city's modernity. As the city evolves, its ever-changing skyline remains a testament to its focus on the future.

FROM LEFT: 2P2PLAY/SHUTTERSTOCK, BLANSCAPE/SHUTTERSTOCK, SERGII FIGURNYI/SHUTTERSTOCK

Perfect Timing

Reach your viewing spot an hour before sunset to watch the city skyline transform from day to night. Sunset reservations at bars are a must.

Light Up the Night

To add some razzle-dazzle to your vista, head to the Event Plaza at Marina Bay to catch free nightly light-and-water show Spectra.

Spend Wisely

Bypass the Marina Bay Sands SkyPark and head to CÉ LA VI, where for a similar price you can enjoy a cocktail and an amazing view.

Supertree Grove (p46), Gardens by the Bay

BEST SKY-HIGH EXPERIENCES

Enjoy your craft-beer tasting paddle at ❶ **Level 33** (p50), the 'world's highest urban microbrewery', along with jaw-dropping Marina Bay views.

Break up your shopping spree and head up to ❷ **ION Sky** (p109), teetering 218m above Orchard Rd, for knockout views in all directions.

Embark on a 30-minute aerial adventure on the ❸ **Singapore Flyer** (p44) for stunning bird's-eye views of the city.

Take to the skies aboard the open-air ❹ **SkyHelix Sentosa** (p191), which rotates slowly 12 storeys above the ground.

Enjoy perfect panoramas from ❺ **CÉ LA VI** (p50), Marina Bay Sands' canti-levered rooftop bar.

HAWKER HAVENS

Hawker centres in Singapore have a history dating back to the 1800s, when street vendors sold quick, affordable meals to the masses. After WWII, many unemployed people turned to hawking, which saw the industry boom and in turn created hygiene, traffic and littering problems. In the 1970s, the government established purpose-built hawker centres to address these issues. Today, hawker centres are culinary hubs that are integral to Singapore's food culture, offering diverse and affordable dishes.

FROM LEFT: BOYCATALYST/SHUTTERSTOCK, KAPI NG/SHUTTERSTOCK, 2P2PLAY/SHUTTERSTOCK

Save Your Seat

Put a packet of tissues on the table in front of your seat to *chope* (save) it. It's common to share tables with strangers.

Choose Your Meal

Join the longest queue for guaranteed good nosh. Take note of your table number if the stall delivers; otherwise, wait in line for your food.

Clear Away

It's mandatory to return your tray and dishes to a cleaning station once you've finished – fines may apply if you don't.

Maxwell Food Centre (p72), Chinatown

BEST HAWKER-CUISINE EXPERIENCES

Head to ❶ **Chinatown Complex** (p72) for a hardcore hawker experience as you try to navigate its labyrinth of more than 260 stalls.

Witness Singapore's chicken-rice war at ❷ **Maxwell Food Centre** (p72). Who makes the best? Let your tastebuds decide!

Tuck into some of the island's best street eats at ❸ **Tekka Centre** (p92), Little India's liveliest hawker centre serving delectable Indian fare.

Sample some new-gen hawker delights, alongside plenty of classics, at lunchtime favourite ❹ **Amoy Street Food Centre** (p80).

Indulge in sunset satay and seafood at ❺ **East Coast Lagoon Food Village** (p141), a breezy beachfront hawker centre in East Coast Park.

Buddha Tooth Relic Temple (p72), Chinatown

SACRED SITES

When it comes to religious worship, Singapore is a wonderful fusion of cultures. The island celebrates a variety of faiths, with Buddhism (31%), Christianity (19%), Islam (16%), Taoism (9%) and Hinduism (5%) all commonly practised. This rich mixture of religions is beautifully represented through the exquisite holy structures found across the island.

Respectful Dress

Modest attire is expected in places of worship. You may also need to remove your shoes, and hats and sunglasses should not be worn inside.

Cameras Down

Refrain from taking photos without permission, especially of devotees praying. Be considerate of your surroundings if you intend to post on social media.

BEST RELIGIOUS EXPERIENCES

Wander through the five-storey ❶ **Buddha Tooth Relic Temple** (p72), home to (reputedly) a tooth of the Buddha discovered in Myanmar.

Marvel at the golden-domed ❷ **Sultan Mosque** (p96) in Kampong Glam, which resembles a scene from a fairy-tale illustration.

Soak up the energy at Little India's colourful ❸ **Sri Veeramakaliamman Temple** (p89), dedicated to the ferocious goddess Kali.

Explore the ❹ **Thian Hock Keng Temple** (p76), Chinatown's oldest Hokkien temple that's guarded by a pair of imposing stone lions.

Visit the ❺ **Armenian Apostolic Church** (p67) and its Memorial Garden, which spotlights Armenians who shaped Singapore.

WITH KIDS

Singapore stands out as one of the best Asian countries for travelling with children. With its safe, clean environment and efficient public transport, it's an easy and convenient destination for families. Children are warmly welcomed everywhere, and the city provides an array of facilities and amenities tailored to kids of all ages.

FROM LEFT: DR DAVID SING/SHUTTERSTOCK, WISNUPRIYONO/SHUTTERSTOCK

Getting Around

Singapore is a breeze to navigate with kids thanks to its excellent footpaths, easily accessible MRT system, and buses with designated stroller entry and parking.

Eating Out

Don't fret if your kids are fussy eaters, as the island has a wealth of cuisine types. High chairs and children's meals are commonly available.

Splash Break

Make sure to pack the kids' swimwear as many parks and attractions have free wet play areas – perfect for cooling down hot tots.

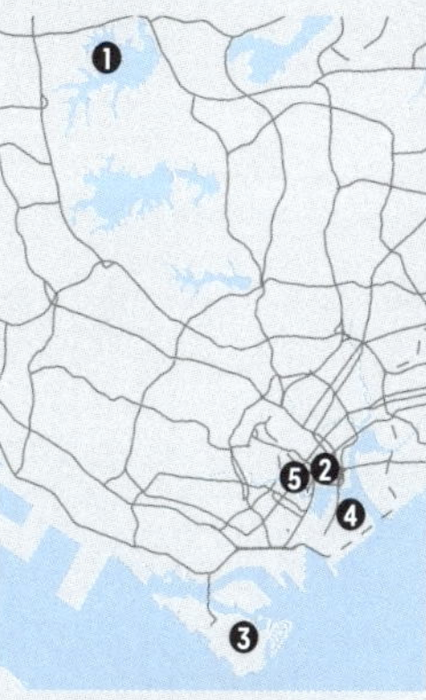

BEST EXPERIENCES FOR KIDS

Go wild at ❶ **Mandai Wildlife Reserve** (p154), home to renowned nature parks such as the Singapore Zoo, Night Safari and Bird Paradise.

Hop aboard ❷ **Singapore DUCKtours** (p55), a remodelled WWII amphibious warcraft, for land and water fun in Marina Bay.

Gear up for thrills and spills on ❸ **Sentosa Island** (p178), brimming with theme parks, amusements, beaches and evening spectaculars.

Enjoy the Children's Garden in ❹ **Gardens by the Bay** (p46), featuring a water-play zone, adventure playground and towering treehouse.

Let imagination soar at the ❺ **Children's Museum Singapore** (p67), packed with immersive shows and interactive fun.

Find more things to do with kids in Singapore on lonelyplanet.com

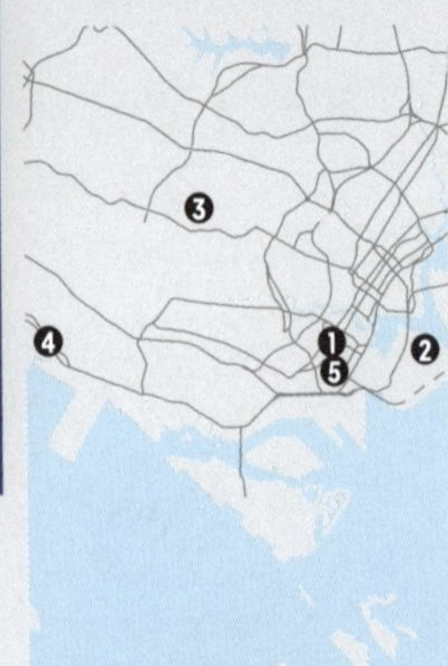

FOR FREE

Despite maintaining its position as one of the world's most expensive cities, Singapore has numerous free or highly affordable activities for everyone to enjoy. From exploring lush gardens and cultural districts to relishing local cuisine and taking in captivating light shows, there are plenty of ways to experience the city's charm without breaking the bank.

BEST FREE EXPERIENCES

Dip in and out of Chinatown's religious sites along South Bridge Rd. Begin at the ❶ **Buddha Tooth Relic Temple** (p72) and continue north.

Catch the free twice-nightly Garden Rhapsody sound-and-light show at the Supertree Grove in ❷ **Gardens by the Bay** (p46).

Spend a morning exploring the ❸ **Singapore Botanic Gardens** (p118), which offers free guided tours and performances.

Relive a touch of 1950s tourism at the quirky ❹ **Haw Par Villa** (p166), an offbeat (and more than slightly scary) theme park.

Explore the ❺ **Singapore City Gallery** (p74), a captivating journey of the nation's cityscape and urban planning through the decades.

Find more free things to do in Singapore on lonelyplanet.com

FROM LEFT: TY LIM/SHUTTERSTOCK, ONLYSHAYNESTOCKPHOTO/SHUTTERSTOCK

Getting Around

The MRT isn't free, but it's incredibly cheap (purchase an Ez-link card); it's the fastest, cleanest and easiest way to navigate the city.

Neighbourhood Streets

Spend a day crisscrossing the island to discover its diverse and colourful neighbourhoods, where daily life is the best show in town.

Green Spaces

Singapore has a wealth of free green spaces, from world-class gardens to coastal parks and hiking trails, for a refreshing respite from the hustle.

KANDL STOCK/SHUTTERSTOCK

Sembawang Hot Spring Park (p159)

UNDER THE RADAR

While most visitors stick to Singapore's well-trodden tourist trails, venturing slightly off the beaten path reveals a host of delights. Explore local neighbourhood haunts, chilled-out island retreats, and forest trails alive with wildlife. Along the way, discover quirky museums and unusual sights, offering a richer, more adventurous perspective of the city.

BEST UNDER-THE-RADAR EXPERIENCES

Embrace the sea breezes and a laid-back vibe at ❶ **Changi Village** (p137), best savoured with a cool drink in hand.

Pick up handmade pottery at ❷ **Thow Kwang Pottery Jungle** (p173) and see Singapore's last remaining dragon kiln.

Cycle around ❸ **Pulau Ubin** (p196), a slightly untamed island with one of Singapore's last surviving *kampongs* (villages).

Kick back with a foot soak at ❹ **Sembawang Hot Spring Park** (p159), and cook an egg in the steaming waters.

Relive your childhood at the ❺ **MINT Museum of Toys** (p65), home to over 50,000 vintage toys from around the world.

Explore the Heartlands

Lively neighbourhoods include Tampines, Jurong, Bishan, Toa Payoh and Ang Mo Kio – exit the MRT and go for a wander.

Discover the Islands

Grab your swimwear and a picnic and spend the day exploring Singapore's Southern Islands. All three are easily accessible via public ferry.

Perfect Days

Thanks to Singapore's small footprint and efficient transport network, you can effortlessly explore and eat your way around all corners of the island in no time at all.

Sri Veeramakaliamman Temple (p89), Little India

TANG YAN SONG/SHUTTERSTOCK

DAY 1

Downtown & Marina Bay

Start with a riverside stroll at the Quays, winding your way back to the Colonial District. Visit the brilliant **Asian Civilisations Museum** (p52) or continue to the **National Museum of Singapore** (p61), the **Peranakan Museum** (p67) or the art-filled **National Gallery** (p52).

Lunch Take the MRT to Little India and head into the **Tekka Centre** (p92) for top-notch hawker fare.

Little India & Kampong Glam

Explore the streets, dotted with spice sellers, sari stores and gold dealers. Admire the colours of **Sri Veeramakaliamman Temple** (p89), then delve into the area's rich history at the **Indian Heritage Centre** (p89). Wander south to Kampong Glam and its fairy-tale **Sultan Mosque** (p96) before hunting down street art at **Gelam Gallery** (p98) and shopping in Haji Lane and Arab Street.

Dinner Head for an early meal of *nasi padang* (rice with curries) at **Hjh Maimunah** (p99) – order the melt-in-your-mouth beef rendang.

Downtown & Marina Bay

As the crowds dwindle, head into the Flower Dome and Cloud Forest conservatories at high-tech **Gardens by the Bay** (p46) before catching the Garden Rhapsody light-and-sound show at the Supertree Grove. Grab a cocktail at rooftop Marina Bay Sand's **CÉ LA VI** (p50) and end your night with sky-high views of the island.

DAY 2

Chinatown, Tanjong Pagar & the CBD

Enjoy a Singapore breakfast set of *kaya* (coconut and egg jam) toast, runny eggs and *kopi* (coffee) at **Ya Kun Kaya Toast** (p79) before glimpsing neighbourhood life at the **Chinatown Heritage Centre** (p72), **Thian Hock Keng Temple** (p76) and **Buddha Tooth Relic Temple** (p72). Look out for murals by local artist Yip Yew Chong. For a bird's-eye view of the metropolis, ascend **Pinnacle@ Duxton** (p79), or learn its story at the **Singapore City Gallery** (p74).

Lunch At the **Amoy Street Food Centre** (p80), queue for Singapore-style ramen from A Noodle Story.

Eastern Singapore

Dive into Peranakan culture in Joo Chiat, stopping at **Koon Seng Rd** (p128) for a photo with the colourful shophouses. Visit the moving **Changi Chapel & Museum** (p137), which recounts the stories of those who endured the Japanese occupation. Afterwards, go for a bike ride at beachfront **East Coast Park** (p134).

Dinner Feast on chilli crab at **Roland Restaurant** (p136) – order plenty of *mantou* (steamed bun) to wipe up the sweet and tangy sauce.

Eastern Singapore

Beeline for neon-lit **Geylang** (p142), a tame red-light district juxtaposed with temples, mosques and some of Singapore's best food. Stop at one of the roadside stalls to try durian, the king of fruits.

DAY 3

Northern & Central Singapore

Join the wildlife ambassadors for Breakfast in the Wild at **Singapore Zoo** (p154). Ride the guided tram to get your bearings, and book animal feeding times. Grab a combo ticket if you want to check out any of the other parks at **Mandai Wildlife Reserve** (p154). Alternatively, head to **MacRitchie Reservoir** (p158) for an evocative jungle escape.

Lunch Grab some chicken rice or laksa at the zoo's **Ah Meng Restaurant** (p155).

Sentosa Island

After all that wildlife, it's time for a wild time on Sentosa, Singapore's island of fun! To cool down, don your swimmers for family-fun water slides at **Adventure Cove Waterpark** (p186), or tackle **Universal Studios** (p182) for a mix of rides and shows. If you're looking to really get your heart racing, **Mega Adventure** (p190) fits the bill, along with **Skypark Sentosa by AJ Hackett** (p190).

Dinner Chow down on Greek fare at **Blu Kouzina** (p189) on Palawan Beach Walk.

Sentosa Island

As late afternoon hits, pull up at one of the island's beach clubs for a sundowner – options include adults-only **+Twelve** (p188) and the secluded and trendy **Tanjong Beach Club** (p188). Finish your evening with some mega light-and-laser-show action at **Wings of Time Fireworks Symphony** (p190).

WHEN TO GO

Visiting Singapore is excellent year-round. Its warm tropical climate means daytime temperatures typically range from 28°C to 31°C.

Located just 137km north of the equator, Singapore lacks distinct seasonal variations and has a warm, humid climate throughout the year. The island has almost daily rainfall, but these showers are typically brief and refreshing. Singapore experiences two official monsoons: the northeast monsoon (December to March) and the southwest monsoon (mid-June to September). February to April is the most favourable time to visit, as this period sees the least rainfall and the lowest humidity. The weather is also pleasant during the transition months of September and October. From May to August, Singapore can be affected by haze caused by smoke from neighbouring countries' wildfires.

Accommodation Lowdown

Singapore isn't cheap, so it's best to avoid the super-peak seasons. School holidays in June and December are busy, as is Chinese New Year. Any large entertainment or sporting event, such as a major concert or the F1 race, will send prices sky-high.

I LIVE HERE

BIRDWATCHING

Jason Chan is a software engineer based in Jurong and an avid birdwatcher.

Sungei Buloh Wetland Reserve is my top spot for bird-spotting, especially during September to May when migratory shorebirds flock here. With several bird hides, you can get an up-close view of these feathered friends in their natural habitat. Keep your eyes peeled for other wildlife, too – monitor lizards, otters and saltwater crocodiles all call the wetlands home year-round.

Regional forest fire haze

FROM LEFT: PUMIDOL/SHUTTERSTOCK, JAVEN/SHUTTERSTOCK

HAZY DAYS

The haze season, which typically occurs from June to October, is caused by winds bringing in tiny particles of ash from forest fires burning in the region. Farmers in neighbouring countries use slash-and-burn methods to clear land.

Weather Through the Year

JANUARY	FEBRUARY	MARCH	APRIL	MAY	JUNE
Avg. daytime max: **25.8°C**	Avg. daytime max: **26.2°C**	Avg. daytime max: **26.7°C**	Avg. daytime max: **27.1°C**	Avg. daytime max: **27.4°C**	Avg. daytime max: **27.3°C**
Days of rainfall: **13**	Days of rainfall: **9**	Days of rainfall: **12**	Days of rainfall: **15**	Days of rainfall: **15**	Days of rainfall: **13**

SINGAPORE SHOWERS

Singapore has an average of 173 rainy days a year. Even though that might sound like a lot, much of the rain falls in sudden afternoon thunderstorms that last only an hour or so.

Religious Festivities

The streets of Chinatown (p68) come alive with lanterns and lion dancers in the run-up to **Chinese New Year**. Shoppers head to the area en masse to pick up festive treats. **January/February/March**

Little India (p88) is ablaze during **Deepavali**, the 'Festival of Lights', which celebrates Rama's victory over the demon king Ravana. The festival culminates in a huge street party on the eve of the holiday. **October/November**

Hari Raya celebrates the end of the Ramadan fasting month. Head to the bazaar at Geylang Serai in eastern Singapore or to Kampong Glam (p96) for nightly feasts. **February/March**

As **Christmas** rolls around, Orchard Rd (p102) and Gardens by the Bay (p46) both light up in spectacular festive displays. **November/December**

Lights, Dance & Go!

Prepare to be wowed at **Chingay**, Singapore's biggest multicultural street parade, featuring lion dancers, floats and performers. Tickets are required. **February**

Nights come alight for the spectacular **Singapore Night Festival**, as buildings become canvases for rainbow light projections and visitors are treated to interactive installations, performance art and comedy shows. **August/September**

For three high-energy days each year, the Esplanade (p44) comes alive with **Baybeats**, Singapore's free alternative-music festival showcasing emerging local bands and rising Asian acts across indie, punk, metal, hip hop and electronica. **August**

The Marina Bay area is transformed into a high-speed race track for the only **Formula One** race at night. Held over three days, the event features nonstop racing action and big-name entertainment. **September**

I LIVE HERE

RESORT LIVING

Amy Tan is a finance analyst who called River Valley home before swapping the city vibes for the beaches of Sentosa.

Living on Sentosa feels like dwelling on a perpetual resort island with golf buggies and beach clubs. The weather is hot year-round, but the sea breeze keeps temperatures down. During December and January the slightly cooler evenings create picturesque sunset scenes at the Marina at Keppel Bay, which I enjoy alfresco with a drink in hand.

Sentosa Island (p178)

A LIGHTNING CAPITAL

With around 163 lightning events per kilometre, Singapore has the highest lightning density in the world. April, May and November are the most lightning-prone months because of the monsoon conditions at this time.

JULY	AUGUST	SEPTEMBER	OCTOBER	NOVEMBER	DECEMBER
Avg. daytime max: **27°C**	Avg. daytime max: **26.9°C**	Avg. daytime max: **26.9°C**	Avg. daytime max: **26.7°C**	Avg. daytime max: **26.3°C**	Avg. daytime max: **26°C**
Days of rainfall: **14**	Days of rainfall: **14**	Days of rainfall: **13**	Days of rainfall: **15**	Days of rainfall: **19**	Days of rainfall: **19**

FROM LEFT: LECHATNOIR/GETTY IMAGES, PHOTO 12/ALAMY

GET PREPARED FOR SINGAPORE

Useful things to load in your bag, your ears and your brain.

Clothes

Loose, light attire Singapore is hot and humid throughout the year, so lightweight and breathable clothing is a must. Neat casual clothes are appropriate for exploring, but remember to dress respectfully when you visit temples. Pack a smarter outfit for fine-dining establishments and clubs, as many of these have dress codes. Many restaurants and shopping malls are air-conditioned and can feel arctic (especially the cinemas), so carry a light wrap or sweater.

Footwear Flip-flops are fine for getting around, but bring trainers or hiking boots if you're visiting any of the nature reserves.

Manners

Spitting or littering in public is both frowned upon and illegal.

Seats are reserved by placing a packet of tissues or an umbrella on the table or chair.

Cleaning away your tray after eating is a must in hawker centres and public dining areas.

Addressing elders as 'uncle' or 'auntie' is a sign of respect and common practice.

Hat and umbrella The Singapore sun can be fierce, so a hat is essential. A small umbrella will shield you from midday rays and sudden downpours, which are common in the late afternoon.

READ

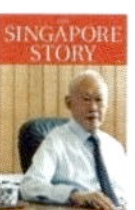

The Singapore Story (Lee Kuan Yew; 1999) Learn the secrets of Singapore's success from the man who masterminded the whole thing.

Singapore: A Biography (Mark Ravinder Frost & Yu-Mei Balasingamchow; 2010) A well-written and handsomely illustrated history of Singapore.

This Is What Inequality Looks Like (Teo You Yenn; 2018) A collection of essays that look behind Singapore's glittering and glamorous image.

Tanamera (Noel Barber; 1981) Part history lesson, part romance novel set in 1930s Singapore.

Words

Singlish is a colloquial blend of English and local languages such as Hokkien, Tamil and Malay. Verb tenses are often simplified or replaced with time indicators, such as *lah* for emphasis. The last syllable of phrases is stressed, leading to syncopated consonants and changed vowel sounds. Pronouns and prepositions are frequently omitted, and word order can be unconventional. Some view Singlish as a cultural emblem that fosters identity; others perceive it as a barrier to mastering standard English. It continues to thrive in everyday conversations, literature and media. See p230 for more about Singlish.

lah – can be added for emphasis to the end of just about every phrase or sentence

can? – is that OK?

can! – yes, that's fine!

alamak! (ah-lah-mak) – exclamation of disbelief or frustration: 'oh my gosh!'

aiyo (ai-yo) – expression of disappointment, annoyance or sympathy: '*aiyo*, why so upset?'

makan (mah-kahn) – to eat: 'you *makan* already?'

shiok (she-oak) – very good: 'this chicken rice is *shiok*'

dabao (dah-bao) – to take away: 'chicken rice, *tabao*'

chope (joh-pe) – to reserve a seat

die, die, must try – yummy dish you must sample

atas (ah-tahs) – snobbish or high-class: 'he is so *atas*'

kaypoh (kay-poh) – a busybody

kiasu (kee-ah-soo) – afraid of losing out

lepak (leh-park) – relax and unwind: 'let's go *lepak* at the beach'

jalan jalan – walk: 'let's go Orchard Rd *jalan jalan*'

WATCH

Ilo Ilo (Anthony Chen; 2013; pictured above) Touching story about a Chinese-Singaporean boy and his Filipino maid. Won the 2013 Caméra d'Or at Cannes.

Apprentice (Junfeng Boo; 2016) Prison drama about Singapore's controversial death penalty and those who undertake the job of executioner.

Ah Boys to Men (Jack Neo; 2012) The first movie in a satirical series about National Service recruits.

Crazy Rich Asians (Jon M Chu; 2018) A peek into the lives of Singapore's mega-wealthy families.

Emerald Hill (Loo Yin Kam; 2025) Netflix drama series set in a Peranakan enclave and following the lives, loves and secrets of the Zhang family.

LISTEN

Genesi (JJ Lin; 2014) Award-winning album by one of Singapore's most famous Mandopop artists.

Life Story (Dick Lee; 1974) Debut that started Lee on his journey to become the 'Father of Singaporean Pop'.

Home (Kit Chan; 1998) Patriotic hit rolled out for National Day in 1998. Brings a tear to the eye of nearly every Singaporean.

Improm2 (Louis Soliano; 2004) Solo album by an icon of Singapore's jazz community. Famous concerts have been performed in his honour.

FROM LEFT: MYPHOTOBANK.COM.AU/SHUTTERSTOCK, DUC HUY NGUYEN/SHUTTERSTOCK

Above: Changi Airport; Right: MRT train

GETTING THERE

Practically a destination in itself, world-class Changi Airport is Singapore's aviation crowning jewel. Named World's Best by Skytrax 12 times, this Asian hub services a plethora of regional and international routes. Buses and trains connect Singapore with Thailand and Malaysia, and ferries with Malaysia and Indonesia.

MRT

The Mass Rapid Transit (MRT) is the best low-cost option. The station is located below Terminals 2 and 3. The trip to City Hall costs S$2.14 and takes around 40 minutes. Change trains at Tanah Merah. Trains run between 5.30am and 11.18pm.

Airport Transfer & Shuttle

Transfers can be booked via the 24-hour Ground Transport Concierge (GTC) counters at all terminals or via the Changi app. Private vehicles include four- and six-seaters (S$55/60 per trip to anywhere in Singapore). The City Shuttle is S$5 per person to the Tanah Merah Ferry Terminal, where boats depart to Indonesia and Malaysia; it operates daily from 10am to 7.52pm.

Taxi & Rideshare

There are taxi ranks at all terminals. A trip to the city costs between S$25 and S$45; surcharges kick in from 5pm to 6am. Grab rideshare can be booked via mobile app; there are pickup points at all terminals. Budget S$25 to S$35.

Bus

Public bus 36 runs from Terminals 1, 2 and 3 and from the Carpark 4B bus stop to Colonial District (S$2.26) and Orchard Rd (S$2.32) and takes 75 to 90 minutes. Buses leave roughly every 10 minutes between 6am and 11pm.

FROM THE AIRPORT TO THE CITY CENTRE

To the City

MRT	40min/S$2.14
Bus	75min/S$2.26
Taxi	20min/S$30

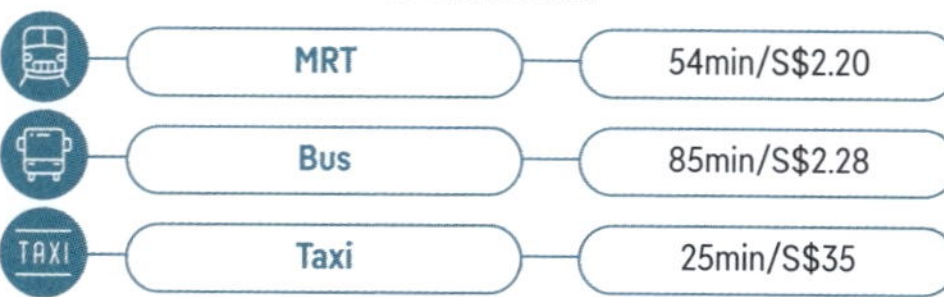

To Chinatown

MRT	54min/S$2.20
Bus	85min/S$2.28
Taxi	25min/S$35

To Orchard Road

MRT	47min/S$2.20
Bus	90min/S$2.32
Taxi	25min/S$40

TIP

It's compulsory for all visitors to complete the Singapore Arrival Card (SGAC), which can be submitted up to three days before arrival via *eservices.ica.gov.sg/sgarrivalcard*, the MyICA app or by scanning a QR code at Immigration. Do it before landing to pass through Immigration smoothly.

OTHER POINTS OF ENTRY

Bus & Taxi

There are two land border crossings between Singapore and Malaysia: the busy Johor-Singapore Causeway and the Second Link at Tuas, which is less congested. From Johor Bahru, buses and taxis cross the Causeway into Singapore. Buses are frequent and affordable, while taxis are faster and more direct. Private bus companies operate services from Kuala Lumpur, Melaka and Penang in Malaysia.

Ferry

The Tanah Merah Ferry Terminal and HarbourFront Passenger Terminal offer regular ferry services to nearby destinations in Malaysia and Indonesia. Larger cruise ships, including international liners, dock at the modern Marina Bay Cruise Centre and the centrally located Singapore Cruise Centre.

Train

The KTMB Shuttle Train *(online. ktmb.com.my)* is the fastest way to cross the Causeway but terminates just within the border at Woodlands Train Checkpoint, requiring onward transport from there. Bookings open 30 days in advance via the website or app and sell out quickly, especially for public holidays and weekends.

FROM LEFT: DR DAVID SING/SHUTTERSTOCK, JO PANUWAT D/SHUTTERSTOCK

Circle Line MRT train

GETTING AROUND

Navigating Singapore is a breeze, thanks to its sleek and widespread public transport system, which includes an extensive network of trains (MRT) and buses. The city enhances accessibility with bike rentals, affordable taxis and car-sharing options, all supported by wide, well-maintained footpaths and abundant green spaces.

MRT & LRT

Six highly efficient Mass Rapid Transit (MRT) lines crisscross Singapore, complemented by several Light Rail Transit (LRT) loops that serve outer residential neighbourhoods. When using the network, it's helpful to remember the name of the last station on your line, as this will guide you to the correct platform for boarding. Trains operate daily from around 5.30am to midnight, with extended hours during major festive seasons. During peak periods, services typically run every two to four minutes, while off-peak frequencies range from five to 12 minutes. Delays are rare, making Singapore's public transport system one of the most reliable in the world.

TIP

Download the CityMapper or MyTransport.SG app to help you get around the island using different modes of transport. Both offer useful features for planning routes, checking bus and train arrival times, and receiving real-time transport updates.

Golden Rules of the MRT

- Keep left when traversing stations, especially on travelators and elevators.
- Queue in designated spots on platforms and allow passengers to alight before boarding.
- Move towards the middle of the carriage and refrain from pushing.
- Give up your seat for those who need it, including pregnant or older travellers and those with a disability.

Bus

Singapore's bus service is modern, safe, affordable and – most importantly – air-conditioned! Designated bus lanes ensure reliable journey times, but expect services during the peak before- and after-work hours to get very busy. Raise your hand to flag down the driver. Tap on with your payment or Ez-link card and tap off when alighting, or you'll pay the full fare to the end of the line. Bus services, like the trains, run mainly between 5.30am and midnight; however, some run 24 hours a day – for specific timings, check *sbstransit.com.sg*.

TIP

Take note: durians are banned on public transport. The famously pungent fruit isn't allowed on Singapore's MRT trains and buses because of its strong smell, which many find overwhelming and unpleasant.

Taxi & Rideshare

Taxis in Singapore aren't quite as cheap as they were before the COVID-19 pandemic, but they remain a convenient way to get around. If you travel outside peak hours and avoid riding during rainstorms, fares are still reasonably affordable. Be aware that various surcharges apply for rides during peak hours, late at night or from the airport. All hailed taxis are metered, but you can also prebook and lock in fares through taxi and rideshare apps like CDG Zig and Grab. Rideshares have clearly marked pickup points at Changi Airport for easy access.

PUBLIC TRANSPORT ESSENTIALS

Travel Fares

If you're in town for more than a day or two, the easiest way to pay for travel on public transport is with the **Ez-link** *(ezlink.simplygo.com.sg)* card. The card allows you to travel by MRT trains, local buses, river taxis, the Sentosa Express monorail and most taxis. Simply swipe the card over sensors as you enter and leave a station or bus. Another option is to get a one-, two-, three-, four- or five-day **Singapore Tourist Pass** *(thesingaporetouristpass.com.sg)*, which offers unlimited train and bus travel plus perks and discounts at stores and attractions. Cash is accepted on buses – the correct fare is required, as no change will be provided. Keep the ticket as proof of payment.

How to Pay: Ez-link vs Bank Card

You can pay for public transport using either an Ez-link card or a contactless bank card, including those linked to mobile wallets like Apple Pay or Google Pay. Fares are usually the same for both, though Ez-link cards offer a small discount over single-trip tickets. Do note that foreign-issued bank cards may attract a small daily administrative fee.

RIDESHARE APPS

Grab is Singapore's leading rideshare app. Choose from standard GrabCar rides for everyday travel or GrabCar Premium for a more luxurious experience. GrabShare enables carpooling with passengers headed the same way, GrabTaxi allows hailing licensed taxis via the app, while GrabAssist caters to passengers with a disability. GrabFamily provides rides equipped with child safety seats – drivers are trained for proper installation, ensuring safety compliance. A small surcharge applies for these services. Booking and payment are seamless through the Grab app, supporting credit/debit cards and GrabPay, the app's digital wallet.

Other rideshare apps in Singapore include Gojek, TADA and Ryde, each offering similar on-demand transport services.

Bike Sharing

There are two main bike-sharing companies in Singapore – HelloRide and Anywheel. They're relatively easy to use: download the app, set up an account, scan the bike's QR code and get pedalling. Most have GPS tracking to locate designated parking areas; failure to park correctly may incur a S$5 fee. Only foldable bicycles that comply with the allowable dimensions may be brought onto trains and buses.

Walking

Neighbourhoods are best explored on foot, although some of the pavements in Chinatown and Little India are tiny and can get very busy. Keep in mind that the weather can be extremely hot and humid year-round, so opt for cool and breathable clothing. A small umbrella is always a wise choice to shield you from the sun or sudden downpours.

Driving

There's little need to rent a car in Singapore – it's usually more trouble than it's worth. Although local drivers are mostly disciplined, traffic can be heavy, road space is limited, and lane changes can be abrupt and unsignalled. Motorcyclists often weave crazily between cars, especially during traffic jams.

Cable Car

Singapore's cable-car system has two lines. The Mt Faber Line travels between Mt Faber, HarbourFront and Sentosa Island. Once on Sentosa, the Sentosa Line runs entirely within the island, linking Merlion station, Imbiah Lookout and Siloso Point, making it easy to explore the main attractions.

Sentosa Monorail, Bus & Beach Tram

The Sentosa Express monorail (7am to midnight) links the mainland to Sentosa Island, departing from VivoCity shopping mall – which is directly connected to HarbourFront MRT station – and stopping at three stations on the island: Waterfront, Imbiah and Beach. There's a one-time fee of S$4 when entering Sentosa by monorail, but travel between the island's stations is then free. Once on Sentosa, a complimentary beach tram (an electric shuttle) runs along Siloso, Palawan and Tanjong Beaches daily from 9am to 10pm. In addition, two free bus routes – Bus A (westbound) and Bus B (eastbound) – operate from 7am to midnight, connecting the island's main attractions.

FROM LEFT: CYNTHIA A JACKSON/SHUTTERSTOCK, PHADUNGSAK SAWASDEE/SHUTTERSTOCK

Mt Faber Line cable cars

PREPARING FOR THE MRT

Buying Tickets

Buy paper tickets for public transport from ticket machines in MRT stations or from bus drivers. Ez-link cards (S$10 including a S$5 non-refundable deposit) are available at MRT station counters and 7-Eleven stores. Top up using cash or cards at station ticket machines. The Singapore Tourist Pass (from S$17 for one day) is available at Singapore Tourist Pass kiosks in Changi Airport and Orchard MRT station, or SimplyGo ticket offices in select MRT stations.

Rush Hour

The MRT can get crowded during weekday peak periods – typically 7am to 9am and 5pm to 7pm. This is somewhat eased by trains running every two to four minutes during peak hours, compared to every five to 12 minutes off-peak. Plan your journey to avoid these busiest windows.

Find the Exit

Singapore's MRT stations often have multiple exits, each leading to different streets, malls or landmarks. Clear signs within the station indicate which exit letter (A, B, C etc) to use for your destination. Many exits list nearby attractions, bus stops or buildings they connect to. Larger stations, like Dhoby Ghaut or City Hall, can be overwhelming, so plan ahead using station maps or apps like MyTransport.SG or CityMapper.

TRAVEL COSTS

Singapore Tourist Pass 1/2/3/4/5 days
S$17/24/29/37/45

Sentosa Express monorail
S$4 to Sentosa Island

Shared-bike hire
From S$1 per 30 minutes, 50 cents for every additional 10 minutes

NEED TO KNOW

In MRT stations, you can be fined for eating or drinking (even water), attempting to board a full train, carrying large bags, being intoxicated, or lingering for more than two hours.

ACCESSIBILITY

Singapore's public transport system is highly accessible and user-friendly for everyone. MRT stations and buses are equipped with lifts, ramps and tactile guidance paths to assist people with a disability or who are vision-impaired. Priority seats and designated wheelchair spaces are clearly marked on all public buses and trains, and announcements are made both visually and audibly to keep passengers informed. All public buses are wheelchair-accessible, and almost all stops are barrier-free. Overall, Singapore's commitment to inclusive design ensures a smooth and convenient travel experience for all.

ELENA ALEKSANDROVNA ERMAKOVA/GETTY IMAGES

Hawker centre fare

DINING OUT

From simple hawker fare to five-star fine dining and everything in between, Singapore has it all. Welcome to the 'island of feasting'.

In Singapore, *makan* (eating) is taken very seriously. Food-enamoured Singaporeans will line up for food, Instagram the hell out of it, and passionately debate whether it is 'die, die, must try' – Singlish slang for 'to die for'. And why wouldn't they be captivated? Singapore's food landscape delights the palate with an incredible variety of flavours and cuisines that represent the nation's multicultural heritage, which has been influenced by Chinese, Malay, Indian and Peranakan traditions. The essence of Singapore's culinary diversity can be found in its treasured hawker centres, where mouthwatering and pocket-friendly dishes await to ignite your foodie experience. But that's just the beginning! The city pulses with a happening culinary scene, featuring a plethora of cafes, restaurants and bistros that infuse their unique creative twists into the mix. Meanwhile, the rapidly evolving fine-dining landscape is positioning itself as one of the best in Asia. One thing's for sure – you'll never have to worry about going hungry in Singapore.

Hawkers of the Future

Singapore's hawker culture is so integral to the nation's identity that in 2020 it was awarded a place on UNESCO's Intangible Cultural Heritage list. But all this is at risk of disappearing as ageing hawkers, who have spent decades perfecting their dishes, edge towards retirement. Younger generations have generally shunned the industry in favour of more white-collar career paths, so there are few successors.

Best Singaporean Dishes

CHICKEN RICE
Tender chicken and fragrant rice poached in chicken broth.

CHILLI CRAB
Crabs in thick chilli sauce served with *mantou* (fried or steamed buns).

NASI LEMAK
Coconut-milk rice with fried fish or chicken, egg, anchovies and chilli.

LAKSA
Rice noodles, chicken and seafood in a spicy coconut broth.

Nonetheless, the government is actively supporting the sector, and a new wave of hawkers is rising, blending tradition with modernity. To sample the dishes of next-generation superstar hawkers, head to the **Amoy Street Food Centre** (p80) or **Timbre+ One North** (p173).

For more on hawker centres, read the essay on p234.

Feeding the Country

As you wander through the wet markets of Singapore, you'll be greeted by bustling stalls overflowing with a wide variety of fruits, vegetables, seafood, meats and cooking essentials. Considering Singapore's small size – a mere 736 sq km, with just 1% allocated for farmland – you might wonder where all this food comes from. The reality is that Singapore relies heavily on imports for more than 90% of its food, making it susceptible to potential shortages and price fluctuations.

In 2019, to address this vulnerability, the Singaporean government devised a '30 by 30' strategy, aiming to produce 30% of the island's nutritional needs locally by 2030. But a series of challenges, from the COVID-19 pandemic to supply-chain disruptions and rising operating costs, stalled progress. In 2025, this target was replaced by a new four-pronged strategy focusing on diversifying imports, boosting local production, stockpiling key items, and strengthening global partnerships through government-to-government food trade agreements.

Singapore is still committed to developing its agri-food sector. New targets aim to produce 20% of the country's fibre needs (leafy and fruited vegetables, bean sprouts and mushrooms) and 30% of its protein (eggs and seafood) by 2035. To support this, the government is exploring a multi-tenant facility where various farms can operate under one roof, sharing resources to reduce production and distribution costs – particularly for land-based aquaculture and indoor greenhouse farming.

Through these measures, Singapore is determined to strengthen its food supply and build long-term resilience – to 2035 and beyond. See p239 for more on how Singapore is rethinking food security.

NARUTO4836/SHUTTERSTOCK

Geylang Serai Ramadan Bazaar

FOOD & DRINK FESTIVALS

Singapore Food Festival (*singaporefoodfestival.com;* September) Month-long showcase of the island's food culture, with food tours and masterclasses.

Singapore Cocktail Festival (*singaporecocktailfestival.com;* May) The island's top bartenders create a festival tipple served throughout the three-week booze fest.

Brewnanza (*brewlander.com;* August) A celebration of unique brews from local and international breweries.

Geylang Serai Ramadan Bazaar (February/March) Come for the food and revel in the colourful sights and sounds.

Moon Cake (Mid-Autumn) Festival (September/October) Takes place at the full moon of the eighth lunar month.

Chinese New Year (February) Secure prosperity by using chopsticks to throw the ingredients of *lo hei* (raw-fish salad) high in the air.

CHAR KWAY TEOW
Stir-fried noodles with cockles, Chinese sausage and dark sauces.

SATAY
Grilled meat skewers dipped in a spicy peanut sauce.

BAK KUT TEH
Pork ribs simmered in a complex broth of herbs and spices.

ROTI PRATA
South Indian fried flaky flatbread perfect for dipping in curry sauce.

PAUL HARDING 00/SHUTTERSTOCK

Long Bar (p63), Raffles Singapore

BAR OPEN

Come nighttime, Singapore sheds its all-business image to reveal a dynamic bar and nightlife scene roaring to life.

From speakeasy cocktail bars to boutique beer stalls to artisan coffee roasters, Singapore has immersed itself in the finer points of drinking. For stunning views, head to the rooftop bars that dot the Colonial District and Marina Bay; aim for a pre-sunset arrival to get the most bang for your buck, because knockout drink prices often accompany those knockout views. You'll find many of Singapore's hottest bars in Chinatown, especially around Amoy St, Club Street, Duxton Hill and Keong Saik Rd. Chinatown's Neil Rd is home to a handful of swinging gay venues. Other popular drinking spots include bohemian-spirited Kampong Glam, culturally steeped Joo Chiat, heritage-listed Emerald Hill Rd, expat enclaves Dempsey Hill and Holland Village, and hyper-touristy Boat and Clarke Quays. The clubbing and dance-party scene centres on Marina Bay and the Quays, attracting A-list DJs and plenty of revellers ready to dance the night away in high-tech nightspots. For a more chilled vibe, head to Sentosa Island's beach clubs – their weekend parties are legendary.

From Kopi to Coffee

While traditional *kopitiams* (coffeeshops) have stood the test of time, serving generations with their comforting *kopi* (coffee), Singapore's speciality-coffee revolution started as a drop in a cup but is now a

Best Singapore Drinking Spots

LONG BAR
The Raffles Singapore institution that's home to the iconic Singapore sling. **p63**

BACKDROP
Percolated cocktails created by master bartender Dario Knox. **p110**

NATIVE
Surprising local ingredients and clever twists in trendy Amoy St. **p84**

NUTMEG & CLOVE
Reinterpreting classic food and cocktails with a modern Singaporean twist. **p63**

full-blown storm. Drawing inspiration from Australia's artisanal-coffee culture, wave upon wave of contemporary cafes are sourcing and roasting their own beans – try **Chye Seng Huat Hardware** (p95), **Alchemist** (p113), **Brawn & Brains Coffee** (p95) and **Common Man Coffee Roasters** (p60). No matter how you like your cup brewed, be it by espresso machine, drip, Aeropress or siphon, you'll easily get your fix on the Little Red Dot.

The Cocktail Revolution

Singapore's cocktail scene has undergone a transformation in recent decades. While the legendary cotton-candy-coloured Singapore sling once reigned supreme, the city-state has emerged as a global mixology hub. In classic establishments, rooftop bars and secret speakeasies tucked away in alleyways, bartenders all over the island are experimenting with exotic ingredients and innovative techniques to craft delightful libations. This evolution is showcased at the **Singapore Cocktail Festival** *(singaporecocktailfestival.com)*, where mixologists mesmerise with their creations, leaving enthusiasts and newcomers alike in a cocktail coma. As boundaries continue to be pushed, Singapore's cocktail culture stands tall, celebrating creativity and innovation in every sip.

Let's Party

Singapore's club scene suffered during the COVID-19 pandemic, with alcohol service ending at 10.30pm and dance floors turning into restaurants. Thankfully, the tables and chairs have now been cleared away and DJs are returning in full force. (Weeknights still remain relatively quiet, though.) Clarke Quay's super-club **Zouk** (p58) has a number of themed spaces for getting your groove on. Thrill-seekers flock to Marquee in **Marina Bay Sands** (p49), where the full-size Ferris wheel and slide are just some of the toys to enjoy while you party the night away. Laneway festivals and dance parties are starting to fill up the calendar – check *timeout.com/singapore* for details.

CARLINA TETERIS/GETTY IMAGES

NEED TO KNOW

Opening times Bars are generally open from around 5pm until at least midnight Sunday to Thursday, and until 2am or 3am on Friday and Saturday.

Entry fees Unless you know someone at the door or get signed in by a member, at the hottest clubs you'll have to join the queue. You can avoid the cover charge for some bars and clubs by going early.

Costs Drinking can be costly in Singapore, mainly because alcohol is highly taxed and also because of the sky-high price of commercial rentals.

Extra charges Regular bars add 19% to your bill: a 10% service charge and 9% for GST. You'll see this indicated by '++' on drink lists. Tipping on top of this isn't customary.

ATLAS
Swanky 1920s cocktail lounge with a 12m-high gin tower. **p100**

LEVEL 33
World's highest urban craft brewery, with stunning Marina Bay views. **p50**

NO SLEEP CLUB
Former pop-up, now a cemented star on Singapore's bar scene. **p84**

LIVE TWICE
Evoking mid-century modern Japan, along with delicious libations. **p84**

FROM LEFT: HITI912/SHUTTERSTOCK, MOSAYMAYZ/SHUTTERSTOCK

Formula One Grand Prix track

SHOWTIME

Singapore's nightlife thrills year-round with live music, theatre and adrenaline rushes, plus festivals, sports spectacles and hot-ticket concerts.

Singapore is rewriting the rulebook as Asia's ultimate entertainment powerhouse, where the world's biggest stars and headline-grabbing spectacles collide. The city isn't just on the global tour map – it's the destination. From international Broadway and West End blockbusters to arena-filling comedians and chart-dominating rock and pop icons, Singapore stages it all with flair. In 2024, it ignited diplomatic fireworks by clinching Taylor Swift's only Southeast Asia shows on her Eras Tour. With sleek infrastructure and flawless logistics, this is a city built for showtime, delivering experiences that glitter as brightly as its skyline. Then comes the adrenaline. The Formula One Singapore Grand Prix turns the city into a neon-lit carnival of speed, glamour and all-night revelry – the very definition of sporting theatre. Add the Singapore Badminton Open, Rugby Sevens, LIV Golf and a roster of elite tournaments, and the Lion City proves it's not just dazzling the stage, it's owning the stadiums too.

Concerts & Theatre

Singapore has several world-class venues that host major international artists and Broadway musicals. But it's not just international luminaries who bask in Singapore's spotlight – there's plenty of homegrown talent too. Among them are the **Singapore Repertory Theatre** *(srt.com.sg)*, with its acclaimed 'Shakespeare in the Park', and thought-provoking production house **Wild Rice** *(wildrice.com.sg)*, whose shows always get the island talking. Both the **Singapore Ballet** *(singaporeballet.org)* and the **Singapore Symphony Orchestra** *(sso.org.sg)* are a source of national pride.

Spectator Sports

The number-one highlight on Singapore's sports calendar is the **Formula**

One Grand Prix *(singaporegp.sg)*, roaring into town each September. Its entertainment lineup ensures pumping off-track performances rivalling the on-track ones. If you're not a rev-head, there are plenty of other sporting tournaments, including the fast-paced **Rugby Sevens** *(svns.com)*; Asia's leading table-tennis event, the **Singapore Smash** *(singaporesmash.com)*; the prestigious **Singapore Badminton Open** *(singaporebadminton.org.sg)*; and the professional golf tournament, **LIV Golf Open** *(livgolf.com)*. The **Singapore Festival of Football** has seen multiple Premier League teams compete at stadiums around the Little Red Dot in July.

Festivals & Outdoor Cinema

Embrace the fun of watching movies under the stars. At Tanjong Beach's **Sunset Cinema** *(sunsetcinema.com.sg)*, DJs weave beats as the sun dips below the horizon – sink into a striped deckchair, slip on wireless headphones and behold cinematic blockbusters. For a city vibe, **Films at the Fort** *(filmsatthefort.com.sg)* is set against the backdrop of historic Fort Canning, where the experience is elevated with gourmet bites and plush inflatable chairs.

Events to plan your trip around include the **Singapore Fringe Festival** *(singapore fringe.com; January)*, **Singapore International Festival of Arts** *(sifa.sg; May/June)*, **Jazz in July** *(esplanade.com/jazzinjuly)*, **Baybeats** *(esplanade.com/baybeats; October/November)* and **Singapore International Film Festival** *(sgiff.com; November/December)*.

LONELY PLANET'S TOP...

Local Acts

Wild Rice Theatre company renowned for bold, socially conscious and innovative storytelling.

Singapore Repertory Theatre Diverse and captivating shows include the popular 'Shakespeare in the Park'.

Singapore Symphony Orchestra Acclaimed ensemble delivering masterful classical and contemporary performances.

Live Performances

Esplanade – Theatres on the Bay Nonstop programme of international and local shows.

Sands Theatre Sets the stage for world-class musicals and concerts.

Simply Jazz by Tin Box Enjoy curated jazz performances in intimate surroundings.

Comedy Masala Get ready to belly-laugh at this weekly stand-up show.

Esplanade – Theatres on the Bay (p44)

ENTERTAINMENT BY NEIGHBOURHOOD

Downtown & Marina Bay	Main hub for global music acts, Broadway shows, festivals and stand-up comics. Sports fans love the Formula One and events at the Singapore Sports Hub.
Chinatown, Tanjong Pagar & the CBD	Witness the centuries-old tradition of Chinese opera performed by the Chinese Theatre Circle and Kreta Ayer People's Theatre.
Little India & Kampong Glam	Little India comes alive during Deepavali with music and cultural shows. Kampong Glam's Bali La is a local favourite for live music and comedy.
Holland Village, Botanic Gardens & Dempsey Hill	The Star Theatre has regular performances and the Shaw Foundation Symphony Stage in the Botanic Gardens hosts free events.
West & Southwest Singapore	Art hub Gillman Barracks stages exhibitions and workshops, while Timbre+ One North pairs live music with scrumptious bites.
Sentosa Island	Home of LIV Golf Open and beach parties throughout the year.

FROM LEFT: TIAGOBAIAO/GETTY IMAGES, REDARTI4/SHUTTERSTOCK

Bugis Street Market (p101)

SHOP

World-class shopping malls, colourful local markets and a wealth of homegrown design talent make Singapore a must-stop for retail lovers.

After enjoying glorious nosh, retail therapy is Singapore's favourite pastime. The city's most famous retail district is Orchard Rd, a glamorous boulevard adorned with opulent malls showcasing global fashion giants, chic high-street brands and a few discount havens – there's something for everyone. For a more local experience, Chinatown entices with cheap deals on clothes and souvenirs along with a good array of antiques. Little India draws shoppers with aromatic spices, exquisite gold jewellery, brightly coloured saris and retail behemoth Mustafa, open 24/7. For local independent boutiques, Haji Lane and the surrounding streets are a treasure trove of finds, as is Joo Chiat, where Peranakan pieces wait to be discovered. For market enthusiasts looking for trendy fashions and electronics, the bazaar in Bugis is the place to trawl for bargains; a little polite haggling is acceptable. Beyond these hubs, head to heartland neighbourhoods, where local stores beg to be explored – who knows what unusual finds you'll turn up!

Local Designers

In recent years, Singaporean designer talent has created a slew of new brands, many with a touch of local flair. For a taster, make a beeline for **Design Orchard** (p107), which houses numerous designers under one roof in Orchard Rd. If your visit coincides with one of the **Boutique Fairs** *(boutiquefairs.com.sg)*, count your lucky fashion stars!

Tourist Refund Scheme

As a traveller in Singapore, you may be eligible to claim the goods and services tax (GST) you've paid on purchases through the electronic Tourist Refund Scheme (eTRS).

Look for the Tax-Free Shopping logo at retailers, or ask before you buy as not all shops participate in the scheme. You'll need to spend S$100 at a single retailer on a single day – up to three same-day receipts can be collated to meet the minimum amount. Before making your purchases, inform the cashier you're a traveller, present your passport (copies are not accepted) and show your ePass, which will be emailed to you by the immigration department once you've entered Singapore. Once your purchase is complete, collect your receipt and keep it safe. You won't receive a physical eTRS ticket, but you can check your transaction via the eTRS Singapore app or at *touristrefund.sg*.

At the airport, proceed to the eTRS self-help kiosk with your goods. For purchases you plan to check in, you need to apply at the eTRS self-help kiosk in the Departures check-in hall before going through Immigration and checking in your luggage. If you're carrying your purchases on board, you need to apply at the eTRS self-help kiosk in the Departures transit lounge, after Immigration. The outcome of your claim will be displayed on the kiosk screen – read it to see whether inspection of your goods is required at the customs counter. Choose how you'd like to receive your refund, and you're good to go.

LONELY PLANET'S TOP...

Independent Stores

Design Orchard (p107) The best of Singapore's homegrown labels under one roof.

Anthony the Spice Maker (p78) Choose from all the traditional flavours of Singapore.

Independent Market (p123) Quirky Singaporean-themed gifts and homewares.

Rumah Bebe (p135) The place to pick up some Peranakan treasures.

Best for Local Fashion

Beyond the Vines (p110) Multidisciplinary design studio that's the epitome of SG cool.

In Good Company (p110) Modular wardrobe essentials for women and men.

Atelier Ong Shunmugam (p123) Womenswear store known for its modern spins on cheongsam.

Benjamin Barker (p110) Menswear studio with impeccably tailored suits and shirts.

SHOPPING BY NEIGHBOURHOOD

Neighbourhood	
Downtown & Marina Bay	Interconnected malls, curated museum gift stores, and in-the-know fashion, books and art.
Chinatown, Tanjong Pagar & the CBD	Chinese antiques, food, medicines, local art and antiques, plus plenty of tourist tat.
Little India & Kampong Glam	Spices, incense and saris in Little India; rugs, perfumes and indie boutiques in Kampong Glam.
Orchard Road	Singapore's luxury-mall-lined shopping epicentre.
Eastern Singapore	Traditional wares, from Peranakan clothing, slippers and porcelain to batik and Malaysian and Indonesian food.
Holland Village, Botanic Gardens & Dempsey Hill	High-end art and fashion in the former military base of Dempsey Hill, and expat shopping hubs Holland Village and Cluny Court.
West & Southwest Singapore	MRT-connected mega-malls at HarbourFront and Jurong East.

SINGAPORE

THE GUIDE

Chapters in this section are organised by neighbourhood. Neighbourhoods are delineated by a specific local character or identity, where you'll find unique specific experiences, local insights, insider tips and expert recommendations.

Chinatown (p68) during Chinese New Year

DEREKTEO/SHUTTERSTOCK

NEIGHBOURHOODS AT A GLANCE

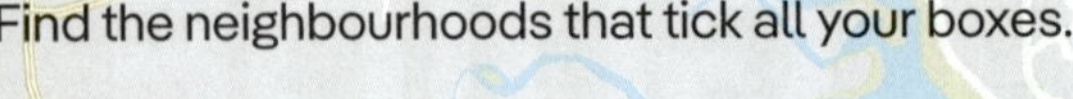

Find the neighbourhoods that tick all your boxes.

West & Southwest Singapore (p162)
A vast area packed with attractions, from quirky theme parks and a sprawling art outpost to scenic hikes along the Southern Ridges.

Holland Village, Botanic Gardens & Dempsey Hill (p114)
Explore hip boutiques, chic eateries and the verdant Botanic Gardens brimming with themed gardens, rare orchids and lush rainforest trails.

Sentosa Island (p178)
Singapore's good-time island, rich in wartime history, now offers unabashed fun – from thrilling attractions to cool beach bars and everything in between.

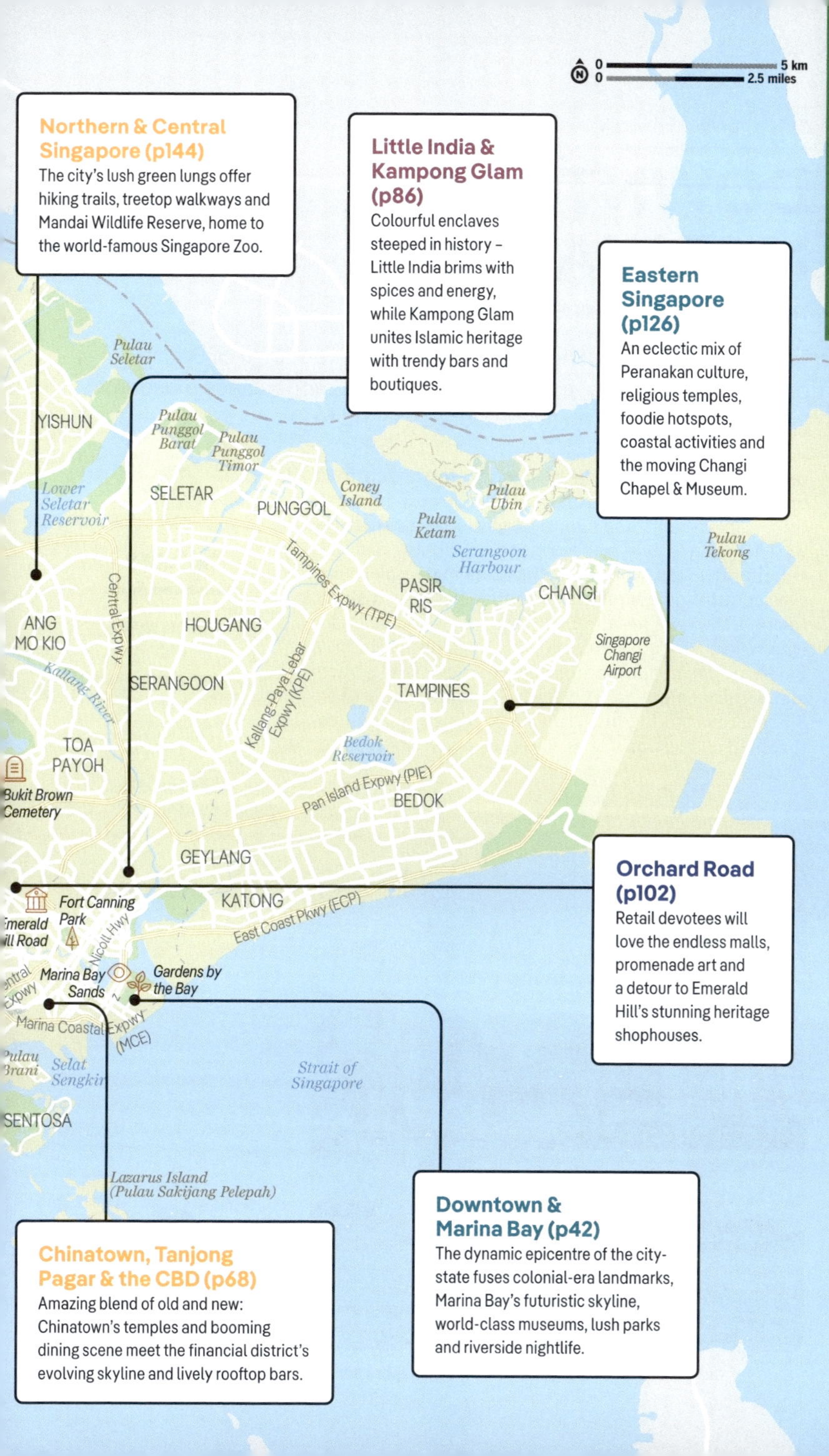

Northern & Central Singapore (p144)

The city's lush green lungs offer hiking trails, treetop walkways and Mandai Wildlife Reserve, home to the world-famous Singapore Zoo.

Little India & Kampong Glam (p86)

Colourful enclaves steeped in history – Little India brims with spices and energy, while Kampong Glam unites Islamic heritage with trendy bars and boutiques.

Eastern Singapore (p126)

An eclectic mix of Peranakan culture, religious temples, foodie hotspots, coastal activities and the moving Changi Chapel & Museum.

Orchard Road (p102)

Retail devotees will love the endless malls, promenade art and a detour to Emerald Hill's stunning heritage shophouses.

Downtown & Marina Bay (p42)

The dynamic epicentre of the city-state fuses colonial-era landmarks, Marina Bay's futuristic skyline, world-class museums, lush parks and riverside nightlife.

Chinatown, Tanjong Pagar & the CBD (p68)

Amazing blend of old and new: Chinatown's temples and booming dining scene meet the financial district's evolving skyline and lively rooftop bars.

Researched by Jaclynn Seah

DOWNTOWN & MARINA BAY

THE DYNAMIC EPICENTRE OF THE CITY-STATE

This is the palpitating heart of Singapore – a melange of British colonial architecture, futuristic skyscrapers, world-class museums, lush tropical parks and lively riverside nightlife.

Downtown Singapore is where the city's story began, from the sinuous Singapore River that winds through its heart. Once a maritime trade hub, the quays lined with gritty warehouses are now transformed into vibrant nightlife and dining areas. Nearby, the bustling marketplace has evolved into today's gleaming central business district. North of the river lies the Civic District, its stately buildings echoes of British colonial rule; just beyond in Bras Basah, the former European Quarter is now the city's arts and culture epicentre. The river flows into Marina Bay, Singapore's striking modern icon of futuristic architecture built on reclaimed land where the sea once stretched.

INCLUDES

Dragon boat racers practising on the Singapore River

See p205 for places to stay in Downtown and Marina Bay.

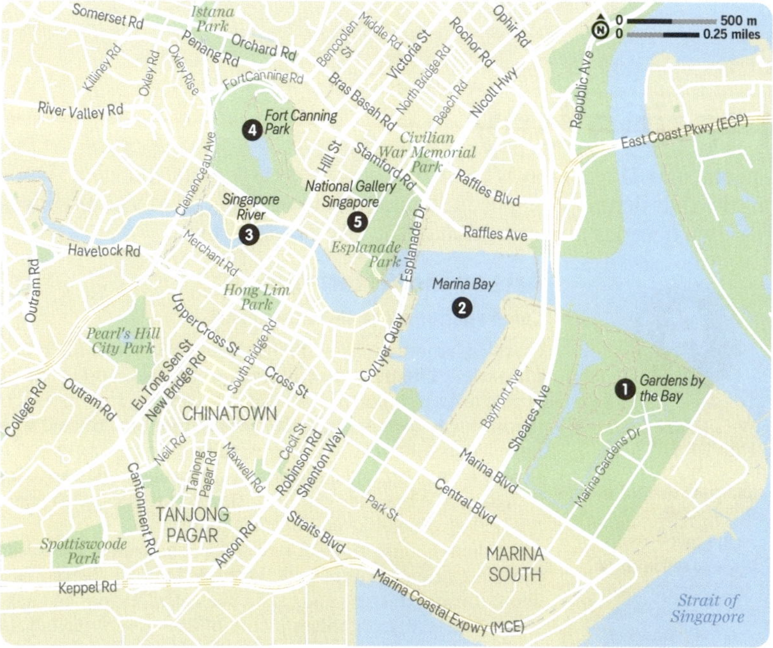

Highlights

❶ Gardens by the Bay
Discover a futuristic botanical garden, climb the Supertrees and enjoy the light-and-music show. **p46**

❷ Marina Bay
Stroll around the waterfront, admire its architectural wonders and soak in skyline views. **p44**

❸ Singapore River
Explore the waterway on foot or by boat, and unwind in nightlife districts along its shores. **p56**

❹ Fort Canning Park
See remnants of war and learn about Singapore's origin story on a hilltop sanctuary in the city. **p64**

◀ ❺ National Gallery Singapore
View the largest collection of Southeast Asian modern art. **p52**

Getting Around

MRT
This area is well connected by MRT lines. City Hall MRT Station serves the Civic District and Marina Bay waterfront. Bayfront Station is connected to Marina Bay Sands and Gardens by the Bay. Clarke Quay and Fort Canning Stations link the Quays.

Walking
The district is easily walkable and many sights are connected by shaded walkways or underground malls.

Bus
Hop on a public bus for longer connections. Use Google Maps and a contactless credit card for affordable and fuss-free travel around the district.

Marina Bay

Spectacular Marina Bay is framed by soaring skyscrapers and iconic landmarks that define Singapore's skyline, a remarkable transformation over just two decades and reflection of the city's rapid growth.

WHY I LOVE MARINA BAY

Jaclynn Seah, Lonely Planet writer

Picturesque Marina Bay is so synonymous with Singapore today that it's wild to think the entire area was once open sea. Massive land reclamation from the 1970s to 1990s created 360 hectares of brand-new land, which then sat mostly empty for years. Growing up in the '80s, I remember it as wide, quiet grass fields. Everything changed in 2010, when Marina Bay Sands and other landmarks rose into the skyline. And the story isn't over – MBS is set to add a fourth tower, and huge swathes of Marina South are waiting to be developed. I can't wait to see what comes next.

Arts on the Waterfront

Catch a performance at the Esplanade

On the northern bank of Marina Bay, the S$600-million **Esplanade – Theatres on the Bay** *(esplanade.com)* is one of Singapore's premier performing art centres and an architectural icon for its distinctive thorny roof ever since it was unveiled in 2002. The aluminium spikes or cladding atop the Esplanade's twin domed shells were an ingenious design to let in light while blocking out heat, though critics say it makes the building look like two upturned durians.

The domes house an 1800-seat concert hall and a 1940-seat theatre. Curious visitors can take guided tours to learn more about the architecture and take a peek at what goes on backstage. The centre organises plenty of free events around its complex, including annual cultural festivals, art exhibitions, indie film screenings and music gigs. The outdoor theatre with the backdrop of Marina Bay waterfront is picturesque in the evenings no matter what's on stage. Find updates and book tickets online or visit the box office on the mezzanine level.

Up, Up & Away!

Go for a ride on the Singapore Flyer

The 165m-high **Singapore Flyer** *(singaporeflyer.com; adult/child S$40/25)* is Asia's tallest observation wheel and provides million-dollar views from Marina Promenade. On a clear day, the 30-minute ride will let you gawk at the high-rise skyline of southeastern Singapore and the iconic buildings of Marina Bay and downtown. Each of the 28 air-conditioned capsules can hold 28 passengers, so you'll rarely have to wait in line; sunset and weekends are busiest. You can also enjoy a four-course dinner in your own capsule with the Sky Dining experience.

EATING IN MARINA BAY: OUR PICKS AT THE ESPLANADE

Boiler: Feast with your friends on fresh seafood spiced with Cajun and Asian flavours in a Louisana-style seafood boil. *11.30am-2.30pm & 5-10.30pm* $$

Supply & Demand: Indulge in modern Italian dishes on the ground floor or sip a sophisticated tipple at the rooftop bar. *hours vary* $$

Malayan Council: Blending traditional Malay recipes and fusion European cuisine into elevated flavour-packed halal dishes. *11am-11pm* $$

Makansutra Gluttons Bay: Satisfying and affordable hawker-centre cuisine in this outdoor food centre by the bay. *4-11pm Mon-Fri, from 3pm Sat & Sun* $

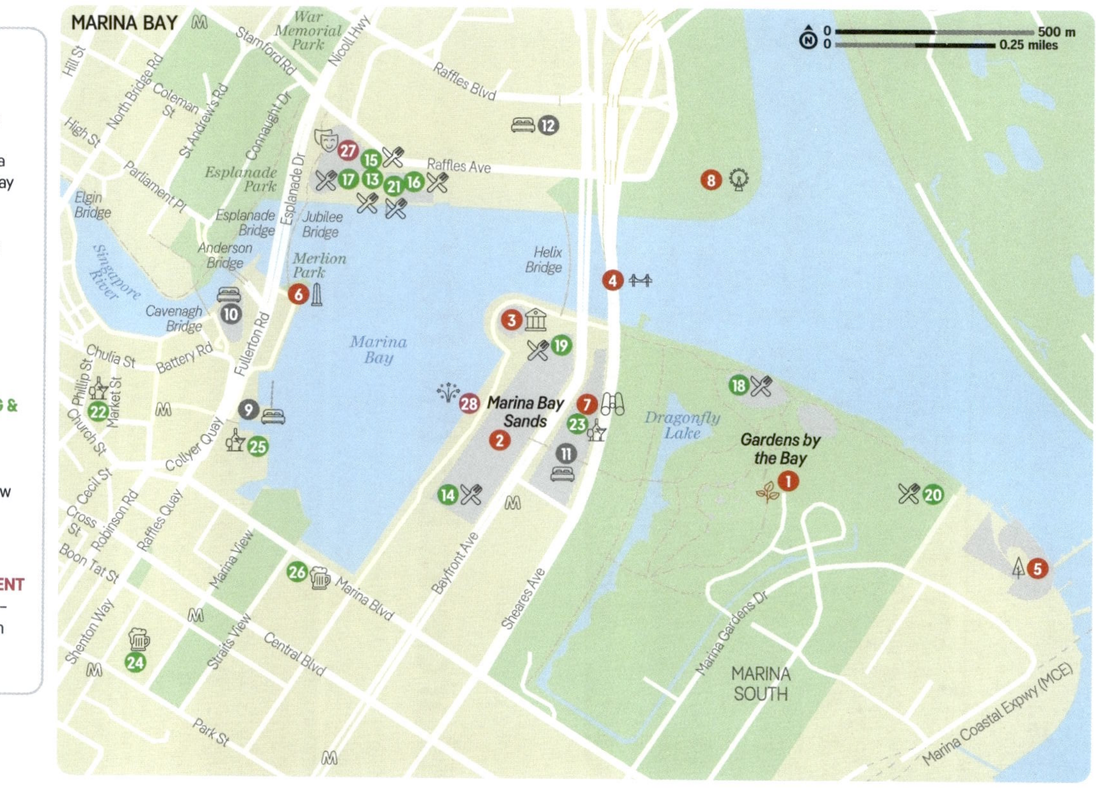

HIGHLIGHTS
1 Gardens by the Bay
2 Marina Bay Sands

SIGHTS
3 ArtScience Museum
4 Benjamin Sheares Bridge
5 Marina Barrage
6 Merlion
7 Sands SkyPark Observation Deck
8 Singapore Flyer

SLEEPING
9 Fullerton Bay Hotel
10 Fullerton Hotel
11 Marina Bay Sands
12 Ritz-Carlton Millenia Singapore

EATING
13 Boiler
14 JUMBO Signatures
15 Labyrinth
16 Makansutra Gluttons Bay
17 Malayan Council
18 Marguerite
19 Rasapura Masters
20 Satay by the Bay
21 Supply & Demand

DRINKING & NIGHTLIFE
22 1-Arden
23 CÉ LA VI
24 Cook & Brew
25 Lantern
26 Level 33

ENTERTAINMENT
27 Esplanade – Theatres on the Bay
28 Spectra

BENNY MARTY/SHUTTERSTOCK

Supertree Grove

TOP EXPERIENCE

Gardens by the Bay

Glimpse the future at this avant-garde botanical garden, punctuated by glass-walled bio-domes, high-tech Supertrees and contemporary sculptures. Sprawling across 101 hectares of reclaimed land in the city centre, it's an ambitious masterpiece of urban planning that cost S$1 billion to build. The mind-blowing display of horticultural and architectural artistry has completely transformed Singapore's cityscape.

DON'T MISS

- Supertree Observatory
- OCBC Skyway
- Cloud Forest
- Flower Dome
- Floral Fantasy
- Heritage Gardens
- Kingfisher Wetlands

Supertree Grove

The centrepiece of Gardens by the Bay, the colossal **Supertrees** tower over the canopy like bionic sci-fi timber. Adorned with 162,900 plants from over 200 species, these steel-clad concrete structures act as vertical gardens. Seven of the 18 Supertrees also generate solar power used to light and cool the conservatories. Their large canopies absorb and disperse heat, and provide shelter for visitors walking beneath.

It's free to roam around the grove and watch the **Garden Rhapsody** light-and-sound show that takes place nightly at 7.45pm and 8.45pm. At the **Supertree Observatory** *(adult/child S$14/10)* you can take in views of Singapore's cityscape

PRACTICALITIES

● gardensbythebay.com.sg ● gardens free ● 9am-9pm (Floral Fantasy from 10am)

from the open rooftop deck. In the air-conditioned indoor viewing space one level below, you can also experience a digital presentation themed around climate change. For knockout views, walk across the 22m-high **OCBC Skyway** *(adult/child S$14/10)* that connects six Supertrees. Get tickets to the observatory and skyway at the Supertree Grove booth.

Planet Sculpture & Heritage Gardens

South of the Supertree Grove lies British artist Marc Quinn's extraordinary sculpture **Planet**. Created in 2008, it features a colossal infant, fast asleep and seemingly floating above the ground. The bronze bubba (modelled on Quinn's son) comes in at a hefty 7 tonnes. Right next to the sculpture, the **Heritage Gardens** are four themed green spaces showcasing plants that are intricately linked to the culture of Singapore's three main ethnic groups and colonial past.

Flower Dome & Cloud Forest

To the far north, two asymmetrical space-age bio-domes act as conservatories for over 217,000 plants from 800 species. The **Flower Dome** holds the Guinness World Record for the largest glass greenhouse, occupying an area equivalent to 75 Olympic-size swimming pools. The innovative megastructure replicates a dry Mediterranean climate, with a temperature of 23°C to 25°C. Free tours run on weekends from 2pm to 5pm. Dine inside the Flower Dome at the Michelin-starred **Marguerite** *(marguerite.com.sg)*, helmed by chef Michael Wilson, for the ultimate back-to-nature experience.

Recreating the tropical montane climate found between 1500m and 3000m altitude, the **Cloud Forest** houses one of the world's tallest indoor waterfalls and a lush mountain clad with plants from around the world. Feel the spray of the 35m-high waterfall, stroll the aerial Cloud Walk and look out for carnivorous Venus' flytraps, delicate blue oil ferns, and mosses. Buy tickets for both bio-domes *(adult/child S$46/32)* online or at the on-site ticket kiosks.

Floral Fantasy

Opened in 2019, the blooming **Floral Fantasy** *(adult/child S$24/16)* interweaves floral artistry and technology. The highlight is 4D simulated-flight ride **Flight of the Dragonfly**, taking you on an augmented-reality journey (minimum height for participants is 1m). The gardens are divided into four landscapes: wander amid flowering plants in Dance, enjoy the sounds of a bubbling brook at Float, and then enter Waltz, where a rain oasis and a poison-dart-frog vivarium await. Last, immerse yourself in the cave-like space of Drift, where 50 species of plant bloom from terraced rock formations.

Kingfisher Wetlands

Home to more than 200 native mangroves, this freshwater sanctuary has water cascades, natural rock pools and a wildlife lookout deck from which you can spot birds and reptiles.

GETTING TO THE GARDENS

The easiest way is to take the MRT to Gardens by the Bay station (Thomson East Coast Line), or take exit B at Bayfront Station (Downtown Line) and cross Dragonfly Bridge towards the main entrance. Guests at Marina Bay Sands can take the overhead bridge across the road. There's a taxi stand at the drop-off point at the main entrance.

TOP TIPS

- The main attractions are each closed on different days once a month for maintenance. Check the schedule online before booking tickets to avoid disappointment.
- If you have kids, don't miss the Children's Garden, featuring a water-play area, a huge tree house and an adventure playground (plus shower and changing facilities).
- There are several food options in the Gardens. Open-air hawker centre Satay by the Bay (p48) dishes up Singaporean favourites such as chilli crabs and satay.
- Walk along the water's edge to **Marina Barrage**, a popular hangout for Singaporean families and kite enthusiasts, particularly at sunset, with great skyline views.

Meet Singapore's Mythical Creature

Take a selfie with Merlion

Across Esplanade Dr from the Fullerton Hotel you'll find a statue of Singapore's mascot, the **Merlion**. The Merlion's fish-like body symbolises Singapore's origins as a fishing village, while its leonine head represents the city's original name, Singapura (meaning 'lion city' in Sanskrit). Spouting water from its jaws, the Merlion is 8.6m high and weighs 70 tonnes. Originally located at the mouth of the Singapore River, the S$165,000 statue was unveiled on 15 September 1972. While the sculpture makes for fun photos, the creature itself isn't worth a special trip to see it – but the Marina Bay views make a visit worthwhile.

MULTIPLE MERLIONS

There are five other Merlion statues scattered across Singapore, though not all are easily found. Look out for the 2m-tall 'Merlion cub' just a few metres behind the original, and another standing tall at **Mt Faber Park** (p176) near the cable car station.

LEGEND OF THE LION CITY

The story behind Singapura's name is one of the country's best-known legends recorded in the Malay Annals *(Sejarah Melayu)*. According to the story, a prince from Palembang, Sang Nila Utama, was sailing past the island when he spotted a striking animal on the shore. His aides identified it as a *singha* (lion), which seemed like an auspicious sign, leading him to found a settlement there and name it after this good omen. However, it's unlikely Sang Nila Utama actually saw a lion as lions have never lived in this region. More likely it was a tiger, as these majestic beasts once roamed freely in Singapore. Unfortunately, they were a threat to the growing population, and the last wild tiger was reportedly shot in the 1930s.

Bird's-Eye Views from Downtown

Sky-high viewpoints around the bay

Singapore's downtown is home to some of the country's tallest buildings, though only a few offer public access to view the city's iconic skyline from above. Housed in the 280m-tall CapitaSpring, the Sky Garden at **1-Arden** *(1-arden.sg)* is a standout option with lush gardens amid sleek architecture on the 17th to 20th floors and F&B outlets on the 51st floor. Garden admission tickets are quite limited *(S$10; 8.30-10.30am & 2.30-6pm Mon-Fri)*; consider booking a table at the restaurant or bar instead.

Among the free elevated spots for panoramic vistas of downtown Singapore is the green roof of Marina Barrage (p47) park, which has a great view of the city skyline and is popular for

EATING IN MARINA BAY: LOCAL EATS

Satay by the Bay: Enjoy yummy satay (grilled meat skewers) and other local hawker dishes with a scenic waterfront view. *9am-10.30pm* $

Rasapura Masters: Perpetually crowded food court in the Marina Bay Sands Shoppes basement, with a handful of 24-hour stalls. *10am-11pm* $

JUMBO Signatures: Feast on Singapore's famous chilli crab and other seafood. *11am-3pm Mon-Fri, noon-3.30pm Sat & Sun, 5.30-10.30pm daily* $$$

Labyrinth: Acclaimed chef LG Han reinvents classic Singaporean flavours at this Michelin-star establishment. *6.30-11pm Wed-Sun & noon-2.30pm Fri-Sun* $$$

TOP EXPERIENCE

Marina Bay Sands

Since its 2010 opening, Marina Bay Sands has become the symbol of Singapore, rising from the southern bank of Marina Bay against a sea of green. Costing US$5.6 billion, the three 55-storey towers resembling propped-up playing cards are designed by Israeli-born Moshe Safdie. The complex includes a hotel, a casino, a theatre, an exhibition hall, a mall and a museum.

VICHY DEAL/SHUTTERSTOCK

Skypark Observation Deck

The 1.2-hectare **Sands SkyPark Observation Deck** *(adult/child from S$35/31; 10am-10pm)* floats like a massive ship grounded atop the hotel's three towers (pictured). While its famous infinity pool is just for hotel guests, the deck is open to the public and has dramatic vistas across the Singapore skyline.

Spectra – a Water & Light Show

Every night, Marina Bay Sands razzle-dazzles with a free water-and-light show, **Spectra** *(8pm & 9pm daily, also 10pm Fri & Sat)*. The 15-minute show features dancing fountain jets, video projections and laser displays, backed by an orchestral soundtrack.

ArtScience Museum

Fronting Marina Bay is the **ArtScience Museum** *(adult/child from $23/18; 10am-7pm)*. With 21 galleries spread over three storeys, it houses exhibitions that push the boundaries of science and technology. A must-visit is the permanent exhibition 'Future World: Where Art Meets Science', created by renowned Japanese digital-art collective teamLab.

Sampan Rides

Take a 10-minute ride along the indoor canal aboard a traditional sampan boat from 11am to 9pm *(non-peak/peak S$11/15)*. It circles the base of **Rain Oculus**, a 22m-wide acrylic bowl that collects the rainwater filling the canal.

TOP TIPS

- Enjoy similar SkyPark views for the price of a drink at rooftop bar CÉ LA VI (p50).
- Visit from Monday to Thursday for fewer crowds and cheaper entrance fees.
- After the 8pm Spectra show, cut through the hotel via the overpass to Gardens by the Bay for Garden Rhapsody at 8.45pm in the Supertree Grove.

PRACTICALITIES

- marinabaysands.com
- hours and prices vary by attraction

SINGAPORE'S TALLEST BUILDINGS

While Marina Bay Sands SkyPark is the most popular viewing deck in Singapore with its unblocked vistas, it stands just 200m high, a fair bit shorter than the 280m-tall skyscrapers found in the central business district just across the bay. The maximum height of these buildings – United Overseas Bank Plaza 1, One Raffles Place, CapitaSpring and Republic Plaza – is due to early restrictions regarding proximity to flight paths.

The current tallest building in Singapore is Guoco Tower at nearby Tanjong Pagar standing 290m high, though the future Alibaba Tower along Shenton Way is set to eclipse this record at 305m in a few years. In comparison, Singapore's highest natural peak, Bukit Timah Hill in the Central Catchment Area, is a paltry 163m high.

CHERRY-HAIZ/SHUTTERSTOCK

Sky Garden, 1-Arden (p48)

picnics and kite-flying. Chill out on the Esplanade (p44) roof terrace in between performances for the Marina Bay skyline. If you're feeling adventurous, climb up to the pavement of **Benjamin Sheares Bridge** from the Active Garden in Gardens by the Bay for views of the Kallang Basin. Finally, the Ng Teng Fong Roof Garden of the National Gallery Singapore (p52) is a great vantage point for the Padang and surrounding colonial-era structures.

DRINKING IN MARINA BAY: BEST ROOFTOP BARS

Cook & Brew: This chic gastro-bar atop Westin Singapore offers a variety of drinks with delicious grub and CBD aerial views. *hours vary Mon-Sat*

Level 33: Slurp house-brewed beer at 'the world's highest urban craft brewery' 33 storeys high, with a jaw-dropping view over Marina Bay. *noon-11pm*

CÉ LA VI: Sip cocktails and enjoy perfect panoramas from Marina Bay Sands' cantilevered rooftop bar. *hours vary*

Lantern: Stylish bar atop the Fullerton Bay Hotel is only four storeys high but offers up-close views of Marina Bay. *3pm-1am Sun-Thu, to 2am Fri & Sat*

CIRCLING THE BAY

Explore Singapore's transformation from entrepot trade hub to cutting-edge metropolis on this scenic loop around Marina Bay.

START	END	LENGTH
Merlion Park	Clifford Pier	3km; 1hr

Snap a selfie with the 1 **Merlion** (p48) statue at the mouth of the Singapore River to kick off your walk. Take in the Marina Bay skyline from the 2 **Jubilee Bridge** (p59) built to commemorate Singapore's 50th anniversary of independence in 2015.

Stroll along the waterfront of the 3 **Esplanade – Theatres on the Bay** (p44), where you might catch a free outdoor performance. Detour around the ongoing construction of the future NS Square before crossing the swirls of the 4 **Helix Bridge** (p59), an homage to DNA structure.

The lotus-shaped 5 **ArtScience Museum** (p49) is great for photos both from a distance and close up. Meander along the Marina Bay waterfront, where the Louis Vuitton and Apple stores seemingly float on water, and enjoy the skyscraper views of the CBD from this side of the bay.

Pop into the 6 **Red Dot Design Museum** as you near the Marina Bay Financial District. The 7 **Promontory** area often hosts festivals and exhibitions with the bay as backdrop.

Pass through the old 8 **Customs House**, once home to the harbour police and now a refined dining destination complementing its neighbour, 9 **Fullerton Bay Hotel** (p205), where you can spend the night basking in bay views.

Finish at 10 **Clifford Pier**, a former jetty and immigrant landing point that's been transformed into a sleek restaurant.

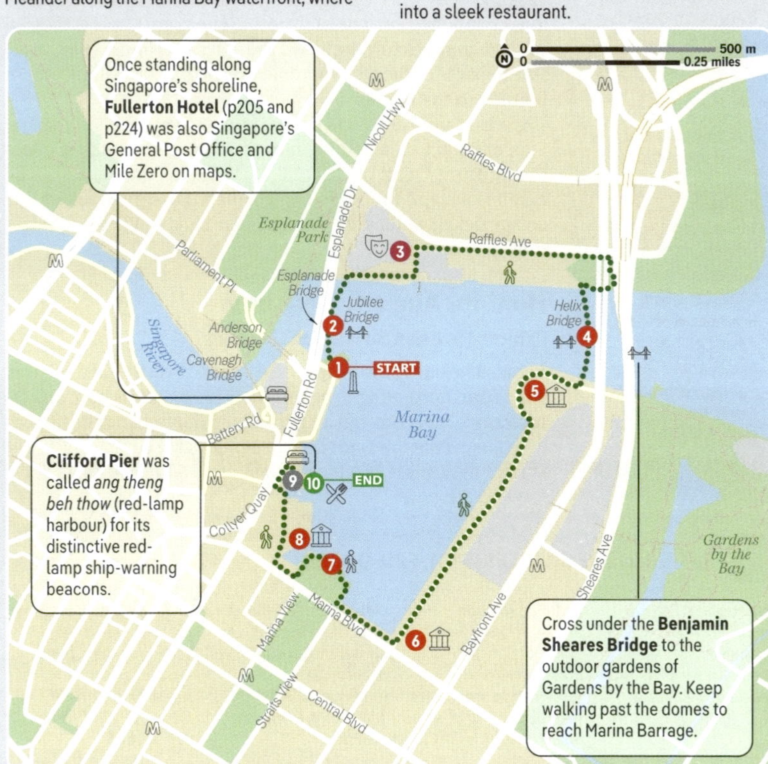

Civic District

Once the seat of colonial administration and where the British lived, the Civic District is now home to Singapore's finest cultural institutions and historic landmarks.

A HISTORICAL LANDMARK

The Asian Civilisations Museum is housed in the neoclassical Empress Place Building, designed by British architect John Frederick Adolphus McNair and completed in 1867 using Indian convict labour. For more than 100 years the building housed colonial British and then Singaporean government offices.

To the west stands a marble statue of Sir Thomas Stamford Raffles, the British East India administrator who played a key role in Singapore's history. This spot, on the north bank of the Singapore River between the Asian Civilisation Museum and Old Parliament House, marks the site where Raffles is believed to have landed on 29 January 1819.

Southeast Asian Contemporary Art

Tour the National Gallery

The S$530-million **National Gallery Singapore** *(nationalgallery.sg; adult/child S$20/15)* occupies the beautifully restored former City Hall and Old Supreme Court buildings, housing the world's largest public collection of Southeast Asian modern art with over 8000 artworks within two national monuments. Permanent exhibition 'Between Declarations and Dreams' showcases 300 artworks that trace the art history of Southeast Asia from the mid-19th century. Those travelling with kids shouldn't miss the gallery's Keppel Centre for Art Education, where kids are encouraged to interact with artworks and create their own masterpieces. There are various themed guided tours held regularly; the Back-of-House tour takes you to parts of the Old Supreme Court that are usually out of bounds to the public.

Much of the National Gallery premises are free to explore – an excellent viewpoint can be found at the sheltered open-air **Padang Deck** on Level 6 overlooking the Padang. The exhibitions and tours require a gallery pass; prebook online or buy tickets at the Coleman Street & Padang Visitor Services Counters on Level 1.

Hunt for Ancient Treasures

Explore the Asian Civilisations Museum

Perched beside the Singapore River, the **Asian Civilisations Museum** *(nhb.gov.sg/acm; adult/child S$15/10)* is both an ethnographic museum and an art gallery showcasing the history of Asian peoples and cultures. Its remarkably curated galleries, spread over three levels, are home to Southeast Asia's most

EATING IN THE CIVIC DISTRICT: FINE DINING

Whitegrass: French techniques meet quality Japanese ingredients for award-winning fusion food. *noon-2.30pm & 6-10.30pm Tue-Sat* $$$

National Kitchen by Violet Oon: Taste Singapore's finest Peranakan flavours in a restaurant helmed by a local celebrity chef. *noon-3pm & 6-10.30pm* $$$

Odette: Elegant plates of modern French cuisine served amid sophisticated decor in the National Gallery. *noon-1.15pm Tue-Sat & 6.30-8.15pm daily* $$$

JAAN By Kirk Westaway: Michelin-star venue serving elevated British cuisine against the Marina Bay skyline. *11.45am-2.30pm & 6.30-10.30pm Tue-Sat* $$$

SIGHTS
1 Arts House
2 Asian Civilisations Museum
3 CHIJMES
4 National Gallery Singapore
5 Padang
6 Raffles Landing Site
7 St Andrew's Cathedral

SLEEPING
8 LYF Funan

EATING
9 Brasserie Astoria Singapore
10 Bricolage
11 Drinks & Co Grill & Cocktails
12 Godmama
13 JAAN By Kirk Westaway
14 National Kitchen by Violet Oon
15 New Ubin Seafood CHIJMES
16 Odette
17 Rempapa
18 Whitegrass

DRINKING & NIGHTLIFE
19 ANTI:DOTE
20 SKAI Bar

ENTERTAINMENT
21 Victoria Theatre & Concert Hall

LAWN OF LEGACY

The 4.3-hectare **Padang** (Malay for 'field') may appear unassuming, but it's steeped in Singapore's history. One of the oldest public recreation grounds, this expansive green field has witnessed pivotal events, from the jubilant victory parade after Japan's WWII surrender in 1945 to the celebrations marking Singapore's merger with Malaysia in 1963. Gazetted as a National Monument in 2021, the Padang today hosts regular sporting events – it's home to the Singapore Cricket Club and Singapore Recreation Club – and Singapore's National Day Parade during milestone years. It's flanked by the neoGothic **St Andrew's Cathedral**, the **Arts House** (formerly the Parliament House and now an arts centre) and the Victoria Theatre & Concert Hall (formerly the Town Hall). Get the best view from the top floor of the National Gallery Singapore.

comprehensive collection of pan-Asian treasures. Objects on display tell stories of the exchange of ideas that flowed from international commerce and maritime trade.

Highlights include the Tang Shipwreck collection, which features over 60,000 Tang dynasty ceramics that sank more than 1000 years ago off the shores of Sumatra; its cargo gives insights into the history of regional trade. Don't miss the ginger-root-form teapot in the Chinese Ceramics collection, modelled upon a tall piece of ginger growing from the earth.

Timeless Tunes in Historic Halls

Catch a performance at Victoria Theatre & Concert Hall

Enjoy concerts, recitals and music performances at Singapore's oldest performing arts venue. The regal **Victoria Theatre & Concert Hall** *(artshouselimited.sg/vtvch)* consists of three structures. The oldest is the Theatre section which began as the Town Hall in 1862, while the 600-seat Concert Hall was added in 1902 to commemorate Queen Victoria's passing. Completed a few years later is the 54m-high **Clock Tower**, linking the two buildings. Stand in the atrium and observe the two distinctly different architectural styles between the theatre and concert hall on either side.

Adventurous folk can sign up for the **Clock Tower Climb** *(S$50)*, a tour where you ascend rickety ladders for a closer look at the five bells that chime the familiar Westminster tune hourly at the top of the tower. You must be 18 or older to join the tour.

THE ORIGINAL RAFFLES

A bronze statue of Sir Thomas Stamford Raffles, British colonial founder of Singapore, stands in front of the Victoria Theatre & Concert Hall. Commissioned in 1919, this is the original version of the more photographed **marble statue** (p52) along the Singapore River.

EATING & DRINKING IN THE CIVIC DISTRICT: OUR PICKS

ANTI:DOTE: This swanky bar in the lobby of the Fairmont Hotel serves 'Cure-all' cocktails and an elegant afternoon tea in a drawer chest. *8.30am-1am*

SKAI Bar: Sip and savour the views through floor-to-ceiling glass from the 70th floor of Swissotel the Stamford. *5pm-midnight Sun-Thu, to 1am Fri & Sat*

Brasserie Astoria Singapore: Elegant, intimate setting with an extensive wine list – perfect for pre-concert drinks at Victoria Theatre. *hours vary*

Drinks & Co Grill & Cocktails: Lively bar at CHIJMES with happy hour till 9pm. Try the Singapore sling. *noon-11pm Sun-Thu, to midnight Fri & Sat*

HIT1912/SHUTTERSTOCK

CHIJMES

A Night Out at CHIJMES

Convent school turned nightlife hub

CHIJMES *(chijmes.com.sg)*, pronounced 'chimes', is a historic complex now housing heaving bars with live music and upscale restaurants. It's open to the public and free to visit – wander through its beautiful fountain-lit courtyards and admire the intricately designed metal staircases and stained-glass windows designed by the renowned Irish architect George Coleman.

Dating back to 1854, the building was originally a convent school named CHIJ (Convent of the Holy Infant Jesus), established by an order of French Catholic nuns. **CHIJMES Hall** was the former Gothic chapel, though now it's a venue for parties and weddings, most notably featured in the 2018 movie *Crazy Rich Asians*. The main building after you enter the complex, **Caldwell House**, is one of the oldest surviving buildings in Singapore. The other buildings play host to restaurants and live-music bars.

BEST GUIDED TOURS AROUND DOWNTOWN

Singapore River Cruise: An old-school wooden bumboat (motorised sampan) takes you on a journey down the Singapore River from Clarke Quay to Marina Bay.

Singapore DUCKtours: Drive around the Civic District on a remodelled WWII amphibious Vietnamese warcraft before taking to the waters of Marina Bay.

Free Walking Tours: Indie Singapore and Monster Day Tours offer free guided walks (tip as you like!) every week exploring the Singapore River and downtown.

Cycling Tours: Jump on a bike with Let's Go Tour Singapore and GoBike Singapore for a cycling tour around various downtown districts.

Fullerton Heritage Tours: The Fullerton Hotel offers free public walking tours of its historical building and other heritage waterfront properties like Clifford Pier and Customs House.

EATING IN THE CIVIC DISTRICT: LOCAL FAVOURITES

Bricolage: Cosy cafe at the Arts House with creative plant-forward dishes and rotating 'pay as you want' set lunches. *11.30am-7pm Thu-Sun* **$$**

Godmama: Contemporary Peranakan fare and fusion cocktails, like *babi assam* (tamarind stew pork belly) and ginger-flower martini. *hours vary* **$$**

New Ubin Seafood CHIJMES: Specialising in *kampong*-style seafood, this homegrown brand delivers elevated local fare. *11pm-1am* **$$**

Rempapa: Casual eatery by a notable Eurasian chef offering nostalgic Singaporean flavours and comfort food. *8am-6pm Wed-Sun* **$$**

The Quays

The stretch of Singapore River before it flows into Marina Bay houses the Quays (Boat Quay, Clarke Quay and Robertson Quay), three distinctive areas transformed from grimy warehouses into bustling nightlife and entertainment districts.

BOAT QUAY'S EVOLUTION

Boat Quay, near the original mouth of the Singapore River, was the commercial heart of early Singapore and remained an important economic area into the 1960s. Its crescent-shaped bend resembling a carp belly, considered auspicious in Chinese geomancy, attracted traders and merchants. For over 150 years, bustling *godowns* (warehouses) and bumboats lined the banks of the quay. Over time, the river became extremely polluted, so the government moved cargo services to a facility in Pasir Panjang. A cleanup campaign between 1977 and 1987 turned the river into what it is today, and Boat Quay is now a conserved heritage district.

Sailing Through History

Cruise down the Singapore River

The **Singapore River Cruise** *(rivercruise.com.sg; adult/child S$28/18)* is an easy way to explore the downtown area without too much effort. A 40-minute ride on a bumboat (motorised sampan) that used to transport goods along the river will take you from Clarke Quay jetty through Boat Quay and make a loop around Marina Bay before returning to Clarke Quay. Sit in the open-air section at the back of the boat for the best views. Lines form around sunset and in the evenings when temperatures are cooler.

Book online or at the Clarke Quay jetty; pay extra if you'd like to catch the Marina Bay Sands' Spectra (p49) sound-and-light show from the water *(adult/child S$42/28)*; boat departures are at 7.30pm and 8.30pm, half an hour before the show.

Singapore's Oldest Places of Worship

Hidden historical shrines in the city

While downtown Singapore is dominated by soaring skyscrapers, some of its oldest places of worship still stand quietly among them. In the shadow of CapitaSpring is the charming **Yueh Hai Ching Temple** *(thengeeannkongsi.com.sg)*, a Taoist temple built in the 1820s by Teochew immigrants from southern China and dedicated to the sea goddess Mazu and patron deity Xuan Tian Shang Di. Take a closer look at the intricate porcelain figurines along its roof, depicting animals and scenes from folklore. It's also a popular place to pray for love.

DRINKING IN THE QUAYS: BEST BARS IN BOAT QUAY

BYD by 1826: Sample fusion fare, craft beers and cocktails at this concept eatery by the Chinese EV company. *11.30am-11pm Sun-Thu, to midnight Fri & Sat*

Dragon Chamber: This Asian-inspired speakeasy has a 93-seat space that contrasts strikingly with its humble fridge entrance. *11am-3pm & 5-10.30pm Tue-Sat*

Quay House: Asian tapas place with dishes and drink flavours influenced by Boat Quay's history as a maritime hub for trading spices. *11.30am-11pm Mon-Sat*

Offtrack: Ranked one of Asia's 50 best bars in 2024; the music is as key as the pan-Asian food and classic cocktails. *6pm-midnight Mon-Thu, 5pm-1am Fri & Sat*

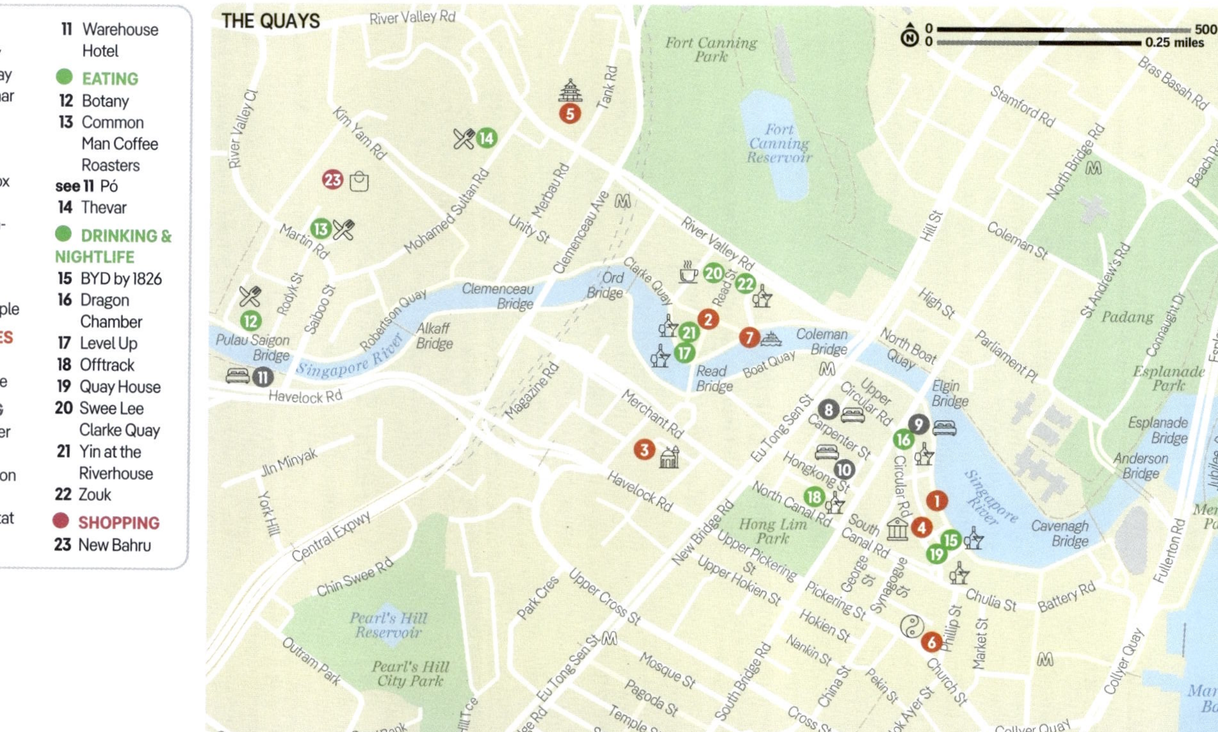

SIGHTS
1 Boat Quay
2 Clarke Quay
3 Masjid Omar Kampong Melaka
4 Singapore Musical Box Museum
5 Sri Thendayuthapani Temple
6 Yueh Hai Ching Temple

ACTIVITIES
7 Singapore River Cruise

SLEEPING
8 21 Carpenter
9 Heritage Collection on Boat Quay
10 KINN Habitat
11 Warehouse Hotel

EATING
12 Botany
13 Common Man Coffee Roasters
see 11 Pó
14 Thevar

DRINKING & NIGHTLIFE
15 BYD by 1826
16 Dragon Chamber
17 Level Up
18 Offtrack
19 Quay House
20 Swee Lee Clarke Quay
21 Yin at the Riverhouse
22 Zouk

SHOPPING
23 New Bahru

CLARKE QUAY'S COLOURFUL COMEBACK

Nowhere in Singapore reflects the island's transition better than lively Clarke Quay (named after Singapore's second colonial governor, Sir Andrew Clarke). In the 1800s it was the destination for goods barges: the area was colloquially known as *cha jung tau* ('harbour for ships carrying firewood' in the Teochew dialect). After the bumboats moved to a new facility in Pasir Panjang, the warehouses and shophouses here were abandoned and the quay fell silent. Gazetted as a heritage district in 1989, the quay became the biggest conservation project along the Singapore River. Historic warehouses were painted in rainbow hues and the area became an open-air pedestrian precinct brimming with nightclubs, hip-hop joints and salsa bars.

Near Clarke Quay lies Singapore's oldest surviving religious building, **Masjid Omar Kampong Melaka** *(masjidomarkampongmelaka.org.sg)*. Built in 1820 by Yemeni-Arab merchant Syed Omar bin Ali Aljunied, the mosque served the early Muslim community that lived in the village along the Singapore River. Now a gazetted national monument, it remains a place of worship and remembrance. Syed Omar and his descendants are buried in its grounds.

Sri Thendayuthapani Temple *(sttemple.com)*, built in 1859 at the western foot of Fort Canning Hill, is also known as the Chettiar's Temple after the Chettiars, an Indian subgroup from Tamil Nadu who were early Singapore's main moneylenders. Today, the temple is best known as the endpoint of the annual **Thaipusam** procession (held in January or February), with devotees carrying *kavadis* (heavy metal frames decorated with peacock feathers, fruit and flowers), often attached to their bodies with hooks or skewers, as acts of faith and penance.

Unboxing Antique Tunes

Singapore's history revealed through music boxes

The **Singapore Musical Box Museum** *(singaporemusicalboxmuseum.org; adult/child S$20/12)* showcases a private collection of over 40 antique music boxes, some more than 200 years old. Peer into the inner workings of the small basic boxes all the way through to cupboard-sized, multi-instrument music makers. One was even destined for the *Titanic* but missed the boat. The museum also highlights Singapore's lesser-known link to the craft, with local artisans taught to make and mend these boxes – look out for the rare Singapore-made piece on display.

Guided tours take about an hour; bookings are essential. The museum is closed on Mondays.

New Bahru School Vibes

Creative cluster in a former school

A short walk from dining district Robertson Quay, **New Bahru** *(newbahru.com)* – Bahru also means 'new' in Malay – is a trendy lifestyle destination occupying the restored grounds of the former Nan Chiau High School. Heritage meets hip in this creative cluster, with old classrooms and hallways in the

DRINKING IN THE QUAYS: COOL HANGOUTS IN CLARKE QUAY

YIN at the Riverhouse: Chinese tapas and sophisticated cocktails housed in Singapore's oldest Chinese mansion. *6-11pm Wed-Sat*

Zouk: Singapore's best-known club with three main rooms (Zouk, Capital and Phuture) is for dancing the night away. *hours vary*

Swee Lee Clarke Quay: A music lover's dream with music retail, vinyl listening stations and live music, along with a chill cafe and bar. *11am-9pm*

Level Up: Nostalgia hits hard at this retro-themed bar filled with old-school arcade games and live music. *5pm-1am Sun-Thu, to 3am Fri & Sat*

SINGAPORE RIVER'S NOTABLE BRIDGES

Uncover Singapore's riverfront history through its iconic bridges on this scenic walk from Marina Bay to Robertson Quay.

START	END	LENGTH
Helix Bridge	Alkaff Bridge	4km; 1.5hr

Begin at the striking ❶ **Helix Bridge** near the ArtScience Museum. Look out towards the coast to spot Bayfront Bridge and the towering Benjamin Sheares Bridge, both buzzing with road traffic.

Head north to the Esplanade – Theatres on the Bay and cross the scenic ❷ **Jubilee Bridge**, built in 2015 to mark Singapore's 50th anniversary of independence. Walk under the adjacent Esplanade Bridge to escape traffic and follow the Singapore River inland.

Near the Fullerton Hotel, stroll across elegant ❸ **Anderson Bridge**, closed to regular traffic but famously part of the F1 Grand Prix race track. Continue towards the Asian Civilisations Museum and cross ❹ **Cavenagh Bridge**, Singapore's oldest surviving bridge, built in the 1860s. Follow the curve of Boat Quay to ❺ **Elgin Bridge** – it's a gazetted national monument together with Anderson and Cavenagh Bridges.

Admire the murals beneath Elgin and neighbouring ❻ **Coleman Bridge** before continuing along the riverbank past Central Mall, with views of Clarke Quay's colourful heritage buildings. Cross the pedestrianised ❼ **Read Bridge** into the heart of Clarke Quay.

Keep west along the river, passing ❽ **Ord Bridge** and the underpass beneath ❾ **Clemenceau Bridge**, until you arrive at Robertson Quay. End your walk at the vibrant ❿ **Alkaff Bridge**, and treat yourself to a riverside drink in this relaxed dining enclave.

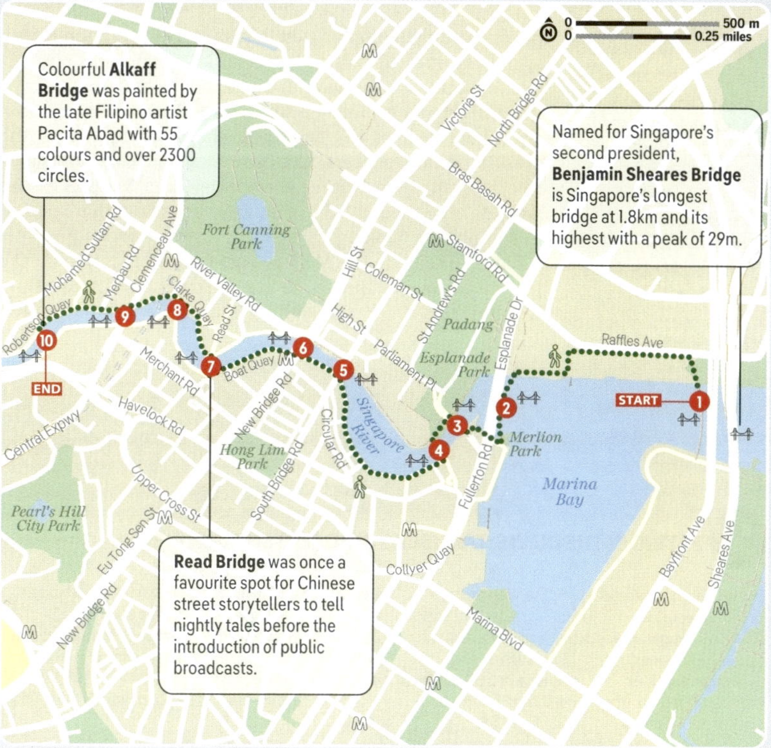

Colourful **Alkaff Bridge** was painted by the late Filipino artist Pacita Abad with 55 colours and over 2300 circles.

Named for Singapore's second president, **Benjamin Sheares Bridge** is Singapore's longest bridge at 1.8km and its highest with a peak of 29m.

Read Bridge was once a favourite spot for Chinese street storytellers to tell nightly tales before the introduction of public broadcasts.

KID-FRIENDLY CULTURAL ACTIVITIES

Children's Museum Singapore (p67): Singapore's first kid-centric museum, complete with immersive shows and interactive displays.

National Gallery Singapore (p52): Kids' imaginations run free at the Keppel Centre for Art Education, a wonderful corner dedicated to nurturing children's creativity.

ArtScience Museum (p49): This high-tech interactive museum impresses both tots and teens with its roaming exhibitions of digital and futuristic displays.

Asian Civilisations Museum (p52): ACM & Me is an engaging, space with lots of hands-on activities to encourage creativity and participation.

Civil Defence Heritage Gallery (p61): Explore the firefighting history of Singapore through interactive exhibits and displays of vintage fire engines, set in the Central Fire Station.

HUNTERGOL HP/SHUTTERSTOCK

Alkaff Bridge (p59), Robertson Quay

peachy orange complex now housing over 40 homegrown brands, from local fashion labels to skilled craftspeople, perfect for picking up a made-in-Singapore keepsake.

Highlight venues include **MAKE by Ginlee** *(makestudio.sg)*, where visitors can customise their own bags with the brand's signature pleats; **Crafune** *(crafune.com)* workshops to craft your own leather accessories; and **Woods in the Books** *(woodsinthebooks.sg)*, a local bookshop that specialises in picture books.

To get here, take the MRT to Fort Canning Station on the Downtown Line or the free shuttle bus every 30 minutes (11am to 9pm) from Pan Pacific Suites Orchard along Somerset Rd.

EATING IN THE QUAYS: OUR PICKS IN ROBERTSON QUAY

Botany: All-day riverside dining; delectable dishes with vegan and gluten-free options taste as good as they look. *9am-10pm Mon-Fri, from 8.30am Sat & Sun* $$

Pó: The Warehouse Hotel's restaurant serves reimagined local comfort foods such as seafood porridge or beef rendang. *7-10.30am, noon-3pm & 6-10.30pm* $$

Common Man Coffee Roasters: The flagship outlet of this household coffee name has exceptional brews alongside savoury brunch meals. *7.30am-6pm* $$

Thevar: Modern Indian cuisine combining European techniques with the flavours of the Malay peninsula. *6-11pm Tue-Sat & noon-3pm Fri & Sat* $$$

Bras Basah

One of Singapore's oldest districts, Bras Basah was once designated as a European Quarter but grew into an unexpectedly diverse community. Today, it's the city's vibrant arts and heritage district, rich in history and culture.

Dive Deep into Singapore's Past

Visit the National Museum of Singapore

It might be the nation's oldest museum – dating back to 1887 – but there's nothing stuffy about the **National Museum of Singapore** *(NMS; nhb.gov.sg/nationalmuseum; adult/child S$24/18)*. Underneath its 19th-century colonial exterior is a high-tech institute that uses cutting-edge multimedia to take you on a journey through Singapore's short but action-packed history.

Spanning six centuries, the permanent exhibition **Singapore History Gallery** on Level 1 charts the development of the island from the time of the settlement's founding as Singapura through its role as a Crown colony to its WWII experience, when it was known as Syonan-To. While it's temporarily closed for upgrading till October 2026, you can check out the special exhibit **Once Upon A Tide**, offering a look at 700 years of Singapore's maritime and trade history with hands-on activities. The Glass Rotunda on Level 2 presents **Singapore Odyssea: A Journey Through Time**, a new immersive multimedia experience. An RFID wristband pairs you with a digital native animal companion that guides you through Singapore's evolving seascape and introduces mythical creatures from regional legends.

Get Snap-Happy on Hill Street

Admire Singapore's architectural pin-ups

Stroll along Hill St at the southern foot of Fort Canning Park to snap photos of some of Singapore's most striking architecture. Dating back to 1909, the **Central Fire Station** sports a distinctive red-and-white brick facade, a characteristic of what is commonly known as 'blood-and-bandage' architecture. The 'blood' points to the exposed red bricks on the facade, while the 'bandage' refers to the plaster layovers that are painted white.

Still an active station, this national monument also houses the **Civil Defence Heritage Gallery** *(scdf.gov.sg)*. Recounting the firefighting history of Singapore, on display are various

THE EVOLUTION OF SINGAPORE'S OLDEST MUSEUM

The National Museum of Singapore is the nation's oldest museum. Originally built as the Raffles Library and Museum, its early collections focused on natural history specimens from the Malayan region, now housed in the Lee Kong Chian Natural History Museum. Renamed as the National Museum upon independence in the 1960s, the focus shifted to documenting Singapore's culture and history.

This elegant neo-Palladian building has been the regal home of the National Museum for over 120 years and designated a National Monument in 1992. It underwent major redevelopment from 2003 to 2006 to restore the complex to its former glory – today the superb neoclassical wing boasts a breathtaking rotunda adorned with 50 panels of stained glass.

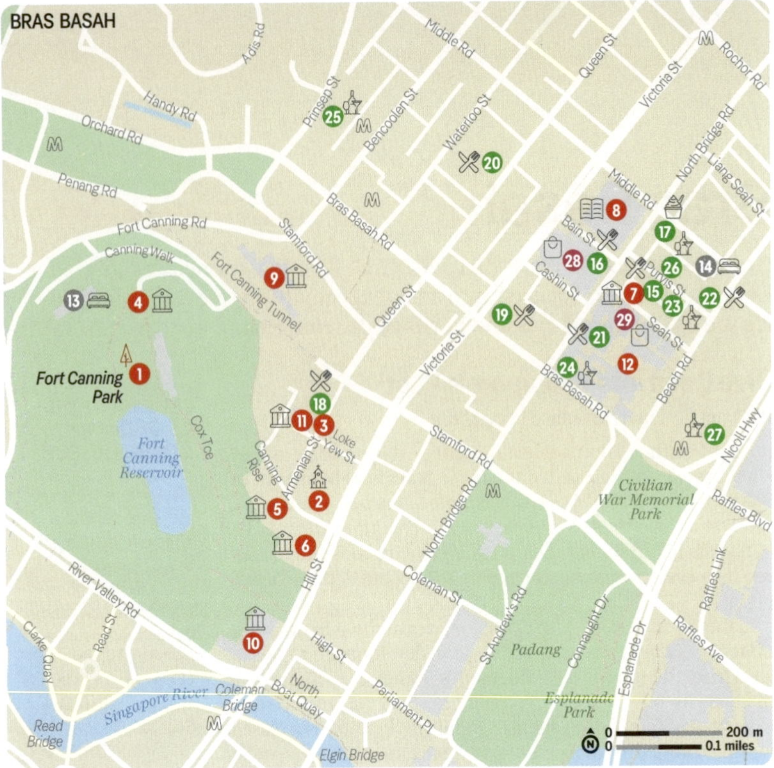

BRAS BASAH

HIGHLIGHTS

1 Fort Canning Park

SIGHTS

2 Armenian Apostolic Church of St Gregory the Illuminator
3 Armenian Street
4 Battlebox
see 6 Central Fire Station
5 Children's Museum Singapore
6 Civil Defence Heritage Gallery
7 MINT Museum of Toys
8 National Library
9 National Museum of Singapore
10 Old Hill Street Police Station
11 Peranakan Museum
12 Raffles Singapore

SLEEPING

13 Mett Singapore
see 12 Raffles Singapore
14 ST Signature Bugis Middle

EATING

15 Garibaldi
16 Narrative Coffee Stand
17 Tom's Palette
18 True Blue Cuisine
19 Wah Lok
20 Waterloo Coffee
21 Yi by Jereme Leung
22 YY Kafei Dian

DRINKING & NIGHTLIFE

23 Draft Land Singapore
24 Long Bar
25 Mama Diam
26 Nutmeg & Clove
27 Quaich Bar Avant-Garde

SHOPPING

28 Bras Basah Complex
29 Raffles Boutique

EATING IN BRAS BASAH: OUR PICKS

True Blue Cuisine: Family-owned award-winning Peranakan restaurant right next to the Peranakan Museum. *11.30am-2pm & 5.30-9.30pm Mon-Sat* **$$**

Wah Lok: For over 30 years, this classic restaurant has been offering stellar Cantonese fare like roast meats, live seafood and delicious dim sum. *hours vary* **$$**

Yi by Jereme Leung: Modern takes on traditional Chinese dishes by a Singaporean chef, including sliced cucumber and poached sea whelk. *11.30am-2pm & 6-9.30pm* **$$**

Garibaldi: At this 20-plus-year-old Italian restaurant, the *osso buco* (braised veal cheek) will keep you coming back for more. *noon-2.30pm & 6-10.30pm* **$$$**

types of fire engines, including the first horse-drawn steam fire engine to arrive in Singapore back in 1884. The interactive stations are great for kids to learn about what firefighters and first responders experience while they're on duty. The station runs free hour-long guided tours; book on the website. The gallery is closed on Mondays.

Just a few metres south is the photogenic **Old Hill Street Police Station**, which often appears in tourism brochures thanks to its eye-catching neo-Renaissance design and rainbow-hued shutters. When it was constructed in 1934, the six-storey building was the biggest and grandest of its kind in Malaya, with over 280 living quarters. During the Japanese occupation it was a notorious interrogation centre. The former police station is now the government office for the Ministry of Information, Communications and Arts.

Relish the Singapore of Yesteryear

Colonial grandeur at the Raffles Hotel

If there's one building in Singapore that has largely remained the same (at least on the outside) since the city's colonial days, it's the **Raffles Singapore** *(raffles.com)*. Built in 1887 as a 10-room hotel fronting the beach (long gone thanks to land reclamation), the island's oldest and most iconic place to stay has undergone just two restorations in its long history – notable in a city where change is the only constant.

Although its resplendent lobby is only accessible to hotel and restaurant guests, this slumber palace is worth a quick visit for its magnificent ivory frontage, famous Sikh doormen and hushed tropical grounds. Whether through its gardens or popping into one of its bars, a visit here offers the chance to time-travel. Guided heritage tours are available for visitors twice a day *(45min; 11.30am & 5.30pm)* and can be booked online *(from S$24)*.

The **Long Bar** is where the hotel's famous Singapore sling was first concocted by bartender Ngiam Tong Boon in 1915 – and is still sold today. It's also the only place you're allowed to sweep your peanut shells onto the floor, a practice that dates back to the 1920s Malayan plantation that the decor is inspired by. The bar only takes walk-in guests so if it gets too crowded, you can pick up Singapore sling and other Raffles-related souvenirs at the **Raffles Boutique** along Seah St.

RAFFLES THROUGH THE YEARS

The Raffles was the brainchild of the Sarkies brothers, immigrants from Armenia and proprietors of two other grand colonial hotels: the Strand in Yangon and the Eastern & Oriental in Penang. One of its most famous stories is about one of the last tigers killed in Singapore – pursued at the hotel and finally shot in the Bar & Billiard Room.

A shabby relic by the 1970s, the property dodged the wrecking ball in 1987 with National Monument designation, reopening in 1991 after a S$160-million facelift. It underwent a two-year major renovation and reopened in 2019 with revamped suites and the addition of technological devices to every room. Thankfully, the hotel's neo-Renaissance facade – and the gravel driveway that once welcomed horse-drawn carriages – have been left untouched.

DRINKING IN BRAS BASAH: OUR PICKS

Nutmeg & Clove: Award-winning bar on Purvis St reinterpreting classic food and cocktails with a modern Singaporean twist. *5pm-midnight*

Mama Diam: A speakeasy bar recalling a traditional *mama diam* (family-run convenience store). *4-10.30pm Sun-Thu, to midnight Fri & Sat*

Draft Land Singapore: Local branch of a popular drinking hole renowned for myriad cocktails on tap. *4pm-late Tue-Fri, from 2pm Sat & Sun*

Quaich Bar Avant-Garde: The definitive bar for all things whisky has more than 500 varieties from all over the world. *5pm-1am Sun-Thu, to 2am Fri & Sat*

TOP EXPERIENCE

Fort Canning Park

Spend a few hours exploring the historical attractions of Fort Canning Park. Over the centuries, this hill has served as the royal grounds of 14th-century Malay kings, the seat of British colonial power, and a key site of Singapore's WWII fight. Today, Fort Canning's lush trails, archaeological sites and preserved structures showcase Singapore's transformation over the centuries.

PHANTOMM/SHUTTERSTOCK

TOP TIPS

- A spiral staircase (pictured above) in the park's north is a popular Instagram spot; you may have to wait in line.
- The Foothills on the south side have galleries and eateries, across the road from Clarke Quay.
- Skip the stairs and access the park from the National Museum's 3rd-storey back entrance.

Learn about Pre-Colonial Singapore

The **Artisan's Garden** is one of Singapore's last archaeological-dig sites, where researchers found evidence of an ancient artisan's workshop dating back to the 14th century. The two-storey **Fort Canning Heritage Gallery** on top of the hill is free to visit and offers excellent context to the gardens and history in the rest of the park.

Botanical Experimentation

A picturesque Gothic Gate leads to a grass slope called **Fort Canning Green**, where the stairs are lined with tombstones of a former Christian cemetery. The grounds of the nearby **Spice Garden** were once part of Singapore's first attempt at a botanical garden (and zoo) and showcase plants that the British tried to cultivate, including cash crops like nutmeg and cloves.

Delve into WWII Bunkers

Take an audio tour of the **Battlebox** *(battlebox.sg)*, delving into the depths of this bomb-proof bunker built into Fort Canning Hill. Wander the eerie underground maze filled with life-size mannequins and dioramas recreating the morning when Singapore fell to invading Japanese forces. Admission is free but bookings are required. An enhanced ticket *(adult/child $20/15)* gives access to two 270-degree projection mapping rooms for an immersive experience of this pivotal historical moment.

PRACTICALITIES

- nparks.gov.sg
- free • 24hr

TOILETROOM/SHUTTERSTOCK

MINT Museum of Toys

A Trip Down Memory Lane

Get nostalgic at the MINT Museum of Toys

MINT may be a museum of toys, but it's really designed for nostalgic parents rather than kids – in fact, **MINT** *(emint.com; adult/child S$30/20)* actually stands for Moment of Imagination and Nostalgia with Toys. Founded by toy collector Chang Yang Fa in 2007, this four-storey building houses his personal collection of more than 50,000 items (around 8000 of which are on display). The toys hail from 40 countries and date as far back as the 1840s; they run the gamut from rare *Flash Gordon* comics to original Mickey Mouse dolls. Beyond the toys, the permanent collection includes two galleries devoted to vintage enamel signs.

Consider paying a little extra for the 'Around the World in 60 Minutes' guided tour to get more context to the displays. There's also a small gift shop selling replica tin toys and old-school games. The museum is closed on Mondays.

A HILL BY ANY NAME

Fort Canning Hill has carried many names over the centuries. Its earliest known name, Bukit Larangan (Forbidden Hill), marked it as a sacred place linked to ancient Malay royalty. When the British arrived in 1819, Sir Stamford Raffles recognised its strategic value and renamed it Government Hill, building the Governor's House at its peak in 1822. At the time, the summit enjoyed an unblocked view of the Singapore River's mouth and the port below. In the 1860s, the hill was reshaped into a defensive fort and renamed Fort Canning after Governor-General Charles John Canning. Though fitted with cannons and fortified walls, it never saw battle and parts of the fort were later demolished. Its underground bunkers housed the British army in the lead-up to WWII.

EATING IN BRAS BASAH: BEST SPOTS FOR A SNACK

Narrative Coffee Stand: A nook in the Bras Basah Complex for those who love their espresso and pour-overs. *8am-5pm Mon-Fri, from 9am Sat & Sun* $

Tom's Palette: House-made ice-cream shop best known for its rotation of innovative flavours like white-chocolate *nori* (Japanese seaweed). *hours vary* $

Waterloo Coffee: Home-based cafe at Waterloo Centre that serves speciality coffee and matcha beverages in cool transparent cans. *8am-9pm* $

YY Kafei Dian: Old-school *kopitiam* (coffeeshop) for homestyle Hainanese fare like the soft toasted *kaya* buns. *7.30am-7pm Mon-Fri, from 8am Sat & Sun* $

FESTIVE TIMES TO VISIT

Singapore Art Week: This visual feast in late January sees a slew of exhibitions and art fairs across most art museums and galleries nationwide.

Singapore Heritage Festival: In late May, expect workshops and other activities at the major heritage institutions in Bras Basah and across the island.

iLight Singapore: Larger-than-life light art installations set Marina Bay and the downtown precincts aglow in this annual festival in June.

Singapore Night Festival: Highlight of the Bras Basah precinct in late August, showcasing building projections, performances, tours and workshops after dark.

Singapore Design Week: See the best of Singapore design centred at the National Design Centre and other galleries across downtown in mid-September.

DEREKTEO/SHUTTERSTOCK

National Library

A Bibliophile's Dream

Visit Singapore's coolest library

Showered with architectural awards before it had even opened, the futuristic **National Library** *(nlb.gov.sg; free)* was designed by Malaysian architect and ecologist Ken Yeang; it's made up of two towers, linked by walkways and covered almost entirely with glass.

The upper floors offer excellent city views and house various collections alongside engaging permanent exhibitions. **The News Gallery: Beyond Headlines** on Level 11 tells Singapore's history through decades of newspaper reporting, and **Book Havens of Bras Basah** in the Immersive Room projects a nine-minute timelapse that charts the neighbourhood's transformation over the last century.

In the basement, the Central Library features the **Singapore Alcove** dedicated to local literature and culture, while young visitors will enjoy the **Children's Biodiversity Library by Singapore Oceanarium**, designed to evoke an underwater world filled with marine life.

Walk Through Time

Discover historical landmarks along Armenian St

Stretching along the eastern base of Fort Canning Park is **Armenian Street**, now a pedestrianised boulevard with several cultural institutions worth checking out.

Make your first stop at the **Peranakan Museum** *(nhb.gov.sg/peranakanmuseum; adult/child S$18/12)* to explore the rich heritage of the Peranakans – people of mixed Chinese and Malay/Indonesian heritage, largely descendants of Chinese traders who married local Malay women. Housed inside a classic Straits Settlements bungalow, the museum has the world's finest collection of Peranakan artefacts, spread out in 10 permanent galleries across three floors. A highlight is the exhibit on the traditional 12-day wedding ceremony, where intricately detailed ceremonial costumes, beautifully carved wedding beds and rare dining porcelain are on display.

PERANAKAN CULTURE

Singapore's Peranakan culture is showcased in the city's shophouses, particularly in the **Katong** (p128) neighbourhood. To imagine life inside these residences, visit **Baba House** (p78) on Neil Rd – the three-storey restored townhouse has a collection of antique furniture, textiles and ceramics.

Further south along Armenian St is the eponymous **Armenian Apostolic Church of St Gregory the Illuminator** *(armeniansinasia.org)*. Consecrated in 1836, this is the oldest church in Singapore designed by its pioneer colonial-era architect, George Coleman. The Armenians were the first Christian community to build a permanent place of worship in Singapore. The **Memorial Garden** highlights notable Armenians in Singapore's history, including Agnes Joaquim who hybridised Singapore's national flower, and the Sarkies brothers who built the Raffles Singapore hotel. The church is free to visit.

At the junction with Coleman St stands the **Children's Museum Singapore** *(heritage.sg/childrensmuseum; adult/child S$17/11)*. Housed in a former primary school built over a century ago, it may be small but it's the first museum in Singapore dedicated to visitors aged under 12. Don't miss the Hidden Chamber, an immersive theatre show in which the Captain opens his secret stash of treasure and shares stories about its origins. Tiny tots (aged two to four) can join the Play Pod, a fun area for free play, while older kids can explore the Maze of Amazement. The museum is closed on Mondays; there are four fixed time slots for entry – at 9am, 11am, 2pm and 4pm.

THE BEST OF BOOK CITY

Known as 'Book City' to older Singaporeans, the **Bras Basah Complex** is overflowing with old-school bookshops and vintage hobby stores.

Basheer Graphic Books: Cosy bookshop stocked with all types of design and graphic books.

Hungry Traveller Bookstore: Vintage bookshop focused on food and travel, with rare cookbooks, travel guides and old maps.

Art Friend: The flagship of Singapore's largest art supply shop is the go-to for artists and arts students around the district.

When I Was Four: Pick up cute Singaporean-flavoured lifestyle products as souvenirs from this Singapore design house.

Tong Tong Friendship Store: Maker of traditional Chinese clothing with bright colourful fabrics and modern styles.

Researched by Morgan Awyong

CHINATOWN, TANJONG PAGAR & THE CBD

TEMPLES, HAWKERS AND TANTALISING TIPPLES

A heritage-rich neighbourhood with some of the island's most contrasting sights, Chinatown still caters to the working class – albeit one that looks very different today.

When British administrator Stamford Raffles carved up Singapore on ethnic lines, Chinese settlers were allocated land west of the Singapore River. Life in colonial Chinatown was tough, characterised by cramped living quarters and harsh working conditions. Despite the district's name, not all of the original inhabitants were Chinese. Historic mosques and Indian temples also dot the neighbourhood's streets.

Today, heritage-listed shophouses sit beside shiny skyscrapers. Gone are the clattering rickshaws and makeshift street-food stalls, replaced by an efficient transport system, organised hawkers and vibrant street art. The area still awakens early, bustling with wet markets and *kopitiams* (coffeeshops). Evenings remain lively with hip bars, trendy restaurants and late-night LGBTIQ+ haunts.

TOP TIP

Chinatown paints the town an auspicious red preceding the Chinese New Year festivities. Enjoy lion dances and street markets. Note that most businesses shutter during the two public holiday dates.

Chinese New Year lanterns

See p205 for places to stay in Chinatown, Tanjong Pagar and the CBD.

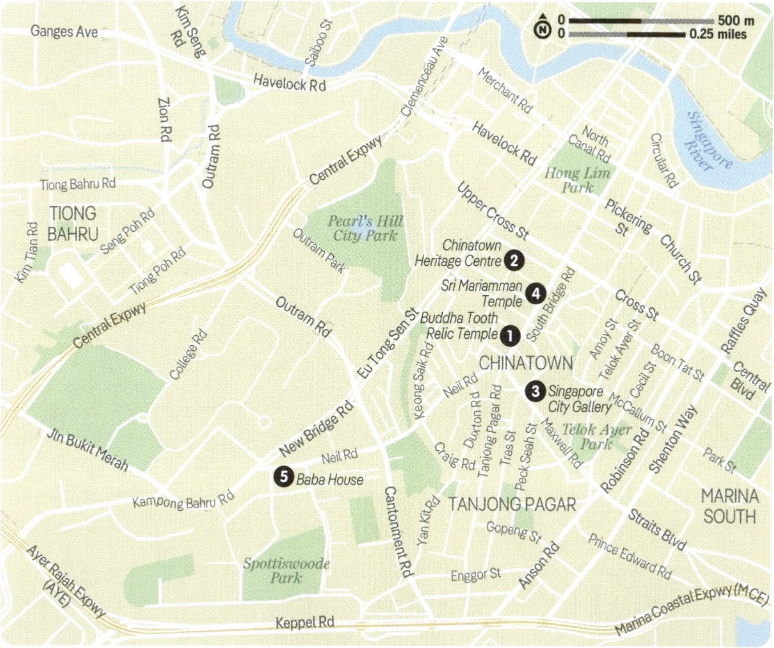

Highlights

❶ Buddha Tooth Relic Temple
Visit a striking Buddhist temple with a rooftop garden. **p72**

❷ Chinatown Heritage Centre
Explore the history of the immigrants who gave this part of town its name. **p72**

❸ Singapore City Gallery
Trace Singapore's growth and glimpse its future. **p74**

❹ Sri Mariamman Temple ▲
Admire Singapore's largest and oldest Hindu temple. **p75**

❺ Baba House
Experience old-style Peranakan life at one of Singapore's most beautiful heritage homes. **p78**

Getting Around

MRT
Well served by three MRT lines, Chinatown station brings you to the heart of the neighbourhood. Pick Telok Ayer station for the eateries and bars towards the CBD, or Maxwell for the southern spots.

Walking
Numerous shophouses offer pleasant shade with their narrow five-foot ways (roofed passageways). Walking also brings you close to the sights and smells to inspire shopping and dining decisions.

Bicycle
While hilly in parts, most of the neighbourhood is flat and easily explorable on wheels. Look out for traffic as there are no dedicated cycling paths and some roads are narrow.

FROM LEFT: FINN STOCK/SHUTTERSTOCK, R.M. NUNES/SHUTTERSTOCK

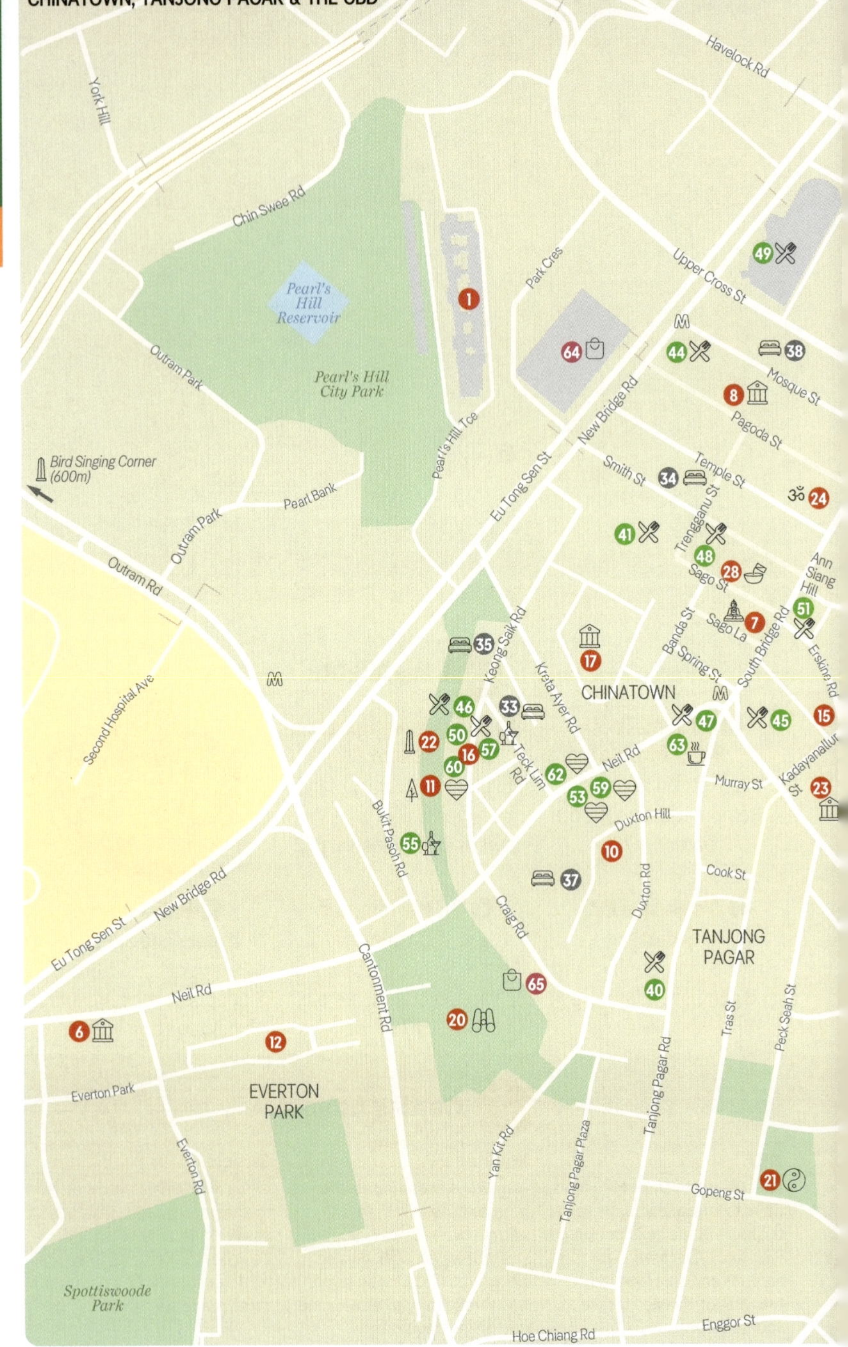
CHINATOWN, TANJONG PAGAR & THE CBD
Havelock Rd
York Hill
Chin Swee Rd
Pearl's Hill Reservoir
Pearl's Hill City Park
Park Cres
Upper Cross St
Outram Park
Mosque St
Pagoda St
New Bridge Rd
Pearl's Hill Tce
Smith St
Temple St
Bird Singing Corner (600m)
Pearl Bank
Eu Tong Sen St
Trengganu St
Outram Park
Outram Rd
Sago St
Ann Siang Hill
Keong Saik Rd
Sago La
Banda St
South Bridge Rd
Kreta Ayer Rd
Spring St
Erskine Rd
Second Hospital Ave
CHINATOWN
Teck Lim Rd
Neil Rd
Kadayanallur St
Murray St
Bukit Pasoh Rd
Duxton Hill
Cook St
Craig Rd
Duxton Rd
New Bridge Rd
Eu Tong Sen St
TANJONG PAGAR
Cantonment Rd
Neil Rd
Tras St
Peck Seah St
Tanjong Pagar Rd
Everton Park
EVERTON PARK
Yan Kit Rd
Tanjong Pagar Plaza
Everton Rd
Gopeng St
Spottiswoode Park
Hoe Chiang Rd
Enggor St

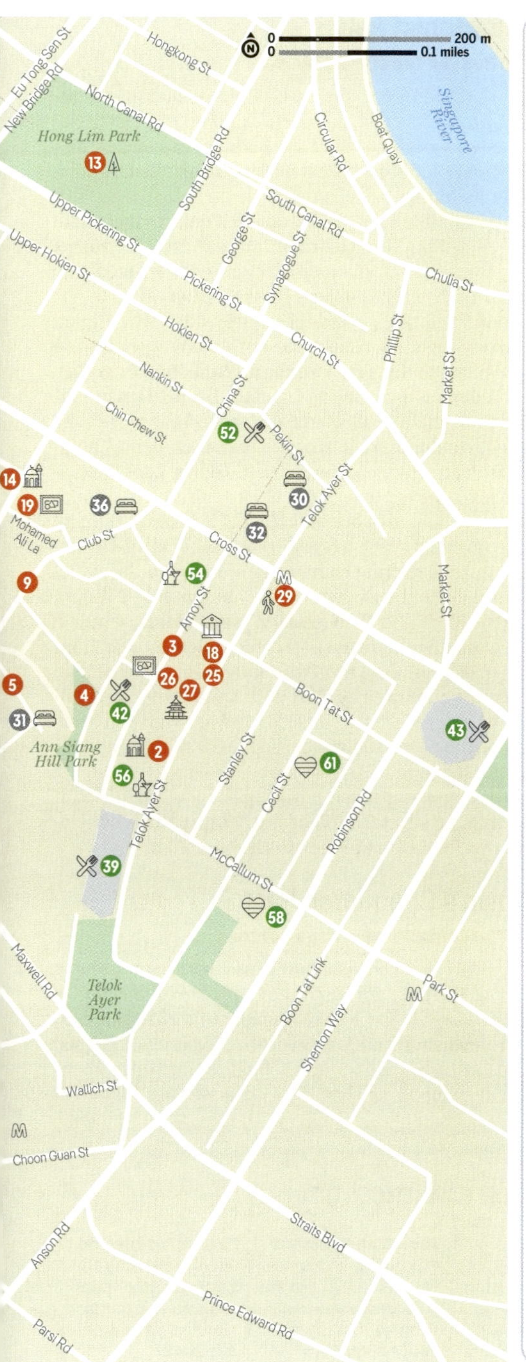

SIGHTS

1 195 PHT
2 Al-Abrar Mosque
3 Amoy Street
4 Ann Siang Hill Water Well
5 Ann Siang Road
6 Baba House
7 Buddha Tooth Relic Temple
8 Chinatown Heritage Centre
9 Club Street
10 Duxton Hill
11 Duxton Plain Park
12 Everton Park
13 Hong Lim Park
14 Jamae Mosque
15 Kada
16 Keong Saik Road
17 Kreta Ayer Heritage Gallery
18 Nagore Durgha Shrine
19 Paper Mask, Mamashop, Lion Dance Head Maker
20 Pinnacle@Duxton
21 Seng Wong Beo Temple
22 Shrine of Sharifah Rogayah
23 Singapore City Gallery
24 Sri Mariamman Temple
25 Telok Ayer Street
26 Thian Hock Keng Mural
27 Thian Hock Keng Temple

ACTIVITIES

28 Food Playground
29 Triad Trails

SLEEPING

30 Amoy Hotel
31 Ann Siang House
32 Clan Hotel
33 Claude Hotel
34 Jyu Capsule Hotel
35 Kinn Studios
36 Mercure ICON Singapore City Centre
37 Mondrian Singapore Duxton
38 Wink @ Upper Cross Street

EATING

39 Amoy Street Food Centre
40 Buko Nero
see 41 Chef Leung's Authentic Hand-Milled Rice Noodle Rolls
41 Chinatown Complex
42 Cloudstreet
see 41 Hawker Chan
see 41 Hill Street Fried Kway Teow
43 Lau Pa Sat
see 7 Lian Xin Vegetarian Restaurant
44 Lim Chee Guan
45 Maxwell Food Centre
see 41 Millennium Glutinous Rice
46 Olivia Restaurant & Lounge
47 Restaurant Born
48 Tai Chong Kok
49 Thye Moh Chan
50 Tong Ah Eating House
51 Tong Heng
52 Ya Kun Kaya Toast

DRINKING & NIGHTLIFE

53 Carnival Haus
54 Employees Only
55 Live Twice
56 Native
57 No Sleep Club
58 Rabbit's Hole
59 Restroom Bar
60 Slippery Slope
61 Sweat Club
62 Tantric
63 Tea Chapter

SHOPPING

see 41 Anthony the Spice Maker
64 People's Park Complex
65 Tong Mern Sern Antiques

HAPPENING 'HOODS

Club Street & Ann Siang Road: Chinatown's bar central, set on sloping streets where the after-work crowd flock. Rooftop joints offer atmospheric toasts.

Amoy Street & Telok Ayer Street: Riddled with temples and shrines, these streets are also a hotbed of hawker treats, hidden bars and K-centric restaurants.

Keong Saik Road: A cluster of boutique hotels in this buzzing enclave is complemented by diverse international eats and top-notch bars.

Duxton Hill: Leafy pocket with cobblestone walkways hiding posh hotels and a small lane at its top with relaxed alfresco drinking and dining.

Sacred Buddhist Relics

Admire the Buddha Tooth Relic Temple

Built in 2007, this hulking, Tang-style Chinese Buddhist **temple** *(buddhatoothrelictemple.org.sg)* is home to what is reputedly the left canine tooth of the Buddha, discovered in a collapsed stupa (Buddhist relic structure) in Mrauk U, Myanmar. While its authenticity is debated, the relic enjoys VIP status inside a 320kg solid-gold stupa in a dazzlingly ornate 4th-floor room. Flanking the room are elevated platforms where devotees and visitors may choose to sit and meditate in proximity to the sacred object. Head up afterwards to the peaceful rooftop garden – accessible only by stairs – where you can spin (clockwise only, please) the world's largest cloisonné prayer wheel inside the **Ten Thousand Buddhas Pagoda**.

More sacred relics await at the 3rd-floor **Buddhism museum**. Housing artefacts collected from around the world, the sequence charts Buddha's journey to enlightenment. The final chamber features crystalline *sariras* (relics) kept in golden reliquaries, believed to be collected after his cremation. A more eclectic mix of artwork and objects is kept on the 2nd floor, while the mezzanine has a startling set of realistic life-sized wax figures depicting eminent monks around the world.

The main floor is the liveliest, split into two halls. Facing South Bridge Rd is the **Universal Wisdom Hall**, where a stream of worshippers deposit assorted lamps as offerings, purchased from kiosks nearby. Two doorways at the sides lead into the **Hundred Dragons Hall** with a showstopping Maitreya Buddha. Carved from a single log and painted with natural pigments, the commanding presence adds to the grandeur in the ornate space.

Respectful attire is a must; cover-ups can be borrowed if needed. For some vegetarian food, visit **Lian Xin**, the temple's very own food court hidden in the basement.

Chinatown's Chequered Past

Delve into the Chinatown Heritage Centre

Explore the gritty backstory of how Chinatown came to be at the immersive **Chinatown Heritage Centre** *(chinatownheritagecentre.com.sg; S$20)*. Newly reopened in 2025 after an extensive refurbishment, it's an evocative experience housed across three restored multistorey shophouses that takes about an hour. The exhibitions shed light on numerous historical

Lady Gaga sat at fan-enshrined table 171 in 2025

EATING IN CHINATOWN: BEST HAWKER CENTRES

Chinatown Complex: The hardcore hawker experience: over 260 stalls, flooded during breakfast and lunch hours (most shuttered by 8pm). *7am-10pm* $

Amoy Street Food Centre: Office crowds flood in during lunch for traditional dishes and next-gen hawker twists. *6.30am-9pm Mon-Sat, to 6pm Sun* $

Lau Pa Sat: Magnificent wrought-iron architecture. On weekday evenings and from 3pm on weekends, Boon Tat St transforms into Satay St. *24hr* $

Maxwell Food Centre: One of Chinatown's most accessible hawker centres; a solid spot to savour hawker staples. *8am-2am* $

TOMMYTLM/SHUTTERSTOCK

Buddha Tooth Relic Temple

chapters, from the perilous voyages of Singapore's early Chinese settlers to the development of local clan associations. It extends to the opium dens and brothels that once defined the area, digging well beneath modern Chinatown's touristy veneer.

The first portion recreates shophouse living in stunning detail, illustrating the stories of fictional characters such as a clog maker through their accommodation. Personal objects and tools for their trade are placed about the cramped quarters, as if they had just left their rooms, while scripted recordings play throughout the space to mimic their presence – their disembodied voices calling out to one another in the unit. Heading up to the top floor, visitors get a glimpse of the challenges early migrants faced upon their arrival, and how clans played an integral role in forming communities. A gallery on customs and festivals follows and is a perfect photo zone. Give one of the traditional toys here a go. The final segment spotlights existing local heritage businesses and hawkers – a handy list for those wishing to explore them later. The retail store includes items from Singaporean makers and is great for some designer souvenirs.

For added exploration into the community's culture, visit the **Kreta Ayer Heritage Gallery** *(chinatown.sg/visit/kreta-ayer-heritage-gallery)*. Just a 10-minute walk away, the small and intimate collection gathers 170 cultural objects. This includes several donated personal items, from Chinese opera make-up and costumes to theatre puppets and calligraphic art. It's open on weekends and free to visit.

WHY I LOVE CHINATOWN

Morgan Awyong, Lonely Planet writer

In short – because I used to live here in the '80s! Up till the age of seven, I spent a good portion of my time with my late paternal grandmother in her shophouse along Boon Tat St. Like with many other owners in the area, the unit was returned to the government for redevelopment. The hodgepodge of small traditional businesses became capital management firms and posh dining spots, but some withstood the pressures of development. From the ornate Thian Hock Keng Temple (p76) to the bustling Amoy Street Food Centre (p80), there are traces of the past all around – often marked by a plaque. While poignant, I have to admit I enjoy the charm of today's striking juxtaposition between everyday heritage and modern gloss.

A BOHEMIAN POCKET

Tucked behind People's Park Complex, **195 PHT** *(195pearlshillterrace.com)* – for 'Pearl's Hill Terrace' – is a creative enclave of artists and businesses taking temporary residence in what was once known as the Upper Barracks. Built in 1934, the neoclassical bomb-proof bunker was a vital police headquarters overseeing the crime-ridden Chinatown area before WWII. Later gazetted as a national historic site in 2008, its reclusive location on a hill lured independent art businesses, drawn by the affordable rent. Apart from ceramic studios, niche cafes and tattoo parlours, there's an eclectic array of statues and graffiti scattered about the complex. Business hours vary greatly and some are by appointment, so it's best to check the official website before visiting.

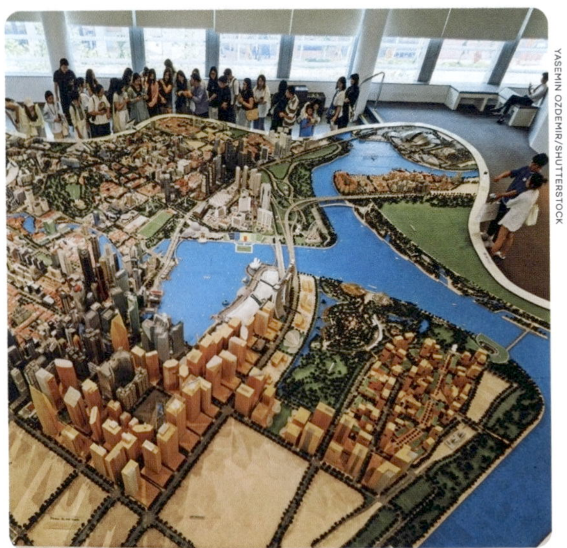

YASEMIN OZDEMIR/SHUTTERSTOCK

Central Area Model, Singapore City Gallery

Plan for the Perfect City

Tour the Singapore City Gallery

Singapore did not just happen. Every centimetre of the sparkling metropolis was painstakingly planned, and this free **gallery** *(ura.gov.sg/Corporate/Singapore-City-Gallery)* provides an insight into the city's rapid evolution and future growth. Five galleries house the permanent exhibits. The first, **Singapore; Vibrant City**, is a dramatic 270-degree panoramic film on a 12m screen offering a 24-hour perspective on the island. Once you've understood what 'home' is for Singapore, continue through the numerous immersive exhibits and galleries, which provide compelling commentary on the government's resolute land-reclamation policies, high-rise housing and meticulous urban planning. There are several interactive stations, which are kid-friendly. The **Central Area Model**, which offers a 3D bird's-eye view of Singapore's central district, is a highlight. It's continuously updated to reflect Singapore's constantly changing urban landscape. You'll end the hour-long visit with a better appreciation of the tiny nation's challenges as it navigates a maturing populace, balancing

EATING IN CHINATOWN: BEST FESTIVE TREATS

Lim Chee Guan: A Chinese New Year favourite, the pork jerky is grilled over charcoal to impart a delectable smokiness to the greasy slabs. *9am-10pm* $

Tong Heng: Handmade Cantonese pastries, four generations on. The creamy diamond-shaped egg tarts are popular for celebrations. *9am-7pm* $

Tai Chong Kok: Lotus-paste mooncakes are a must when mid-autumn comes around; these confectioners still make them from scratch by hand. *9am-8pm* $$

Thye Moh Chan: The assortment of flaky Teochew biscuits are quintessential traditional gifts for Chinese weddings and births. *10am-9pm Sun-Thu, to 9.30pm Fri & Sat* $

important social, climate and conservation initatives with visionary masterplans for its gleaming future.

An excellent example of this constant evolution is the new **Kada** *(kada.sg)* just across Kadayanallur St from the gallery's entrance. Formerly a mission hospital dating from 1923, the structure survived a WWII air raid and went on to become – at varying periods – a wartime hospital, dispensary, polyclinic, and even corporate office for local retail giant Tangs. Look out for Singapore's oldest grill-door lift, originally installed in 1929 and structurally preserved. The refreshed space features an interior triangular air well where patrons sit with their coffee on the ground floor. The lifestyle and wellness destination opened in early 2025 to a motley of speciality cafes, international eateries, a gym with cold plunge facilities, co-living rooms for long-stay guests, and a health clinic offering AI-led screenings.

Historic Hindu Sanctuary

Visit the Sri Mariamman Temple

Sri Mariamman Temple *(smt.org.sg)* stands as Singapore's oldest Hindu temple, originally constructed in 1823 from wood and palm fronds and rebuilt in 1843 using bricks. The strikingly vivid 1930s *gopuram* (tower) at the entrance serves as a defining feature of the temple's South Indian Dravidian architectural style. The temple's perimeter walls are adorned with sacred cow sculptures, while the *gopuram* is embellished with plasterwork depictions of Brahma, Vishnu and Shiva, representing the trinity of creator, preserver and destroyer. That said, the complex is actually dedicated to the goddess Mariamman, known for her power in curing epidemic illnesses and diseases. For the early Indian settlers who had travelled far on congested ships, this was a sanctuary to pray for their health as well as to find refuge. Historically, it was also the Registry of Marriages for the Hindu community and the only authorised venue for some time.

Leave your shoes at the door and step in to explore more ornate sculptures and murals, with each more colourful than the next. Metal barriers define the areas between priests and visitors, and *pujas* (worship) are frequent at this busy temple, with sandalwood incense and jasmine flowers intermingling in the air. Feel welcome to join in and receive blessings. Priests here are aware of the temple's fame and are happy to guide you through the steps. Alternatively, you could hang back and follow everyone else's lead, often ending with a dot of *kumkum* (sacred powder) between your brows to signal your connection to

ORNATE HINDU TEMPLES

Little India has other magnificent temples to discover along Serangoon Rd, including the main **Sri Veeramakaliamman Temple** (p89) and **Sri Srinivasa Perumal Temple** (p90). Equally resplendent is **Sri Senpaga Vinayagar Temple** (p128) at Katong in the east.

TRIAD TRAILS

No country is without its gangs, even stoic Singapore. While Geylang (p142) is known for sanctioned prostitution, it was Chinatown that featured the most vice before the 1950s. Emerging from the clannish secret societies, opium dens were found along Pagoda St, and gambling groups and brothels spread from Smith St to Keong Saik Rd. This hive of triad activities became so rampant it led to the establishment of Pearl's Hill Police Operational Headquarters in the 1930s to diminish their power. Multiple operations in the 1950s and '80s, along with new legislatures, sealed their fate. For an in-depth exploration, **Triad Trails** *(triadtrails.architectsoflife.sg; S$60)* is a two-hour walking tour led by former gang members, offering firsthand insight layered over familiar monuments – you won't find this in local school books.

MARRIAGES FOR THE DEARLY DEPARTED

Tucked discreetly behind metal gates next to Tanjong Pagar MRT station, little **Seng Wong Beo Temple** is often overlooked by tourists. The temple is devoted to the Chinese city god, whose divine role encompasses safeguarding the city's prosperity and guiding departed souls to the underworld. However, Seng Wong Beo holds a unique distinction as the sole temple in Singapore that conducts ghost marriages. This ritualistic practice is intended to aid parents in arranging marriages for their departed children in the afterlife. A visit to the temple unveils intriguing customs and beliefs deeply rooted in Chinese folklore and spiritual traditions.

the divine. Each October the temple hosts the eye-opening **Thimithi festival**, during which Hindu devotees showcase their faith by hotfooting it over glowing coals.

Where Hokkien Mariners Prayed

Explore the Thian Hock Keng Temple

Chinatown's oldest and most important Hokkien **temple** *(thianhockkeng.com.sg)* is often a haven of tranquillity. Built between 1839 and 1842 without nails or screws, it's a beautiful place dedicated to Mazu, the goddess of the sea. It was the favourite landing point of Chinese sailors before land reclamation pushed the sea far down the road. The temple's design features are richly symbolic: the stone lions at the entrance ward off evil spirits, while the painted depictions of phoenixes and peonies in the central hall symbolise peace and good tidings, respectively. When you arrive, avoid entering the doorway on the left. With a tiger carving beside it, it alludes to the Chinese saying, 'sending lambs to the tiger's maws' – an inauspicious way to begin your visit. Presumably, this was the temple's cheeky way of controlling the direction of foot traffic!

The main hall holds the statue of the sea goddess, while others within the compound venerate the likes of the goddess of mercy and Confucius. During restoration works in 1998, one of the roof beams revealed a scroll written by the Qing emperor Guangxu bestowing blessings on Singapore's Chinese community. The scroll is now on display at the National Museum of Singapore. Hunt for unexpected figurines holding up the beams of the roof, like the one representing the Indian Chulias who contributed to its construction (ask for the free brochures at the front counter or scan the five QR codes found about the grounds).

Before you leave, step out and look across to the building opposite. Peer up and you'll see two eye-like structures keeping watch over the temple as that site is still owned by the Hokkien clan. On the outside rear wall, don't miss the 44m **mural** by artist Yip Yew Chong of Singapore's Hokkien immigrants.

The Minarets of Chinatown

A trio of Islamic sights

As Chinatown was the landing spot for most of Singapore's new immigrants, it's unsurprising that its streets are filled

EATING IN CHINATOWN: BEST FINE DINING

Cloudstreet: An unmissable 2½-hour gastronomic experience. Inventive intepretations thrill with their flavours and textures. *6.30pm Tue-Sat & noon Fri & Sat* $$$

Buko Nero: This husband-and-wife affair is artful Italian with Asian-inspired twists from their market runs. *noon-3pm Thu-Sat & 6-11.30pm Tue-Sat* $$

Olivia Restaurant & Lounge: Be transported to Barcelona with tantalising dishes inspired by Catalan and Mediterranean cuisines. *6-10.30pm daily & noon-2pm Tue-Sun* $$$

Restaurant Born: Eye-catching plates at the intersection of Chinese and French cuisine served within a heritage rickshaw depot. *6-11pm Tue-Sat & noon-3pm Fri* $$$

AURELIEN DUCOS/SHUTTERSTOCK

Thian Hock Keng Temple

with places of worship representing an early narrative of spiritual diversity. Both South Bridge Rd and Telok Ayer St are its best examples, with the major religions represented along the same row. For mosques, the mint-green **Jamae Mosque** *(masjidjamaechulia.sg)*, completed between 1830 and 1835, stands as one of Singapore's oldest. Offering insight into the Islamic faith, it was built by the Chulias, who were Tamil Muslims from the Coromandel Coast of Southern India. Above the entrance, a pair of seven-stepped minarets sandwich a detailed palace miniature. The early mixture of influences from trade has given the main prayer hall its neoclassical Tuscan columns and Chinese glazed tiles below its windows. Posters on wooden podiums expand upon the mosque's multiple religious and community functions.

Less than 10 minutes away on foot, at Telok Ayer St, you'll find another pair of mosques managed by the same committee, Majlis Ugama Islam Singapura (MUIS). Often missed because of its modest facade and the narrow road before it, the **Al-Abrar Mosque** *(muis.gov.sg/mosque)* was built in the 1850s. It serves the saturated office populace in the CBD and is often busy with a constant flow of devotees. In contrast, the **Nagore Durgha Shrine** *(ndsociety.sg)* nearby is a spot of calm. Built between 1828 and 1830, the memorial is dedicated to the titular 16th-century patron saint of seafarers and served for a while as a supplementary place of worship. It's now a small heritage centre showcasing a curated selection of objects from Indian Muslim forebears, housed in a beautifully latticed structure with three minarets believed to symbolise the masts of ships.

TRACES OF THE PAST

Heritage educator **Ho Yong Min** *(@urbanist.singapore)* gained online popularity for posting little-known info-nuggets behind some of Singapore's familiar spots. He loves Chinatown for the everyday ways that heritage still persists in often overlooked places.

Ann Siang Hill Water Well: This is the last remaining well of many that used to dot the area, giving the district its name, 'Bullock Cart Water'.

Duxton Plain Park: A forgotten railway track is now a peaceful park. Part of a route that once ran through the city, it gives this green space its unusual linear format.

Shrine of Sharifah Rogayah: In the same park is a green-and-yellow monument honouring Sharifah Rogayah, granddaughter of Habib Noh – a direct descendant of the Prophet Mohammad and known for his regional miracles.

ANTHONY THE SPICE MAKER

If you're gripped by some of the Singaporean dishes you've sampled and are keen to replicate the aromas and flavours at home, a stop at this little spice **treasure trove** *(anthonythespicemaker.com)* is a must. Helmed by Anthony, a second-generation spice maker, and his daughter, the shop is stocked with numerous packets and jars, each containing a heady spice or blend quintessential to local cuisine. It can be bewildering to the novice, so if you need help choosing, the staff are all too happy to assist you in making the perfect flavour selection. The Curry Powder Singapura and the Meat Rendang Blend are standouts.

RICHARD LIM/ALAMY

Baba House

Chinatown's Peranakan Heritage

Marvel at the Baba House

Beautiful blue **Baba House** *(babahouse.nus.edu.sg)*, one of Singapore's best-preserved Peranakan heritage homes, is a must-visit for those seeking to delve into Singapore's history and traditions. Built in the 1890s, this three-storey prewar terrace house on Neil Rd was the ancestral home of shipping tycoon Wee Bin. The house was acquired by the National University of Singapore, which set about renovating it so it best matched how it would have looked in 1928, when the Wee family believes the building was at its most splendid.

The cobalt-blue facade is one of the few remaining frontages to be adorned with a high degree of Chinese-style plaster and brightly coloured porcelain ornamentation. Step inside and marvel at the meticulously maintained period furniture and antiques, as well as the building's elaborate architectural details. You'll learn the stories of the house and its former occupants, whose original family photos still grace the walls.

The ornate bedrooms on the 2nd floor are a sight to behold: look out for the *tenong* (wedding-gift box), which takes pride of place. The 3rd-floor gallery features information on the research and materials used in the house's restoration and several artefacts uncovered during

MORE PERANAKAN PLACES

Other stunning examples of Peranakan shophouses can be found along Petain Rd in **Jalan Besar** (p95) and Koon Seng Rd in **Joo Chiat** (Katong; p128). To learn more about this fascinating culture, drop by the **Peranakan Museum** (p67).

on-site excavations. Temporary exhibitions on Peranakan themes are also held here.

Due to signs of wear, the site is undergoing conservation evaluation and repair. It's scheduled to reopen some time in 2027. At the time of writing, we experienced an interim 'exposed' tour which focused on structural discoveries after the furniture was removed. Subsequently, when actual works begin, this will be replaced by a guided walking tour that highlights only the exterior, but will be accompanied by other significant Peranakan pit stops in the neighbourhood. See the website for updates.

Public Housing Panoramas

Rooftop views from Pinnacle@Duxton

For killer city views at a bargain, head to the 50th-floor rooftop of **Pinnacle@Duxton** *(pinnacleduxton.com.sg; S$6)*, the world's tallest public residential buildings. The project consists of seven 50-storey apartment towers connected by two levels of Skybridge, which provide a 360-degree sweep of the city, port and sea. It's one of an ever-growing number of bold architectural statements that make up Singapore's skyline.

Find the discreet staffed ticket booth at level one, Block G in the south. If you don't have an Ez-link transport card or cash in hand, the digital kiosk accepts credit cards and issues QR code tickets. Take lifts A or B up to the 50th floor and scan the ticket at the gate to pass (it may be fiddly). Chilling out is encouraged, with patches of lawn, modular furniture and sunloungers. Only 150 visitors are allowed each day. Sunset is the best time to visit.

Breakfast of a Nation

Local start to your day

If you want to immerse yourself in the Lion City, start your day with a Singaporean breakfast set. Not quite the standard version of eggs and toast many would know, this 'breakfast set' is made up of two barely boiled eggs (yolks runny and whites teetering on translucent), grilled slices of bread filled with pats of salty butter and a generous spread of sweet, custardy *kaya* (coconut and egg jam) – all washed down with a cup of strong *kopi* (coffee). To eat, crack the eggs into the bowl, add a dash of soy sauce and a good shake of white pepper, mix till just combined, then dip in the *kaya* toast and enjoy. A great place to experience this beloved Singapore staple is **Ya Kun Kaya Toast** *(yakun.com)* – the original shop location on China St is the best. The Singaporean coffee humour posters deserve a giggle. For another take, Keong Saik Rd's old-timer **Tong Ah Eating House** serves thicker slices, still hand-toasted on charcoal.

SHOPHOUSE STREETS & EATS

Off the usual tourist trail, the streets behind Neil Rd are filled with shophouse gems and dotted with galleries, street art and hip coffeeshops – they're definitely worth a meander. Keep your eyes peeled for heritage murals by Singaporean artist Yip Yew Chong painted on the sides of shophouses along Everton Rd. Afterwards, head to **Everton Park** HDB (Housing & Development Board). Camouflaged within the three parallel blocks of public housing flats is a secreted enclave, where third-wave coffee pundits and design hunters congregate, sipping single-origin blends and noshing on bakery bites. The humble setups also mean prices are comparatively lower – just like their ceilings.

RESERVATIONS ONLY

If you notice a packet of tissues on the tables at the hawker centres, don't take them – they're not free giveaways. This culture of *chope* (reservation) has formed over the last few decades due to the density of diners during peak hours at the popular spots, and is a way to secure a seat for yourself before ordering food from a stall that might be a few lanes away. Tissue packets (and the occasional umbrella) have become an unofficial social signal ever since. Don't knock it until you've experienced the stress of finding a seat as a solo diner while having a steaming hot dish in hand.

An Evolving Hawker Scene

Sample dishes from next-gen hawkers

Hawker culture is deeply intertwined in the culinary DNA of Singapore, a fact rightfully recognised when this dimension of the city's food scene earned a place on the UNESCO Intangible Cultural Heritage list in 2020. But as the older generation of hawkers head into retirement, many Singaporeans worry that this integral part of their national identity will be lost. Taking up the challenge, a new breed of hawkers is dishing out great meals on the cheap while infusing traditional recipes with new twists.

At Chinatown's **Amoy Street Food Centre**, a hotbed of next-gen hawkers, you'll find **A Noodle Story** (stall 01-39), where young chefs Gwern Khoo and Ben Tham have perfected their version of Singapore-style ramen. It's Japanese ramen meets *wanton mee* (dumpling noodles) – pure bliss in a bowl topped with a soy-flavoured hot spring egg. The constant line confirms its popularity, as does the sign warning customers that the stall often sells out before closing time. Other shout-outs go to **Lagoon in a Bowl** (01-48), where the charred sous-vide

EATING IN CHINATOWN: TRADITIONAL HAWKER STALLS

Hill Street Fried Kway Teow: Slurp up silky rice noodles in a savoury-sweet sauce with flavours of cockles, Chinese sausage and pork lard. *9am-5pm Tue, Thu & Sat* $

Hawker Chan: It won, and then lost, a Michelin star, but the soy-sauce chicken rice is definitely worth lining up for. *10.30am-3.30pm Tue-Sun* $

Millennium Glutinous Rice: The addictive parcels of sweet or salty glutinous rice, aromatic with fried shallots and peanuts, sell out in hours. *from 7am Mon-Sat* $

Chef Leung's Authentic Hand-Milled Rice Noodle Rolls: Quivering rice rolls swimming in a light sauce, prepared by a Raffles Hotel chef alumni. *6.30am-noon Thu-Sun* $

RAINIEC/SHUTTERSTOCK

Chinatown hawker stall

salmon 'swims in a lagoon' of naturally dyed blue butterfly-pea rice; and **Coffee Break** (02-78), a humble drink stall run by a trio of siblings who took over the reins from their father – they serve good old Singaporean *kopi* with a twist. Black-sesame latte and ginger milk tea, anyone?

With luck, these resourceful individuals will ensure that Singapore's food scene continues to evolve and captivate locals and visitors alike.

Tea-Drinking Rituals

Learn the fine art of tea

In Singapore, the art of tea drinking has evolved to embrace a diverse array of formats. Traditional teahouses coexist with trendy bubble-tea shops, all catering to various tastes and wallets. If you'd like to take your tea tasting to another level, book a tea-appreciation journey at **Tea Chapter** *(teachapter.com)* along Neil Rd, a serene teahouse near Maxwell MRT station where you can dive deep into the intricate art of Chinese tea ceremonies.

Head upstairs and be greeted by atmospheric little booths. The 2nd level features upright seating that requires a surcharge of S$5 per table. The 3rd floor has Japanese-style floor seating. Don't feel intimidated if you're new to tea rituals – the staff will be happy to demonstrate and explain the multiple steps. You'll feel peckish as you linger, so order some dim sum or snacks. The tea eggs and fish fillet are recommended, while the Dragon Well Noodles, with a broth made from tea leaves, is quite special.

If the experience captures your heart, teas and beautiful tea sets are available for sale at the retail shop on the 1st floor, so you can recreate your newfound appreciation at home.

A HAWKER GRAND DAME

Talk about aging gracefully – propped up by frilly green cast-iron arches and crowned with a pavilion-shaped clock tower, **Lau Pa Sat** is still turning heads at 130 years old. First built as a coastal wet market in 1824, it moved locations several times before the elegant Victorian-style structure was completed in 1894. With its proximity to the growing business district, planners swapped the peddlers to hawkers in 1972. It has served as an iconic round-the-clock food destination ever since, and so cherished was its design that during MRT construction in the 1980s it was carefully dismantled and rebuilt like a puzzle. As you wander beneath its octagonal hall enjoying local delights, the lighthearted chime of bronze carillon bells sing every 15 minutes.

A QUIET MORNING IN TIONG BAHRU

A walking tour is the best way to soak up the vibe in Singapore's first public housing estate.

START	END	LENGTH
Tiong Bahru Market & Food Centre	Bird Singing Corner	1.4km; 2hr

Begin at the newly renovated 1 **Tiong Bahru Market & Food Centre** and explore the wet market and hawker-centre hub. Head southeast along Eng Hoon St and browse stylish staples at local clothing brand 2 **Graye**, before ducking into 3 **Tiong Bahru Bakery** for its famous croissants.

Continue southeast to Tiong Poh Rd and cross to check out 4 **Qi Tian Gong Temple**, dedicated to the monkey god. From here, it's a short stroll southwest to 5 **Ah Chiang's**, a retro *kopitiam* (coffeeshop) with fresh charcoal-fired porridge. As you wend your way towards Yong Siak St, take note of the area's 1920s industrial-inspired architecture built to resemble transport from that era. Once you reach Yong Siak St, try inventive flavours from homegrown ice-cream brand 6 **Creamier**, and pick up designer souvenirs at the quirky 7 **Cat Socrates**.

Follow the road north as it curves towards old-school corner noodle shop 8 **Hua Bee** for lunch. When it turns 3pm, another chef takes over. 9 **Dirty Supper** prides itself on its grill and whole-animal cooking with a rotating menu. Head northeast along Seng Poh Rd and turn into Seng Poh La to view the mural 10 **Bird Singing Corner**, reminiscent of days long gone.

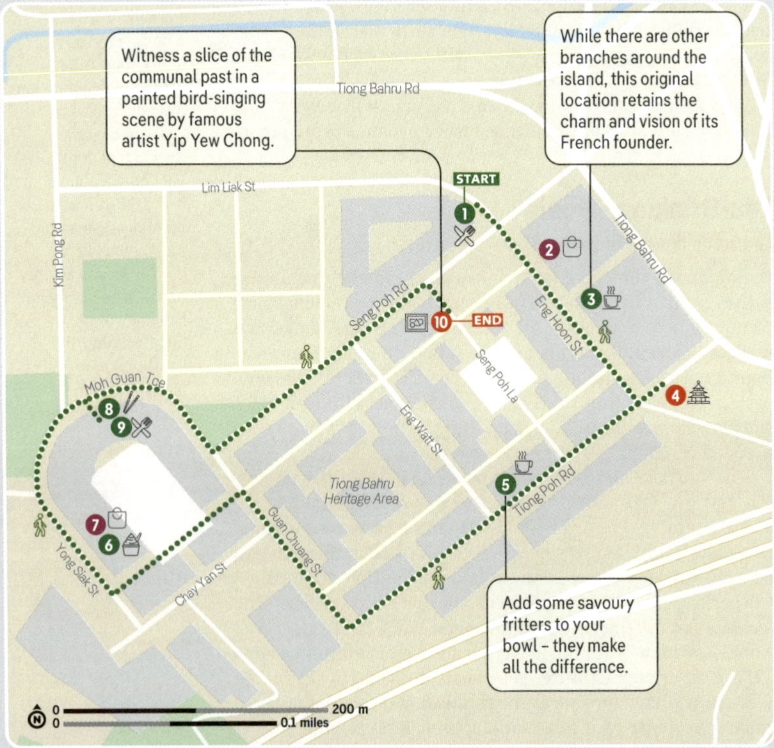

Heritage-Scene Street Art

Old-school Singapore artworks

Amid Singapore's relentless progress and the transition from old to new, local self-taught artist Yip Yew Chong is keeping a touch of yesteryear alive with his incredibly detailed, 3D Singapore-heritage-scene artworks. Originally a white-collar worker by day and an artist at weekends, YC took the leap in 2018, leaving his finance career behind to dedicate himself fully to his art. Public murals have since been popping up all over the city, with the highest concentration in culturally rich Chinatown.

Begin your visual journey with one of his most impressive murals to date, a 44m **masterpiece** adorning the rear wall of Thian Hock Keng Temple that tells the story of the area's Hokkien immigrants. From here, it's a short walk to Mohamed Ali La, where **Paper Mask, Mamashop, Lion Dance Head Maker** is another YC creation, and then onwards to Temple St and Smith St, where numerous walls have been brought to life. Don't miss the colourful and dramatic *Cantonese Opera* at the junction of Temple St and South Bridge Rd. Hip 'hood Tiong Bahru also features numerous murals. Bird Singing Corner, the most prominent, can be found on Song Poh La, but make sure to head up the alley next to it to discover *Pasar* and *Fortune Teller*. Many of YC's murals incorporate interactive elements – an empty chair here, a bench spot there – inviting the viewer to become part of the heritage scene while they take pictures. Check Yip's website *(yipyc.com)* for locations, or just follow the Instagrammers and misty-eyed Singaporean elders.

WHERE STREET ART BEGAN

Visit the artwork that boldly tore apart the rule book at Mexican restaurant **Piedra Negra** (p98) on Haji Lane in Kampong Glam. The colourful Aztec mural ignited a city-wide embrace of wall art with attitude.

THAT SMOKING LADY

Typically, any representation of Samsui women would be celebrated as these early female labourers are beloved locally for their grit, matching male counterparts equally in workload and strength. But the kerfuffle for the behemoth piece at Erskine Rd lay in its depiction. American artist, Sean Dunston, had chosen to paint her young – the audacity! – with an offending cigarette in hand and a pose some deemed too sultry. A handful of complaints were enough to spark a national debate and official investigation. In the end, the work survived intact, but not unconditionally. Authorities fined the building owners for bypassing approval procedures, and a small plaque has been added – warning passerbys of the dangers of smoking.

Bustling Neighbourhood Watch

Local-favourite shopping spot

Look up and you'll easily spot the iconic **People's Park Complex** *(peoplesparkcomplex.sg)* – the building's striking brutalist design has loomed over the heart of Chinatown since the 1970s. Before it was painted the national colours of red and white for Singapore's 60th birthday in 2025, it was a landmark hard to miss with its unusual green-and-yellow combination. A six-storey podium of shops and offices plus a 25-storey residential block, the complex was Southeast Asia's first mixed-use building. It was heralded as an architectural marvel of its time, and it's now an integral part of Singapore's skyline. Wtih an eclectic mix of market stalls, shops, eateries and residential apartments, the complex is a hive of activity inside. All the pursuits it plays host to meld together in a dynamic blend of culture, commerce and community.

Exploring People's Park is akin to embarking on a cultural odyssey, cloaked in the heady scent of Tiger balm. Wend your way from the market stalls on the ground floor to the cheap, no-frills reflexology booths (just what your tired feet

PINK IN THE CITY

Chinatown's pocket of vibrant gay-owned businesses is clustered along Neil Rd. While Singapore isn't exactly a leading queer destination, there's no hostility from the public. In fact, partygoers often have supper at the nearby Maxwell Food Centre, and the older hawker folks happily feed the pink brigade. Otherwise, they'll be at the bars for a spot of karaoke. **Tantric** is a stalwart in the scene, offering eclectic playlists for over a decade. **Restroom Bar** and **Carnival Haus** spill over with go-go boys, DJ nights and drag shows. **Slippery Slope** churns circuit-style music after 10pm. Head further into the CBD for the two biggest dance clubs – trendy **Rabbit's Hole** and the massive **Sweat Club**, where three halls play K-pop, EDM and DJ-led sets.

ordered) on the upper levels, passing traditional Chinese medicine dispensaries and the treasure trove of shops selling everything from textiles to electronics to Chinese antiques. To fuel up, the adjacent food centre is an unpretentious venue for legit hawker fare.

People's Park is also a neighbourhood hub for cultural events and celebrations, which adds to the complex's continual buzz: this is the perfect spot to get a glimpse of local life. Shutterbugs should head up to the rooftop – aka the car park on Level 6 (follow the signs) – as the enormous residential tower and its orderly array of windows serve as a dramatic backdrop. The corner of the car park is also the perfect vantage point for the city's skyline views.

Antique Gem Hunting

The treasures of Tong Mern Sern Antiques

In contrast to all the gentrified shophouses along Craig Rd is the slightly worn-around-the-edges **Tong Mern Sern Antiques** store. An Aladdin's cave packed to the gills with dusty furniture, books, records, woodcarvings, porcelain and other

DRINKING IN CHINATOWN: COOL COCKTAIL SPOTS

Native: Tipples with surprising regional ingredients and clever twists, on the upper floor of an Amoy St shophouse. *6pm-midnight Mon-Thu, to 1pm Fri & Sat*

No Sleep Club: A pop-up that's now a star on Singapore's bar scene; its owners are Singaporean cocktail legends. *4pm-midnight Tue-Sat, noon-6pm Sun*

Live Twice: Teleport to 'cinematic' mid-century modern Japan with plush seating and sharp delicious libations. *6pm-midnight*

Employees Only: Look out for the 'psychic' sign, and push past into this local outpost of the famous New York City cocktail bar. *5pm-1am*

TANG YAN SONG/SHUTTERSTOCK

People's Park Complex (p83)

bits and bobs, Tong Mern Sern is a hunting ground for Singapore nostalgia and treasure. Moreover, it doubles as a workshop where long-forgotten pieces of history are restored and repaired for a new lease on life. There's no pushy sales pitch; instea-d, you're welcome to engage in conversation about your own recently discovered curios. The tongue-in-cheek banner hung above the front door proclaims: 'We buy junk and sell antiques. Some fools buy. Some fools sell.' Best have your wits about you.

Cooking Up the Classics

Learn authentic local recipes

You've been gorging on Singapore's famous food, so why not learn to make it yourself? **Food Playground** *(foodplayground.com.sg; courses from S$120)* is a hands-on cooking school that explores Singapore's multicultural make-up through cuisine, as you prepare classic dishes such as laksa, nasi lemak (coconut rice) and *char kway teow* (stir-fried rice noodles with cockles, Chinese sausage and dark sauces). Courses usually run for three hours and kick off with an informative history of the dishes and an introduction to local ingredients. Instructors are stay-at-home mothers trained by founder Daniel Tan at the Sago St shophouse. As participants prepare their three-course meal, this imparts more open-hearted interactions during the lessons – more like cooking with a skilled relative than a strict chef. The best part, though, is undoubtedly when everyone tucks into their freshly cooked lunch. Classes book out early, so make sure to reserve your spot online.

FOR EVERY SINGAPOREAN

Singaporeans exercise free speech on most matters but you'll notice that protests are rare. While the government does adopt a soft approach in this area, topics on religion, race and politics are still tightly regulated in the public space. This censorship has an exception in the form of **Hong Lim Park** – kind of. Home to the Speakers' Corner, the open green space allows individuals to air their frustrations after first registering with authorities. Seen as a way to vet and curtail, response to the initiative since 2000 has been mostly tepid. There's one exception: in June, the spectacular **Pink Dot** event championing LGBTIQ+ rights takes over the site. While foreigners are barred from entering due to bureaucracy, you can still witness the sparkling celebrations from the park fringes.

Researched by Morgan Awyong

LITTLE INDIA & KAMPONG GLAM

COLOURFUL ENCLAVES STEEPED IN HISTORY

A multisensory journey unapologetic with colour and culture, Little India and Kampong Glam will grab you by the collar with their uninhibited charms.

Little India, originally a settlement for Indian immigrants, is today a bustling commercial and cultural hub. Its main thoroughfare, Serangoon Rd, hosts businesses, restaurants and religious landmarks. The southern portion is particularly lively, offering a sensory feast for visitors. Affordable, authentic Indian cuisine is the star attraction, along with shopping and temple-hopping.

A short walk southwest on Ophir Rd or a quick MRT ride to Bugis station leads to Kampong Glam. It's an intriguing snapshot of the intergenerational Islamic community: storybook mosques, third-wave cafes and eclectic boutiques dotted around brightly painted lanes. The epicentre, Haji Lane, comes alive in the late afternoon with live music and bar patrons spilling onto the pavement.

INCLUDES

Sri Veeramakaliamman Temple (p89)

See p206 for places to stay in Little India and Kampong Glam.

0 500 m
0 0.25 miles
Newton Rd
Moulmein Rd
Central Expwy (CTE)
Thomson Rd
Balestier Rd
Towner Rd
McNair Rd
Serangoon Rd
Bendemeer Rd
Kallang Bahru
Kallang River
Owen Rd
Rangoon Rd
Cambridge Rd
KALLANG
Boon Keng Rd
Tessensohn Rd
Race Course Rd
Beatty Rd
Keng Lee Rd
Dorset Rd
Gloucester Rd
Petain Rd
Lavender St
Kallang Ave
Lor 1
Kampong Java Rd
Birch Rd
Jln Besar
Tyrwhitt Rd
Bukit Timah Rd
Race Course Rd
Serangoon Rd
Kitchener Rd
Hampshire Rd
King George's Ave
Kallang Rd
Cavenagh Rd
Sri Veeramakaliamman Temple
Kampong Kapor Rd
Syed Alwi Rd
Buffalo Rd
LITTLE INDIA
Indian Heritage Centre
Rochor Canal
Crawford St
Mackenzie Rd
Mt Emily Park
Rochor Canal Rd
Victoria St
North Bridge Rd
Sungei Rd
Edinburgh Rd
Wilkie Rd
Mt Sophia Rd
Selegie Rd
Short St
Albert St
Arab St
Jln Sultan
Sultan Mosque
Beach Rd
Prinsep St
Ophir Rd
Haji Lane
Nicoll Hwy
Bencoolen St
Parkview Square
KAMPONG GLAM
Republic Ave
Istana Park
Orchard Rd
Middle Rd
Penang Rd
Waterloo St
Queen St
Victoria St
North Bridge Rd
Rochor Rd
Fort Canning Rd
Bras Basah Rd

Highlights

❶ Indian Heritage Centre Discover a cultural treasure showcasing the origins and rich heritage of Singapore's Indian community. **p89**

❷ Sri Veeramakaliamman Temple Visit Little India's Hindu temple paying homage to the fierce goddess Kali. **p89**

❸ Sultan Mosque ▼ Admire the golden-domed hub holding Kampong Glam together. **p96**

❹ Haji Lane Explore a vivacious, narrow lane that's splashed with graphic murals and bursting with shops. **p98**

❺ Parkview Square Find an immersive museum and swanky bar within the art deco tower claiming old-world opulence. **p99**

Getting Around

MRT

The two neighbourhoods are well connected by the MRT. Take the blue Downtown Line to Little India station to start exploring, and head to Bugis for all things Kampong Glam.

Walking

The area is composed mostly of sheltered shophouses; walkways may be cramped with goods. Go in the morning or late afternoon for the most shade and take a hat or umbrella.

Bicycle

Cycling allows you to cover more ground, but stay vigilant as the roads tend to be chaotic. Dense traffic and erratic pedestrians are challenges, and parking might be limited.

Little India

Dive into the heady assault of fragrant spices and perfumed flowers in Little India. Atmospheric temples and irresistible dishes give you reason to pause at every turn, whetting your appetite and stirring your curiosity.

SIGHTS
1 Abdul Gafoor Mosque
2 Former House of Tan Teng Niah
3 Indian Heritage Centre
4 Sri Srinivasa Perumal Temple
5 Sri Veeramakaliamman Temple

ACTIVITIES
6 Ayush Ayurvedic

SLEEPING
7 Serangoon House
8 Vagabond Club
9 Wanderlust

EATING
10 Asylum Coffeehouse
11 Brawn & Brains Coffee
12 Chye Seng Huat Hardware
13 Community Coffee
see 7 Gupshup
14 Komala Vilas
15 Kunthaville
16 Lagnaa Barefoot Dining
17 Locanda
18 Moghul Sweets
19 MTR 1924
20 Sakunthala's
21 Sungei Road Laksa
22 Tekka Centre

SHOPPING
23 Little India Arcade
24 Mustafa Centre
25 Thandapani Co

Atmospheric Hindu Sanctuary

Pray at the Sri Veeramakaliamman Temple

Little India's most colourful **temple** *(srivkt.org)* is dedicated to the ferocious goddess Kali. Adorned with a garland of skulls, she is depicted tearing apart her victims while engaging in serene family moments with her sons Ganesh and Murugan. The bloodthirsty consort of Shiva has long been revered in Bengal, the birthplace of the labourers who constructed the building in 1881. Its most notable feature, the entrance *gopuram* (tower) with intricate carvings of Hindu deities, was added in the 1980s. The striped red walls pay homage to its earlier incarnation. Visitors are welcome inside the temple during designated hours and the temple is at its most evocative during the four daily *puja* (prayer) sessions. Upon entering (leave shoes at the door), you're enveloped in the aroma of incense, the rhythmic melodies of temple music and the chants of prayers. Multiple sanctums hold various deities from the pantheon framed by ornate doorways; some of these can be incredibly life-like.

Photography is allowed, but be mindful that this is an active site of worship. The temple hosts various religious ceremonies, festivals and cultural events year-round, drawing crowds from all walks of life. Processions with hoisted deities on sedans are common, regaled by the live playing of traditional instruments. Even spectators will be mesmerised by the electric vibes.

A Vibrant Living Tapestry

Explore the Indian Heritage Centre

Discover the origins and rich heritage of Singapore's Indian community at this cutting-edge **museum** *(indianheritage.org.sg; adult/student/child under 6yr S$10/8/free)*, a remarkable S$12-million investment. It is thoughtfully divided into five captivating themes, each offering a unique perspective on Indian culture and its profound influence in Singapore. Start your journey from the 4th floor, where a 10-minute video presentation gives a timeline overview of the Indian diaspora in Singapore and how it evolved in trade, lifestyle and culture.

As you explore the extensive collection of historical artefacts, maps, archival footage and multimedia displays,

SAY A LITTLE PRAYER

Surrounded by the scent of incense and flowers and lured by the hypnotic chants, you might feel inspired to join an ongoing *puja* – and you can! These worship rituals may seem daunting, but simply following the lead of other participants is often enough. *Pujas* usually begin with a cleansing ceremony with sprinkled water or mantras before more prayers follow. Silent participation is totally acceptable. If you've purchased an offering from the temple or nearby vendors, lay it on the altar with others. The session concludes when a lamp is brought in front of devotees. Hold your palms over the flame and bring them to your forehead to 'transfer' the blessings. Some priests may offer shared *prasadam* (blessed food) or dot a *kumkum* (sacred powder) to close the ceremony.

EATING IN LITTLE INDIA: BEST ON A BUDGET

Komala Vilas: South Indian vegetarian restaurant serving wafer-thin *dosas* (lentil-flour pancakes), best finished with a cup of masala tea. *7am-10.30pm* $

Sungei Road Laksa: Join the queue for a fragrant bowl of charcoal-cooked laksa – your taste buds will thank you. *9.30am-4pm Thu-Tue* $

Sakunthala's: The fish-head curry is a tangy signature, and the lamb and fish biryani are heady platters of seasoned meat and fluffy rice. *11am-10.30pm* $

MTR 1924: Devour the crispy *dosas* and house speciality *rava idly* (semolina cake with cashews and spices). *8.30am-3pm & 5.30-9.30pm Tue-Sun* $

HOW LITTLE INDIA CAME TO BE

Named by the Singapore Tourism Board in the 1980s, Little India was once simply known as Serangoon for the main thoroughfare in the precinct. Served by two waterways in the 19th century – the Kallang River and Rochor Canal – the district was a bustling transport and commerce zone driven by cattle. So integral was this animal that entire industries grew around it, with milkmen dispensing fresh milk from their animals at residence doorsteps and women making rounds selling homemade *thairu* (yoghurt). One of the earliest landmarks was the former Tekka Market, erected in 1915 at the junction of Serangoon and Bukit Timah Rds. Built to ease retail congestion in the smaller shophouses, it was moved to today's location in 1981 and remains the activity hub of the area.

you'll delve into the early interactions between South Asia and Southeast Asia, learn about Indian cultural traditions and gain appreciation for the invaluable contributions of Indian Singaporeans to the nation's development. One of the museum's standout attractions is a remarkable 19th-century Chettinad doorway, richly detailed with an astonishing 5000 intricate carvings – a glimpse of the exquisite craftsmanship from the past. The museum's architecture draws inspiration from the *baoli* (Indian stepped well), with its main facade mirroring the pattern of the flights of steps in the well that lead down to the water table. You'll be able to experience this as part of the route when descending to the 3rd floor, with views of the busy streets nearby – a perfect photo op. Aside from its exhibition galleries, the centre also houses a rooftop garden and activity spaces. Pop-ups happen around festivals like **Deepavali**, usually in October or November. As the sun sets, the building's translucent facade undergoes a magical transformation, revealing the vibrant mural that lies behind it like a kaleidoscopic tapestry.

Towering Multicoloured Shrine

Admire the Sri Srinivasa Perumal Temple

Dating from 1855 and sitting on land purchased from the East India Company, this **temple** *(sspt.org.sg)* is dedicated to Vishnu, the Hindu god who restores the balance between good and evil. Remaining unchanged until the 1950s, the redeveloped structure was completed in 1965 and its opening officiated by Enche Yusoff Bin Ishak, the first president of Singapore. In 1966, a 20m-tall *gopuram* was added, enhancing its grandeur. A little scrutiny reveals an array of Hindu deities and celestial beings on the five-tiered design – some re-enacting mythological scenes like a frozen frame of film. Step inside to find statues of Vishnu, Lakshmi and Andal, and Vishnu's bird-mount, Garuda, creating a divine sanctuary enriched with history and artistry. Other popular deities here include Hanuman the monkey god and Ganesha the elephant-headed god.

During the annual **Thaipusam festival**, the temple is the starting point for a colourful, wince-inducing street parade. To show their unwavering faith and devotion, many participants pierce their bodies with hooks and skewers yet exhibit little signs of pain or bleeding. Some become *kavadi* (burden) carriers, carrying milk pots or resting large structures upon themselves in exchange for blessings or to serve penance. The most

DRAVIDIAN BEAUTIES

For more examples of the South Indian Dravidian architectural style, visit the **Sri Mariamman Temple** (p75) in Chinatown. Equally resplendent with detailed carvings is **Sri Senpaga Vinayagar Temple** (p128) in Katong.

KEVIN HELLON/SHUTTERSTOCK

Sri Srinivasa Perumal Temple

elaborate ones are generously topped with feathers that bounce jauntily, even as the piercings dig in. Despite the graphic nature, the event is one of celebration with live music and spirited community worship.

A Maze of Bargain Buys

Shop at the behemoth Mustafa Centre

Long revered as Singapore's epicentre of bargain shopping, the labyrinthine **Mustafa Centre** *(mustafa.com.sg)* stocks it all. From gold jewellery to electronics, fabrics to fashion, luggage to beauty products, its six levels are claustrophobically packed to the brim. With roots as a humble garment shop in Campbell La in 1971, the business-savvy family owners relocated to their current location in just two years. By 1995, after swallowing up neighbouring shophouse units, the main building was complete. The final four-storey extension was added in 1997.

BEST STREET ART IN LITTLE INDIA

A Ride Through Race Course Road: In an alley beside 50 Race Course Rd, an errant jockey has kicked up a vendor's wares – a nod to the former racetrack nearby.

Madame Mogra, Jasmine of the City: Gawk at the blooming jasmine at 27 Chandar Rd. Walk into the alley to find a migrant worker earnestly nurturing the plant.

Village Curry: Tucked into the restaurant it's named after; sit by food vendors preparing classic dishes like *prata* (flatbread) as you eat.

Mayura: Find this massive scene behind the shophouses of Belilios La – the three strutting peacocks are a dazzling backdrop.

Boy with a $100 Bill: Blink and you'll miss this cheeky boy dangling a large bill to tempt passers-by beside Perak Hotel.

EATING IN LITTLE INDIA: MAKE IT FANCY

Kunthaville: Nibble through a six-course tasting menu rooted in family recipes, in a charming classic Colombo tearoom. *11am-2pm, 3-5pm & 6-10pm Tue-Sun* **$$**

Lagnaa Barefoot Dining: Slip off your shoes, choose your spice level and be treated to home-style Indian cooking and a chatty host. *11.30am-midnight Tue-Sun* **$$**

Gupshup: Go on a flavour carousel finessed by chef Jolly of MasterChef India fame. Scrumptious street-snack-inspired entrées. *noon-3pm & 5-10pm Tue-Sun* **$$$**

Locanda: Switch things up with some Italian classics, featuring mains like toothsome house-speciality pasta. *noon-3pm Fri-Sun & 6-11pm Tue-Sun* **$$**

CANDY-COLOURED CHINESE VILLA

Near Tekka Centre stands the rainbow-coloured two-storey **former house of Tan Teng Niah**, a Chinese businessman, that harks back to a bygone era when Chinese industries were a fixture of this neighbourhood. It's believed to be the sole surviving building of its kind in the area – the rest were demolished to make way for more modern developments. Tan Teng Niah operated numerous local businesses, including a rubber smokehouse and several confectionary factories. Willy Wonka would have approved of this technicoloured tribute in the 1900 monument. The building was restored and conserved in the 1980s and designated for commercial use. While it's not possible to enter, its psychedelic facades are a favourite subject for photographers and social media fodder.

Open around the clock daily, it's one of those reliable places you can procure a wheelchair or gold chain at 3am. Within the commercial hub are also moneychangers and a supermarket with a wide range of Indian and international foodstuffs, including direct-from-India brands that migrants snap up. The upper floors carry household sundries and stationery. Expect listed discounts of 10% to 50% off retail rates outside, and rare or limited-edition products not sold elsewhere on the island. The whole experience can be overwhelming, especially with the narrow aisles and constant foot flow, but there's a method to the madness. If you don't like crowds, skip the post-work peak hour and don't even think about visiting on a Sunday. Otherwise, set aside an hour or two and accept that you'll most likely get lost in the endless rows of products – even as something catches your eye. In a pinch? The online directory may save you from the mall's grasp. Once you're done, head outside to **Mustafa Cafe** on Syed Alwi Rd for a warming cup of masala tea or refreshing mango lassi.

Eat, Shop, Repeat

Little India's main market

Located right next to Little India MRT station, the **Tekka Centre** is often hailed as the beating heart of Little India. The multiuse building encompasses a wet market, a food centre and a range of shops – it's loud, busy and a riot of colour. Begin your exploration in the wet market, Singapore's most extensive. Its stalls are laden with tropical fruit, Asian vegetables, aromatic herbs and a galaxy of spices. Keep an eye out for **Lim's Coconuts & Sundry Products**, where you can watch an old-school grating machine churn out fluffy white coconut pulp. The aroma is intoxicating. The wet market also offers a wide selection of meats and seafood, often presented in 'original condition' – meaning you should expect to witness lots of cutting, chopping and slicing. If that isn't your cup of tea, best navigate this area with caution. It's advisable to wear closed and sturdy footwear, as the floor can be wet and slippery. Once you've feasted your eyes and maybe made a few purchases, head to the hawker area to fill up on some delicious Indian fare. Join the queue for real-deal biryani, paper-thin *dosas* (lentil-flour pancakes), fluffy *roti prata* (Indian flatbread) and delectable *murtabak* (stuffed savoury pancakes). Wash it all down with some creamy *teh tarik* (pulled tea). Venture up one floor to find a rainbow-coloured sea of Indian sari and textile stores, not to mention a small battalion of skilled tailors. This is probably the most budget-friendly place to pick up an Indian outfit. While prices are marked, some well-mannered bargaining is always worth a try.

Still up for more? Across Serangoon Rd, the **Little India Arcade** *(littleindiaarcade.com.sg)* is filled with wall-to-wall shops, pungent aromas and Hindi film music. For sweet treats, head to **Moghul Sweets** – the *gulab jamun* (syrup-soaked fried dough balls) and *barfi* (condensed milk and sugar slice) are highlights.

ON FOOT IN LITTLE INDIA

Be prepared for a sensory workout as you soak up the local daily rituals – both practical and spiritual.

START	END	LENGTH
Farrer Park MRT	Tekka Centre	3.4km; 4hr

From 1 **Farrer Park MRT**, head northeast along Race Course Rd to 2 **Sakya Muni Buddha Gaya Temple**. Peek inside at its 15m-tall Buddha, then cross the street to colourful Taoist 3 **Leong San See Temple**.

Head northeast for a look at technicolour 4 **Sri Vadapathira Kaliamman Temple**. Backtrack along Serangoon Rd to the striking 5 **Sri Srinivasa Perumal Temple** (p90), Singapore's first temple for Lord Vishnu. Cross the street and continue southwest, where blessings give way to bargains at 6 **Mustafa Centre** (p91). Further on, pop into 7 **Sri Veeramakaliamman Temple** (p89), Little India's main Hindu temple, then head along Veerasamy Rd.

Turn into Kampong Kapor Rd to find the whitewashed 1929 8 **Kampong Kapor Methodist Church**. Go south along Upper Weld Rd and into Perak Rd. At Dunlop St, turn right to admire 9 **Abdul Gafoor Mosque** (p95), a storybook fusion of Arab and Victorian architecture.

Backtrack northwest along Dunlop St through a colourful jumble of shophouses, then cross over Serangoon Rd and head along Kerbau Rd to eye up the kaleidoscopic 10 **former house of Tan Teng Niah**. Walk down the side alley to Buffalo Rd, a thoroughfare lined with produce and colourful garlands. Finally, slip into the 11 **Tekka Centre** for some cheap and tasty food.

An inner courtyard, accessible via a narrow corridor in the far right of **Leong San See Temple**, hides a small pond.

Observe or join in the sensory feast of *puja* (prayer), dedicated to the goddess Kali, at the **Sri Veeramakaliamman Temple**.

Book tours at the **Abdul Gafoor Mosque** for a comprehensive walk-through, or enjoy the new Heritage Centre.

START
END
Rangoon Rd
Sing Ave
Tessensohn Rd
Race Course Rd
Serangoon Rd
Lavender St
Beatty Rd
Petain Rd
Owen Rd
Burmah Rd
Birch Rd
Roberts La
Kinta Rd
Race Course La
Kitchener Rd
Jln Besar
Verdun Rd
Desker Rd
Rowell Rd
Syed Alwi Rd
Hindoo Rd
Kampong Kapor Rd
Norris Rd
Chander Rd
Veerasamy Rd
Cuff Rd
Kerbau Rd
Upper Dickson Rd
Buffalo Rd
Upper Weld Rd
Bukit Timah Rd
Clive St
Dunlop St
Dickson Rd
Madras St
Perak Rd
Selegie Rd
Sungei Rd
Rochor Canal Rd
Mayo St
Rochor Canal
0 200 m
0 0.1 miles

WHY I LOVE LITTLE INDIA

Morgan Awyong, Lonely Planet writer

Of the three ethnic enclaves in Singapore, Little India feels the most untouched by gentrification. As decades pass, heritage businesses and artisans in Chinatown and Kampong Glam are teetering on the edge of extinction as hip cafes take over. Over at Little India, generational vendors still expertly string jasmine flowers into fresh garlands and ink floral henna tattoos with aplomb at every other lane. Some may avoid Sunday for the ceaseless throngs, but it's also an opportunity to observe the diversity of the Indian diaspora. Whether it's the hardworking migrant labourers picking out bargains from a street stall at Dunlop St or a local family leaving fruit offerings at the temple altar, the traditional ways of culture and commerce continue to thrive in the everyday.

CINTAKU25/SHUTTERSTOCK

Abdul Gafoor Mosque

Ancient Indian Therapies

Revive yourself with Ayurveda

If the frenetic pace of Little India has left you feeling frazzled, surrender yourself to the tranquil rejuvenation of Ayurveda, the Indian system of medicine based on ancient writings that rely on a natural and holistic approach to physical and mental health. Its treatments can feel wonderfully spa-like.

Experience the wonders of Abhyangam, a renowned treatment where warm medicated oils are massaged into your body with long, calming strokes, soothing you from head to toe. For a deeply relaxing encounter, indulge in Shirodhara, where warm oil is rhythmically poured onto your forehead (the third eye), inducing a meditative-like state and revitalising your mind and body. To get the blood pumping, the invigorating Elakizhi treatment involves warming poultices (herbal bags) in medicated oils and using them to massage your entire body, stimulating circulation and awakening your senses – it's pure bliss. A herbal steam bath, where you sit in a large wooden box up to your neck, is recommended as an accompaniment to most treatments to help detoxify and purify the body.

There are numerous centres scattered throughout the area; our pick is **Ayush Ayurvedic** *(ayurvedasg.com; 50min treatments from S$70)*. After a consult with a doctor, you're ushered into a treatment room. Made of wood and with a raised bevel around the edges, the bed catches residual oil used during therapy. Depending on your concerns, sessions last from 15 minutes to an hour. You'll feel the beneficial effects straight after, but typically a few sessions are necessary for the best results.

Aromatic Spice Haven

Pick up some spices at Thandapani Co

Stroll down to Dunlop St, situated just behind the Indian Heritage Centre, and seek out the legendary spice store **Thandapani Co**, which the founder named after his favourite deity. Not much has changed here since the shop opened in the 1960s; it's still adorned with hessian bags packed with chillies, cardamom, fennel seeds and other Indian culinary staples. It's considered one of the best spice vendors in the city and certainly the most extensive. Visit and you'll be rubbing shoulders with home cooks and professional chefs alike, all stocking up on speciality ingredients that are difficult to find anywhere else on the island.

Whimsical Mosque Masterpiece

Explore the Abdul Gafoor Mosque

A compelling mix of Saracenic, Moghul and European elements, this **mosque** *(facebook.com/masjidabdulgafoor)* turns heads with its commanding symmetry and exquisite details. Built in 1907 and restored several times over, the final result is awe-inspiring. Every facet of its Corinthian columns and balustrades is outlined in deep palm green, accompanied by beautiful cinquefoil arches and mini-minarets that add to its magical castle effect. Rising above the entrance and speckling of stars against the white walls is a sunburst pattern. It radiates, in elegant Arabic calligraphy, the names of 25 major Islamic prophets. Within, a central cupola dominates the prayer hall, made majestic with spiralling columns, coloured glass windows and a glittering chandelier. A new **Heritage Centre** invites visitors to explore the mosque's rich history and gain insight into the Islamic faith through a small selection of religious artefacts.

VISIT THE PERANAKAN MUSEUM

If the ornate Petain Rd shophouses have piqued your interest in Peranakan history, visit the **Peranakan Museum** (p67) for a deep dive into the colourful backstory of this Singaporean ethnic community, mainly descended from Chinese migrants who married Malay locals.

CAFFEINATED THROWBACKS

Jalan Besar ('big/wide road' in Malay) was once known for boxing matches and hardware shops. Beginning as a betel-nut and fruit orchard, it saw milestone developments in the form of New World Park (1923), Grand Theatre (1958) and Jalan Besar Stadium (1929), which used to be a key site for important matches. Only the latter remains. These days, Jln Besar is a blend of charming heritage architecture and artisan cafes. This neighbourhood has several Peranakan beauties, but none can rival the row of lavishly adorned double-storey terraces along Petain Rd. Experiencing a renaissance around the 2010s, **Chye Seng Huat Hardware** *(cshhcoffee.com)* kickstarted the coffee revolution. While past its heyday, the hip coffee joints and bakeries in this neighbourhood (mostly along Tyrwhitt Rd) offer a charming off-itinerary break.

EATING & DRINKING IN JALAN BESAR: BEST CAFES

Chye Seng Huat Hardware: Sharp shots and nitro cold brews come with wraps and pasta in this art deco institution with a roastery. *8.30am-10pm* $$

Asylum Coffeehouse: Coffee with a selection of pastries; the 'Singapore series' comes with flavours like *keluak*, a Peranakan ingredient. *8am-4.30pm* $

Brawn & Brains Coffee: Another old-guard institution, this award-winning cafe is a crowd favourite for its laid-back vibe and wide food selection. *hours vary* $$

Community Coffee: Minimalist and cool; it invites you to experiment with its delicious single-origin brews. *9am-6pm Mon-Sat, from noon Sun* $

Kampong Glam

Try not to get whiplash as you walk about Kampong Glam. Between its gleaming mosque, spontaneous street art and aesthetic cafes in rustic shophouses, the riot of contrasts will have your head swivelling.

BURYING THE ROYALS

The mausoleum for Sultan Alauddin Alam Shah may be at the Sultan Mosque, but some other members of his royal family are located a little north, just 10 minutes on foot at the junction of Victoria St and Jln Sultan. Sometimes referred to as the Sultan Mosque's little cousin, **Malabar Mosque** *(malabar.org.sg)* partially stands on Singapore's oldest Muslim cemetery and guards the Royal Mound. Visit the site and spend a brief moment looking at the heritage wall, or simply take in the splendidly tiled cerulean facade of the building. The mosaic of blue-and-white lapis lazuli tiles weave an intricate geometric tessellation across the entire exterior like lace and make for a photogenic landmark.

Kampong Glam's Golden-Domed Hub

Visit the Sultan Mosque

Singapore's grandest **mosque** *(sultanmosque.sg),* seemingly pulled from an *Arabian Nights* storybook, is nothing short of enchanting. Founded in 1824 by Sultan Hussein Shah, it was one of his key requests to Stamford Raffles and the East India Company, made in conjuction with the signing of a land treaty and allowing his continued sovereignty over the area. In 1932, the original single-storey brick mosque was replaced with the present building, designed by an Irish architect.

Gazetted as a national monument in 1975, it showcases Indo-Saracenic style and boasts two majestic golden domes and two eight-storey minarets that can be seen from afar. Additional cupolas and decorative mini-minarets add to the drama, softened by the swaying palm trees nearby. Exquisite arabesque mouldings trail down the front of the two facades. In an inclusive move by the sultan, the green base of the gleaming dome is made of glass-bottle ends donated by lower-income devotees during its construction. Its scale also meant that a part of North Bridge Rd was moved to accommodate the compound. This rear annex houses a splendid mausoleum where the grandson of the sultan and other members of the royal family are buried.

Visitors are welcome from 10am to noon and 2pm to 4pm every day except Friday. Non-Muslims should refrain from entering the main prayer hall, but it's separated by wide grills so that one can still appreciate its inner beauty. All visitors are expected to dress suitably (cloaks and skirts are available at the entrance).

Grand Seat of Royalty

Tour the Malay Heritage Centre

The area of Kampong Glam is the historic seat of Malay royalty, resident here before the arrival of Stamford Raffles. The *istana* (palace) on this site was built for the last sultan of Singapore, Ali Iskandar Shah, between 1836 and 1843. Its buttery-yellow buildings were converted into the **Malay Heritage Centre** *(malayheritage.gov.sg)* in 2015, and the museum's galleries explore Malay-Singaporean culture and history, chronicling the early migration of traders to Kampong Glam and the evolution of Malay-Singaporean cinema, theatre, music and publishing.

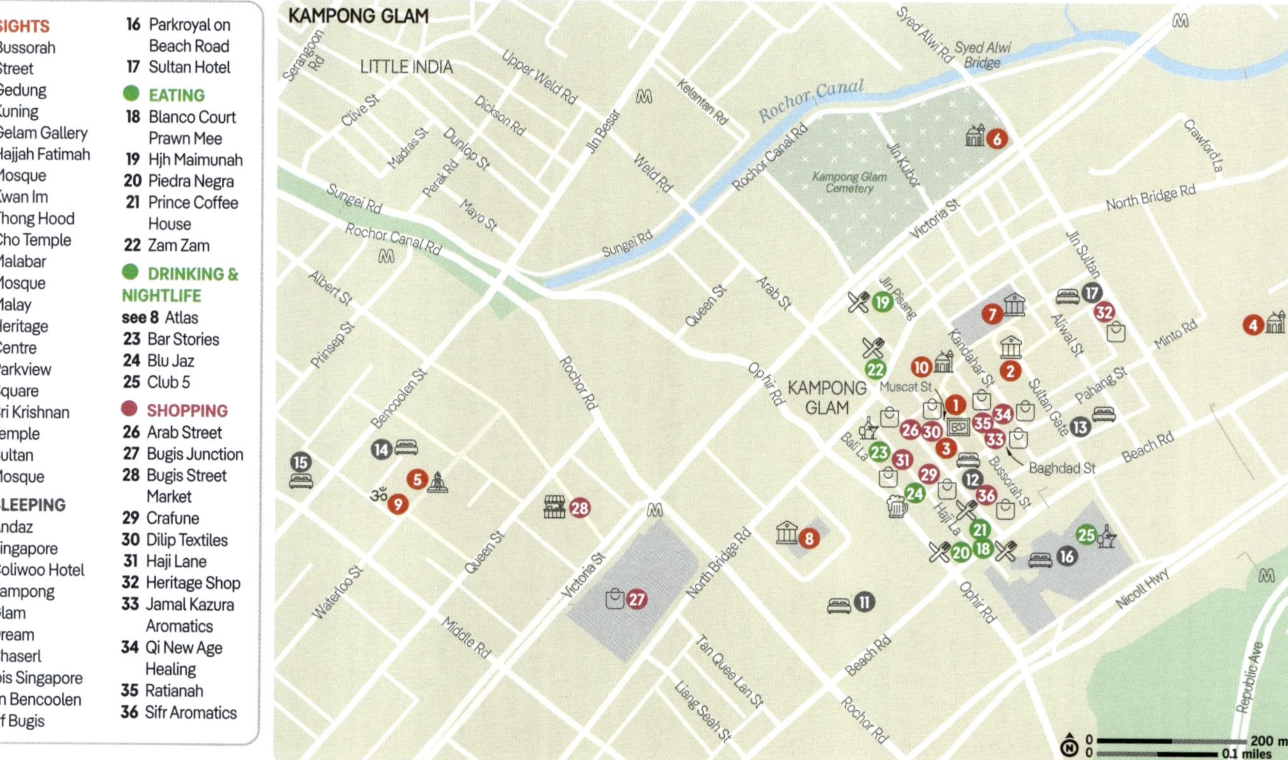

- **SIGHTS**
- 1 Bussorah Street
- 2 Gedung Kuning
- 3 Gelam Gallery
- 4 Hajjah Fatimah Mosque
- 5 Kwan Im Thong Hood Cho Temple
- 6 Malabar Mosque
- 7 Malay Heritage Centre
- 8 Parkview Square
- 9 Sri Krishnan Temple
- 10 Sultan Mosque

- **SLEEPING**
- 11 Andaz Singapore
- 12 Coliwoo Hotel Kampong Glam
- 13 Dream Chaserl
- 14 Ibis Singapore on Bencoolen
- 15 lyf Bugis
- 16 Parkroyal on Beach Road
- 17 Sultan Hotel

- **EATING**
- 18 Blanco Court Prawn Mee
- 19 Hjh Maimunah
- 20 Piedra Negra
- 21 Prince Coffee House
- 22 Zam Zam

- **DRINKING & NIGHTLIFE**
- see 8 Atlas
- 23 Bar Stories
- 24 Blu Jaz
- 25 Club 5

- **SHOPPING**
- 26 Arab Street
- 27 Bugis Junction
- 28 Bugis Street Market
- 29 Crafune
- 30 Dilip Textiles
- 31 Haji Lane
- 32 Heritage Shop
- 33 Jamal Kazura Aromatics
- 34 Qi New Age Healing
- 35 Ratianah
- 36 Sifr Aromatics

SINGAPORE'S LEANING TOWER

Venturing away from the city along Beach Rd, you'll come across **Hajjah Fatimah Mosque** *(masjidhajjahfatimah.sg)*, erected in 1846. The historic place of worship is one of the few in Singapore to be named after a female figure. It pays homage to Hajjah Fatimah, a Melaka-born philanthropist whose residence is believed to have stood on the site. Distinguished by its peculiar architecture, the mosque combines Middle Eastern and British styles; its most notable features include a bulbous dome and a Moorish wooden balcony alongside European-style pilasters and a church-tower-like minaret. The holes in the tower once held lanterns to light the way for sailors. The minaret's distinctive lean, approximately six degrees from the centre and visible from the front, has granted the mosque the moniker of 'Singapore's Leaning Tower'.

For a time, one could still admire the facade and stroll the open garden grounds after its closure for a revamp. At the time of writing, you could only peek at it through Sultan Gate. It was slated to reopen in April 2026 with outdoor galleries and interactive activities.

Back-Alley Street Art

Snap photos at Gelam Gallery

A hub of art and culture, Kampong Glam teems with emerging designer boutiques, vivid street art and trendy coffeeshops. But it's not just the prominent areas that steal the limelight here. The back alleys either side of pedestrianised Bussorah St have come to life with the opening of **Gelam Gallery**, Singapore's first permanent outdoor art space. Rear walls have been transformed into canvases and now feature artworks created by more than 30 artists. Some are painstaking full-wall renderings while others are intricate entities that might be easily missed. This artistic ensemble showcases the work of newly graduated students from esteemed institutions such as the Nanyang Academy of Fine Arts (NAFA) and LASALLE College of the Arts, as well as pieces by experienced local and international artists. Dustbins and the occasional chair or broom might litter the scene, but it's all part of the charm. Come early if you want to take pictures, as delivery vehicles park along the roadways.

A Street-Art Revolution

The piece that started it all

Historically, Singapore's government held a disapproving view of street art and graffiti. However, over the past decade there's been a notable shift in its stance. One might think Yip Yew Chong, a prominent figure in the local street-art scene, is the reason for this, having earned affection from Singaporeans for his heritage-themed works gracing various neighbourhoods. In fact, it was the Aztec murals at **Haji Lane**'s Mexican restaurant **Piedra Negra** *(piedra-negra.net)* in 2010 that were the catalyst for agencies relaxing the rules, after the unsanctioned pieces proved popular with international visitors. If you search the tiny street on social media, it's bound to make an appearance.

Today, the street art born in Kampong Glam has spread across the island. Indeed, it's even the main consideration when organisers wish to enliven an area or initiative. But even as newer pieces pop up in neighbourhoods like Chinatown and Joo Chiat, they lack the spontaneity and organic freedom of Haji Lane's street canvas. Walk the narrow lane lined with pastel-hued shophouses that host an eclectic mix of quirky boutiques, vintage shops, hole-in-the-wall craft-beer bars and thematic photobooths. Although establishments seem to change rapidly – likely due to sky-high rents – you'll be relieved to find that generic chain stores haven't taken over the area. Instead, up-and-coming independent designers and charming cafes clamour for a foothold, ensuring there's always something new to check out.

KLANARONG CHITMUNG/SHUTTERSTOCK

Haji Lane

One block over, **Arab Street** shifts gears with stores that showcase more traditional wares, including fabrics, carpets and scarves. Artworks extend all the way to Aliwal St for avid explorers. After walking all day, return after dark to the black-light neon creations at **Blu Jaz** *(blujazcafe.net)* and throw back a pint.

Art Deco Extravaganza

Step inside Parkview Square

Resembling a structure plucked from the *Batman* series, this magnificent bronze **tower** *(parkviewsquare.com)* with brooding gargoyles is known locally as the Gotham City Building. Its art deco exterior is inspired by the Chanin Building in New York City, and its open-air plaza has an array of statues and sculptures – most notably a majestic golden crane poised to take flight, pointed towards its home temple in China, in tribute to the poem displayed below. Stroll about the compound and see if you can spot luminaries like Sun Yat-Sen, Isaac Newton, Shakespeare and Mozart, or instantly recognisable pieces by

BEST BUYS IN KAMPONG GLAM

Dilip Textiles: A one-stop shop for vibrant block-printed table linens in various styles at affordable prices.

Sifr Aromatics: Perfume emporium specialising in custom blends. Immerse yourself in a treasure trove of olfactory delights, contemporary or traditional.

Crafune: Come for the locally made elegant leather goods, stay for a crafting workshop and take home your own creation.

Heritage Shop: Plenty of thingamabobs, some from a bygone era. Pick up a one-of-a-kind tiffin carrier or pastry mould – it might even have a story attached.

Ratianah: Classic or contemporary, the *kebayas* (pinned blouses) and sarongs here exude timeless elegance. Tailored options are available.

EATING IN KAMPONG GLAM: OUR PICKS

Hjh Maimunah: Pick and point dishes to add them to your rice – that's *nasi padang* (rice with curries) for you. *7.30am-7.30pm Mon-Sat* $

Prince Coffee House: Nostalgia hits this 1977 eatery where the original staff still serve their pies and Hainanese pork-chop rice. *11am-8.30pm Wed-Mon* $

Blanco Court Prawn Mee: The intense prawn broth is a delight best savoured with yellow noodles for that chewy goodness. *7.30am-4pm Wed-Mon* $

Zam Zam: Serving must-eat *murtabak* (stuffed savoury pancakes) since 1908; the large portions mean you can order a medium for two. *7am-11pm* $

SOUL-SEARCHING

Kampong Glam's anti-mall crowd has nourished the eclectic offerings of the neighbourhood, giving rise to some unforeseen trends. Floating in with crystals, tarot and breath meditations, a holistic wave began with Going Om and Sanctum before 2010. Along the way, other venues like The Song of the Self, Life by Design and 3 of Cups took root, though all of them have since closed. The legacy remains in the form of casual roadside readings in the evenings at Haji Lane (weekends are best) and **Qi New Age Healing** *(crystals-newagehealing.com)* centre at Kandahar St, offering consultations, workshops and all the tools of the magical trade.

TANG YAN SONG/SHUTTERSTOCK

Atlas

Dalí and Fernando Botero. They belong to the family landlords at Chyau Fwu Group, a signal of their love for sharing art.

The building has a **museum** *(adult/child S$25/15)* – managed by Groundseesaw – on the 3rd floor. Focusing on immersive visual art, the projections have drawn from the captivating works of Klimt, Van Gogh and Monet. You're encouraged to soak up the visual feast for up to 80 minutes.

The visual indulgence doesn't stop there. The jaw-dropping interior of Parkview Square's 15m-high lobby is as grand as they come. Adorned with marble floors, gilded brass and intricate frescoes, it sets the stage for the centrepiece – the upscale **Atlas** *(atlasbar.sg)* bar with a jaw-dropping 12m-high gin wall and opulent setting. Be prepared to make reservations way in advance. The skyscraper's success also has some whispered geomancy lore. Allegedly, the site was chosen to receive the 'wealth' energies funnelled into the island by neighbouring structure, the Gateway – designed by world-famous IM Pei.

DRINKING IN KAMPONG GLAM: BEST BARS

Bar Stories: A menu-free speakeasy; just mention your likes and dislikes, and boom! – your perfect cocktail. *5.30-10.30pm Tue-Sun*

Blu Jaz: Chilled-out local favourite that pumps with regular live gigs, jam sessions and comedy nights. *11.30am-1.30am Sun-Thu, to 2am Fri & Sat*

Atlas: Glamorous art deco venue; order a gin-based tipple from the staggering collection. *3pm-midnight Mon, noon-midnight Wed & Thu, to 2am Fri & Sat*

Club 5: Dim, laid-back den, heavy with local influence – why eat chicken rice when you can drink it? *4pm-midnight Mon-Thu, to 2am Fri & Sat, 3-10pm Sun*

Two Shopping Worlds Apart

Hit the Bugis Street Market and Bugis Junction

Steel yourself: **Bugis Street Market** is that rare messy retail phenomenon in Singapore that's both rowdy and rollicking. Regardless of their wares, shops here vie for your attention with bright lights and blaring music, while food stalls have the olfactory advantage with their sugarcane, fried snacks and grilled pork jerkies. And yes – there are durians, too, at this perpetual *pasar malam* (night market).

Even though the main route takes all of five minutes to complete, the sea of shoppers will slow your pace to a crawl. Either that, or you'll be swept away into the smaller maze-like corridors, lured by a bargain garment or kitschy mobile-phone accessory. If you're somewhat of a tomb raider, with some luck, you might find the escalators to the upper levels (good luck locating them again on your way down!), providing air-conditioned relief and beauty services such as manicures and ear piercings. Our best advice here: come with no agenda and surrender to the chaos.

The front of the street, with its illuminated billboard, faces its swankier counterpart, **Bugis Junction**. It alludes to the area's past as a nightlife destination, especially between the 1950s and the 1980s when transgender and drag performers walked the streets, some doubling as escorts for visiting foreign sailors. The actual street is now the mall's main paved glass-roofed arcade – just as popular with locals and tourists, but for its glossy storefronts and buffet of international eats. Fun fact: the ship-and-sail logo of the shopping haven pays tribute to the native Bugis people who were famed seafarers in the past.

Best-of-Luck Temple

Seek good fortune at Kwan Im Thong Hood Cho Temple

Amid the lively sounds of *chien tung* (Chinese fortune sticks) shaking in their tins, lies one of Singapore's most bustling **temples** *(facebook.com/kwanimthonghoodchotemple)*. Devoted to the popular goddess of mercy, Kuan Yin (Guan Yin), it's a cherished destination for those seeking good fortune. So revered is this institution that on the eve of every Chinese New Year, devotees huddle around the main incense pot and race to be the first to plunge their sticks into the urn to claim the fresh blessings of the year. The temple's colourful facade exemplifies the craftsmanship popular in the late 19th century, with grand pagoda rooftops and ornate carvings showcasing a rich array of motifs including dragons, phoenixes and water lilies – if you can make them out through the thick incense smoke. The entrance buzzes with elderly vendors, some peddling chrysanthemums and lotuses as fresh offerings, or fortune tellers eager to share sagely advice from palm and face readings. Up the street, believers rub the belly of a bronze Buddha Maitreya, hoping for extra luck. In a very Singaporean case of religious pragmatism, worshippers also offer prayers at the polychromatic Hindu **Sri Krishnan Temple** *(facebook.com/SriKrishnanTemple)* next door. You can never have too many blessings, right?

HERE IN THE PAST

Sarafian Salleh *(@sarafian_)* is a heritage activist and author of *Tuah Bugis* – the ideal candidate to talk about the area. His extensive research revealed these historic insights:

Al-Ahmadiah Press: Now the **Sultan Hotel**, the former press house produced notable early publications like *Mutiara*, and was owned by a member of the royal family from the Riau Islands.

Gedung Kuning: Sitting upon old royal grounds, the mustard-yellow, Palladian-style mansion was once the go-to place for *tali pinggang* – a utility belt used for hajj (Islamic pilgrimage to Mecca).

Bussorah Street: Located before the mosque, this used to be the spot to purchase items in preparation for hajj, including nonalcholic perfumes from **Jamal Kazura Aromatics**. Nearby, Haji Lane had hostels for travellers.

Researched by Ria de Jong

ORCHARD ROAD

WORLD-FAMOUS RETAIL AND ENTERTAINMENT STRIP

Singapore's glitziest strip, Orchard Rd heaves with luxury boutiques, mega malls, fancy hotels and chic cafes. It's a nonstop showcase of style and shopping.

Now world-famous, Orchard Rd began in the 1830s as a dusty, tree-lined track leading to orchards and spice plantations. Nearly a century would pass before it began its transformation into the epitome of modern consumerism we see today.

Following Singapore's rapid post-independence growth, the area boomed with commercial activity and is now home to a vast array of brands – from local designers to international couture. While cultural highlights like the heritage shophouses of Emerald Hill and the presidential residence, the Istana, add historical charm, Orchard Rd's heart beats for shopping. You can shop until you drop, pick yourself up and shop some more.

TOP TIP

Orchard Rd is hugely popular, so plan to visit malls early – around 10am – for a peaceful hour or so of browsing sans the hordes.

ION Orchard Mall (p107)

See p207 for places to stay in Orchard Road.

FROM LEFT: I VIEWFINDER/SHUTTERSTOCK, SORBIS/SHUTTERSTOCK

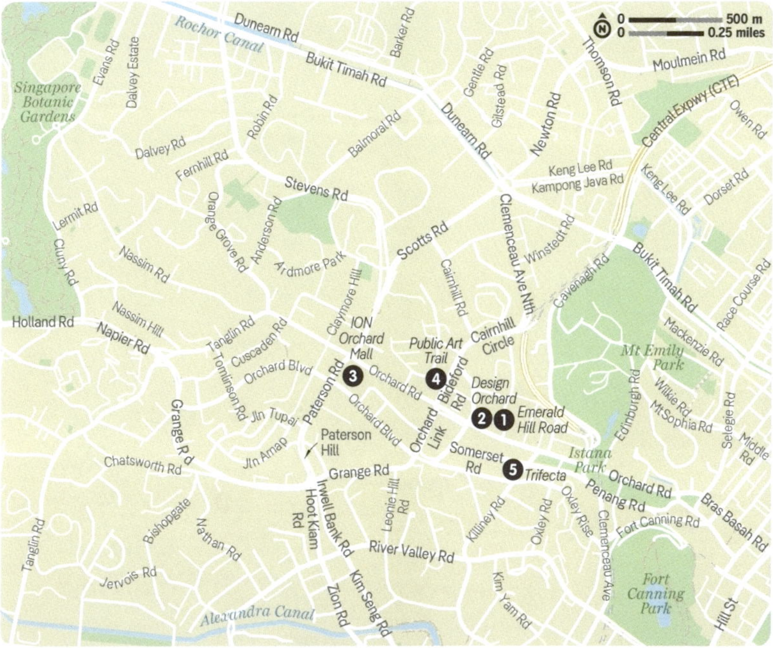

Highlights

❶ Emerald Hill Road
Explore a quiet enclave filled with Peranakan architecture and happy-hour bar specials. **p106**

❷ Design Orchard ▶
Find all of Singapore's best design talent under one roof. **p107**

❸ ION Orchard Mall
Start you shopping spree in Singapore at this mall with sky-high viewing deck. **p107**

❹ Public Art Trail
Bypass Orchard Rd's shopping malls and instead see some priceless beauties streetside. **p111**

❺ Trifecta
Trade the shops for thrills and spills at this multi-sport lifestyle facility. **p110**

Getting Around

MRT
The Orchard Rd area is serviced by four MRT stations – Orchard Blvd, Orchard Rd, Somerset and Dhoby Ghaut – eliminating the need for an exhaustive walk along its entire length.

Bus
Numerous buses traverse Orchard Rd, which flows in a one-way direction towards the city. Bus stops are found on the left side of the road.

Walking
Should you choose to explore the tree-lined pavement, you'll find expansive, impeccably maintained paths. If weather conditions pose a challenge, many malls are interconnected via underground walkways.

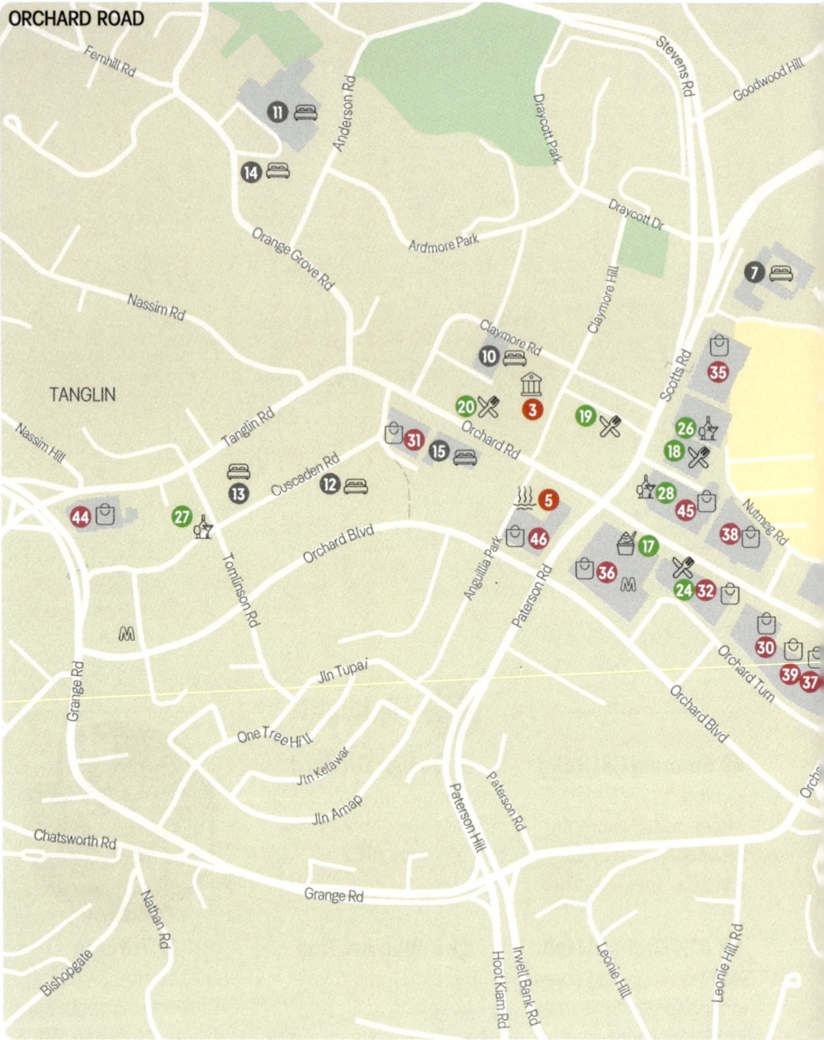

ORCHARD ROAD

TANGLIN
Fernhill Rd
Anderson Rd
Draycott Park
Stevens Rd
Goodwood Hill
Draycott Dr
Ardmore Park
Orange Grove Rd
Nassim Rd
Claymore Hill
Claymore Rd
Scotts Rd
Tanglin Rd
Orchard Rd
Nassim Hill
Cuscaden Rd
Nutmeg Rd
Orchard Blvd
Anguillia Park
Paterson Rd
Tomlinson Rd
Orchard Turn
Grange Rd
Jln Tupai
One Tree Hill
Jln Kelawar
Jln Arnap
Paterson Hill
Chatsworth Rd
Nathan Rd
Bishopgate
Hoot Kiam Rd
Irwell Bank Rd
Leonie Hill
Leonie Hill Rd

HIGHLIGHTS
1 Emerald Hill Road

SIGHTS
see 33 Cathay Gallery
see 36 ION Sky
2 Istana
3 Thai Embassy

ACTIVITIES
see 29 Elements Wellness
4 Head Spa by Goyo
see 42 Kenko Wellness Spa
5 Natureland
see 13 Remède Spa
6 Trifecta

SLEEPING
7 Goodwood Park Hotel
8 JEN Singapore Orchardgateway
9 Lloyd's Inn
10 Pan Pacific Orchard
11 Shangri-La Hotel
12 Singapore EDITION
13 St Regis
14 Standard
15 Voco Orchard

EATING
16 Alchemist The Heeren
see 12 FYSH
17 Ice Cream Carts
see 42 Imperial Treasure Super Peking Duck
see 36 ION Orchard Food Opera
18 Kakushin
see 43 Kopitiam Food Hall Plaza Singapura
19 Les Amis
20 Merci Marcel
21 Newton Food Centre
22 Orchard Bak Chor Mee
see 42 PS. Cafe
see 41 Signs a Taste of Vietnam Pho
see 39 Takashimaya Food Village

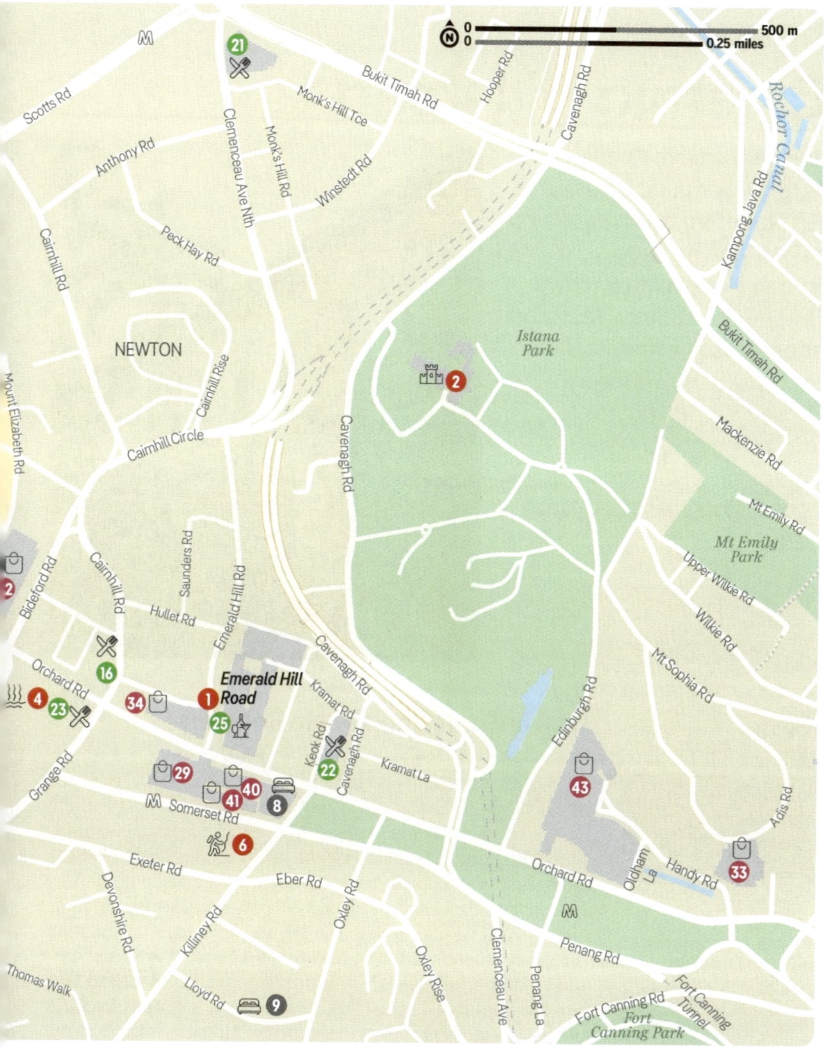

see 36 Taste Paradise at ION Orchard
see 36 Violet Oon
see 35 Wasabi Tei
23 Wild Honey
24 Wisma Atria Food Republic

DRINKING & NIGHTLIFE

25 Alleybar
see 15 Backdrop
26 Brix
see 36 CMCR On The Go @ Ion Orchard
27 Manhattan
28 Other Room
see 35 Piccolo by Hei Kim
see 36 Puzzle Coffee

ENTERTAINMENT

see 29 Cow Play Cow Moo
see 29 K Bowling Club

SHOPPING

see 29 2nd STREET
29 313@somerset
see 35 ANA Book Store
see 36 Benjamin Barker
30 Beyond the Vines
31 Books Ahoy
32 BookXcess
33 Cathay
see 36 Curious Creatures
34 Design Orchard
35 Far East Plaza
see 36 In Good Company
36 ION Orchard Mall
37 Kinokuniya
see 42 Le Petit Society
38 Lucky Plaza
39 Ngee Ann City
40 Orchard Central
41 Orchardgateway
42 Paragon
43 Plaza Singapura
44 Tanglin Mall
45 Tangs
46 Zall Bookstore

TOP EXPERIENCE

Emerald Hill Road

Just steps from Orchard Rd's glitzy malls, Emerald Hill Rd offers a striking blend of heritage and style. This former Peranakan enclave features beautifully restored shophouses, intricate tiles and shuttered windows. By day, it's perfect for a leisurely stroll; by night, it comes alive with buzzing cocktail bars and laid-back cafes.

FANDISTICO/SHUTTERSTOCK

Shophouses

TOP TIPS

- Download a self-guided Orchard Heritage Trail tour from *roots.gov.sg*, which includes Emerald Hill.
- The nearest MRT station is Somerset.
- Early morning is the best time for photos, when the road is quiet and the light is soft.

Take in Some Shophouse Beauties

Like most of the surrounding area, Emerald Hill was filled with spice plantations and orchards before it became an enclave for wealthy local Peranakan and Chinese families. Many of their fine terrace houses still line the road, and you can appreciate exquisite architectural details as you meander along. Several houses are beautifully accentuated by the Chinese baroque influences evident in their facades, wall embellishments and ceramic floor tiles. Special mentions go to **No 56** (one of the oldest buildings here, constructed in 1902), **Nos 39 to 45** (extensive frontages and a grand Chinese-style entrance gate) and **Nos 120 to 130** (art deco features dating from around 1925). Look out for little metal signs along the street that provide snippets of local history.

Lights, Camera, Action

Emerald Hill recently provided the evocative setting for the 2025 Singaporean period drama *Emerald Hill – The Little Nyonya Story*. Set in the 1950s to 1970s, the series follows the fates of three young Nyonya women from the affluent Peranakan Zhang family living along this picturesque street.

Watering Holes

At the Orchard Rd end, century-old shophouses now host lively bars, popular with the after-work crowd thanks to generous happy-hour deals.

PRACTICALITIES

- roots.gov.sg
- free
- 24hr

Malls, Malls, Malls

Where to go for what

Among renowned shopping temples, **ION Orchard Mall** *(ionorchard.com)* reigns supreme, with a plethora of luxury shops and restaurants. Little ones to adorn? Head for **Paragon** *(paragon.com.sg)*, where you'll find upscale designer threads for tiny tykes, toy shops and an indoor playground. Impressive **Ngee Ann City** *(ngeeanncity.com.sg)* hosts all the usual players, plus a branch of the prestigious Japanese department store Takashimaya.

If high-street labels are more your style (and price range), you'll find branches in the basement levels of luxury malls, but if you'd like to see your fashion in daylight, head to **313@somerset** *(313somerset.com.sg)*, **Orchard Central** *(fareastmalls.com.sg/orchard-central)* and **Plaza Singapura** *(plazasingapura.com.sg)*. For one-of-a-kind clothing boutiques and homewares, explore expat-focused **Tanglin Mall** *(tanglinmall.com.sg)*.

Despite the glitz and glamour of Orchard Rd, some budget-friendly shopping spots still exist. **Lucky Plaza** *(luckyplaza.com.sg)* and **Far East Plaza** *(fareastplaza.com.sg)* – the latter hidden slightly off the main drag on Scotts Rd – are filled with cheap-and-cheerful fashion boutiques, beauty spas and suit makers.

Discover Singaporean Talent

Souvenirs shopping at Design Orchard

Celebrating Singaporean craftsmanship and design innovation in a building conceptualised by renowned home-grown firm WOHA, **Design Orchard** *(designorchard.sg)* is a world-class platform for all things local. **DORS** *(dors.com.sg)* operates the ground floor and brings together 80 brands ranging from beauty products to fashion to home furnishings – this is a great spot to pick up a souvenir of your time in the Lion City. Budding designers populate the 2nd floor's incubation spaces, studios and meeting areas intended to nurture the next generation of Singapore's retail stars. At sunset, head to the roof and watch the shopping and work crowds hotfooting it below.

SINGAPORE'S ICONIC DEPARTMENT STORE

A pivotal moment in the evolution of Orchard Rd unfolded in 1958 with the debut of CK Tang, the precinct's inaugural department store. Conceived by the visionary Tang Choon Keng, once a peddler selling his wares from a roadside rickshaw, it foresaw Orchard Rd's remarkable ascent.

The original edifice drew inspiration from Beijing's Imperial Palace. In its 1982 reconstruction, the distinctive green-tiled roof and red colonnades seamlessly integrated into Tang Plaza, accompanied by a 33-storey pagoda-like tower. This tower and the five-floor department store below have become an enduring retail landmark, solidifying **Tangs** *(tangs.com)* as a Singaporean institution, anchored on this iconic shopping strip.

EATING IN ORCHARD ROAD: FOOD COURTS

Takashimaya Food Village: Sprawling subterranean food hall with a 'who's who' of Japanese, Korean and other Asian delights. *10am-9.30pm* $

ION Orchard Food Opera: An upscale setting, Food Opera showcases local cuisine surrounded by colonial-era heritage. *10am-10pm* $

Wisma Atria Food Republic: Transport yourself to post-independence Singapore and indulge in street food and regional delicacies. *10am-10pm* $

Kopitiam Food Hall Plaza Singapura: An extensive collection of hawker stalls dishing up delectable international and local fare. *10am-10pm* $

ORCHARD ROAD'S FINAL BUILDING BLOCK

Visitors often wonder why the **Thai Embassy** occupies such a large and prominent space amid Orchard Rd's staggeringly expensive real estate. The story goes that back in the 1990s the Thai government was offered S$139 million for the embassy's 17,500-sq-metre plot – but the offer was declined because selling the land would be disrespectful to the memory of the revered King Chulalongkorn (Rama V; 1853–1910), who reportedly picked the land up for a mere S$9000 in the 1890s. And so the embassy remains to this day, newly renovated and drooled over by developers who yearn for its coveted location.

Palace of the Nation

Visit the home of the president

Official residence and workplace of Singapore's president, this magnificent neoclassical **landmark** *(istana.gov.sg; adult/child S$20/10)* is set on over 40 hectares of manicured grounds. Known as the **Istana** (Malay for 'palace'), the grand white-washed building was constructed by the British between 1867 and 1869 and served as Government House. The building was renamed Istana Negara Singapura (Palace of the State of Singapore) when the Lion City achieved internal self-government in 1959, and then shortened to Istana on 9 August 1965, when Singapore separated from the Federation of Malaysia to become an independent nation. This date is celebrated annually as the National Day of Singapore. Most visitors will only see the heavily guarded main gates fronting Orchard Rd, but five times a year these are flung open and the public is welcomed inside. Open-house days are set to coincide with public holidays, but check the website to confirm before you set off.

Singapore's Silver-Screen Past

Discover cinematic history at the Cathay Gallery

Before stepping inside the **Cathay** *(thecathay.com.sg)*, pause to admire the original facade of what was Singapore's first skyscraper, officially opened in 1939. This landmark played a crucial role in wartime communications – first for the British and, later, under Japanese occupation. After the fall of Singapore, the Japanese military infamously displayed the heads of looters and dissenters outside the building as a grim warning to all. Commissioned by Dato Loke Wan Tho, founder of the Cathay Organisation, the building housed a grand 1321-seat cinema renowned not only for screening Hollywood blockbusters but also for premiering local and regional productions, helping cement Singapore's reputation as a film hub.

In 2006, the site was redeveloped into – you guessed it – a shopping mall, but its ties to the silver screen endure through the **Cathay Gallery** *(thecathay.com.sg/thecathaygallery; free)*. This small but captivating museum celebrates the Loke family's legacy and Singapore's film heritage. Spend around an hour exploring its collection of vintage film posters, antique cinema seats and early projection equipment that bring the golden age of Singaporean cinema to life.

EATING IN ORCHARD ROAD: BRUNCH & LUNCH SPOTS

Merci Marcel: Outdoor tables are coveted at this French-inspired spot; book for lunch or arrive early. *8am-midnight Tue-Sat, to 11pm Sun & Mon* $$

Wild Honey: Longtime Orchard Rd favourite with all-day breakfasts inspired by all corners of the globe. *9am-9.30pm Sun-Thu, to 10.30pm Fri & Sat* $$

Violet Oon: Elegant Peranakan restaurant serving heritage favourites like dry laksa. Plant-based menu available. *noon-10pm* $$$

PS. Cafe: Stylish nook in Paragon known for its international menu with an Asian twist as well as decadent desserts. *10am-10pm* $$

HIT1912/SHUTTERSTOCK

Istana

Savour a Beloved Singaporean Treat

Seek out a legendary ice-cream cart

Amid all the glitz and glamour of Orchard Rd, you'll still spot a few out-of-place-looking, weather-beaten ice-cream **carts** under beach umbrellas, parked by the kerb. Join the queue and savour a beloved local, nostalgic snack: a thick slab of ice cream hugged by a slice of soft, rainbow bread. Pay in cash, then wander on – with sticky fingers, smiling and refreshingly cooled.

Sky-High City Views

Observe shoppers from above at ION Sky

If you're feeling high after splashing some moolah at ION Orchard, prepare to get a lot higher! **ION Sky** *(ionorchard.com)* is perched 56 levels up and offers an impressive view of the surrounding areas; on clear days, you can see Malaysia in the north and Indonesia in the south. If you download the ION Sky app, local landmarks are easily identifiable through augmented reality – pretty cool. Best of all, access is complimentary

SERENE SPAS

Natureland: Well-known chain for everything from sports massage to body scrubs. The Orchard Rd branches are open to 1am.

Elements Wellness: These serene retreats dot Orchard Rd malls, offering holistic spa, TCM and advanced facial and body treatments.

Kenko Wellness Spa: Renowned island-wide for foot reflexology; the Paragon branch is ideal for easing tension and reviving tired feet.

Remède Spa: Splurge at this swanky St Regis hotel spa and get in the Bastien's Duo – a decadent four-hand synchronised massage.

Head Spa by Goyo: Indulge your scalp and tresses with this luxurious Korean head spa treatment, delivering deep relaxation and revitalisation.

EATING IN ORCHARD ROAD: ASIAN EATS

Signs a Taste of Vietnam Pho: Vietnamese spot in Orchardgateway's basement, serving fragrant pho and fresh rice-paper rolls. *11am-8.30pm* $

Orchard Bak Chor Mee: Late-night institution known for minced-pork noodles in tangy sauce, topped with crispy pork lard and vinegar. *7pm-5.30am* $

Wasabi Tei: Hidden in Far East Plaza and known for ultra-tender sashimi and melt-in-your-mouth black cod. *noon-3pm & 5.30-9.30pm Mon-Sat* $$

Taste Paradise at ION Orchard: Classy dumpling house offering handmade noodles, buns and traditional *xiao long bao* (soup dumplings). *hours vary* $$$

HOMEGROWN BRANDS

Beyond the Vines: Comprehensive, multidisciplinary design studio offering womenswear, menswear, bags and lifestyle products.

In Good Company: A lauded local fashion label known for modern, geometric wardrobe essentials for both men and women.

Benjamin Barker: Menswear studio sporting impeccably tailored suits and shirts, alongside accessories to elevate your dapper ensemble.

Le Petit Society: Stylish, comfortable kids wear and family collections that blend playful design with quality fabrics.

Curious Creatures: Contemporary demi-fine and fine jewellery for every occasion. Permanent jewellery and piercing appointments available.

PHTTRT/SHUTTERSTOCK

View of the city from ION Sky (p109)

from noon to midnight. Visit between noon and 4pm with a same-day receipt of S$50 or more from ION Orchard, and you'll be treated to a complimentary welcome drink (subject to availability). To reach this under-the-radar spot, take the lift from Level 4, near the concierge.

Swap Shops for Slopes

Get your heart racing at Trifecta

If the idea of endless shopping fails to excite you, prepare for an adrenaline-pumping experience at **Trifecta** *(trifecta singapore.com)*, near Somerset MRT station. Embark on a thrilling journey where mountains, waves and even snow (well, a lifelike surface mimicking snow) await. This mega-sport destination allows you to ski, snowboard, skate and surf all within the urban heart of Singapore.

At the **Surf Arena**, brace yourself for Asia's grandest standing wave pool, measuring an impressive 9.34m in length and capable of generating waves 60cm deep and towering up to 1.5m. It's an ideal playground for both youthful adventurers (check the minimum age requirements per activity) and those

DRINKING IN ORCHARD ROAD: COCKTAIL BARS

Backdrop: Master bartender Dario Knox introduces percolated cocktails to the world. *6pm-2am Wed, Thu & Sun, 7pm-3am Fri & Sat*

Manhattan: Inspired by the Golden Age, this grand hotel bar is a must for fine libations. *5pm-midnight Mon-Thu, to 1am Fri & Sat, 6pm-midnight Sun*

Other Room: Speakeasy-inspired watering hole in the Singapore Marriott's lobby for lively late-night tipples. *6pm-2am Mon-Thu, to 3am Fri & Sat*

Alleybar: Heritage bar on Emerald Hill Rd, known for its Singaporean-inspired cocktails and lively after-work crowd. *5pm-1am Sun-Thu, to 2am Fri & Sat*

A TRAIL OF PUBLIC ART

Discover exquisite pieces of public art scattered throughout Singapore's most glamorous shopping district.

START	END	LENGTH
Paragon Shopping Mall	Conrad hotel	1.8km; 45min

Along the front of Paragon Shopping Mall, you'll find six sculptures by Sun Yu-li – 1 **Celebrations, Endearment, Courtship, Development, Friendship and Relaxation** – alongside 2 **BELLOWS** by Daniel Brandimarte and 3 **Noeud Rouge** (Red Knot) by Jean-Michel Othoniel.

Across the road, in the public plaza of the marble-and-granite landmark Ngee Ann City, Liu Ji Lin's pair of 4 **Harmony** sculptures flank the central fountain. Steps away, outside ION Orchard, stands the striking 5 **Urban People** by Kurt Laurenz Metzler, and around the corner is Kumari Nahappan's monumental 6 **Nutmeg & Mace** – a tribute to the area's past as fruit orchards, nutmeg plantations and pepper farms.

Cross Paterson Rd via the underground ION Paterson Link that joins ION Orchard to Wheelock Place. Back in the daylight, head west along Orchard Rd towards the voco Orchard hotel, where Aw Eng Kwang's imposing sculptures, 7 **Wei Chi Jing De and Qin Shu Bao**, stand as stone sentinels at the entrance. On the hotel's facade, Gerard D'Alton Henderson's bold relief, 8 **Eulogy to Singapore**, commands attention.

Nearby, St Regis hotel's entrance plaza features three remarkable works: Anthony Poon's 9 **Sense Surround**, 10 **Reclining Woman** by Fernando Botero and 11 **Dragon-Riding Bodhisattva** by Li Chen. Finally, cross Tomlinson Rd and head south to admire Stephanie Scuris' 12 **Harmony Fountain**, greeting guests at the Conrad hotel entrance.

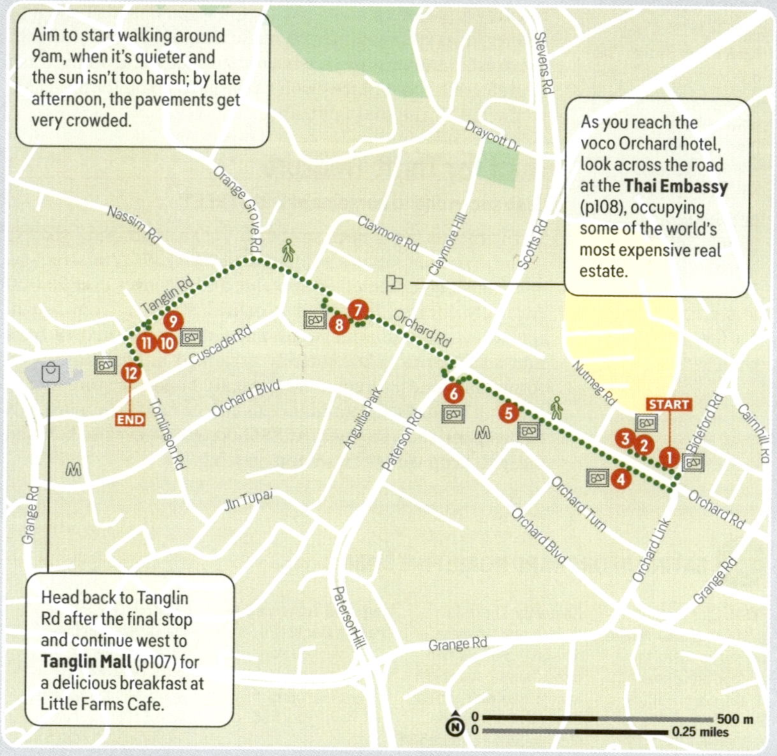

Aim to start walking around 9am, when it's quieter and the sun isn't too harsh; by late afternoon, the pavements get very crowded.

As you reach the voco Orchard hotel, look across the road at the **Thai Embassy** (p108), occupying some of the world's most expensive real estate.

Head back to Tanglin Rd after the final stop and continue west to **Tanglin Mall** (p107) for a delicious breakfast at Little Farms Cafe.

START
END

BEST BOOKSHOPS

Zall Bookstore: A two-storey literary oasis in Wheelock Place featuring over 30,000 books, mostly in Chinese. Check out the cafe and art gallery.

Kinokuniya: Browse more than 500,000 books and magazines in Singapore's largest, most comprehensive bookshop in Ngee Ann City.

BookXcess: A haven for book lovers inside the OCBC bank branch at Wisma Atria, where you can spend hours searching for your next read.

ANA Book Store: This gem of a secondhand bookshop is on the 5th floor of Far East Plaza. Dive into vintage comics, timeless novels and more.

Books Ahoy: A charming children's bookshop at the Forum, brimming with toys, puzzles, games and books for all ages and interests.

young at heart. There are plenty of introductory classes to get you started, but note that slots fill quickly, so be sure to book online in advance.

HQ of Hawker Favourites

Fill up at Newton Food Centre

One of Singapore's most famous hawker centres, **Newton** even had a starring role in the 2018 cinema hit *Crazy Rich Asians*. This place has been cranking out hawker fare since 1971. Popular with locals and tourists alike, its smoky open-air inner courtyard is the place to sit. Make sure to secure yourself a table – take note of the number, as some stalls deliver – before scouting out the 100-plus stalls for some delectable grub. Hawker heavyweights here include **Heng (01-28)** – it's not your traditional sweet carrot cake, but give it a go; **Alliance Seafood (01-27)**, for saucy chilli crab with a side of fried *mantou* (steamed buns); **TKR (01-33)**, with sticks of pork, mutton and chicken satay charred to perfection; and **Hup Kee Fried Oyster Omelette (01-73)**, serving crispy-edged omelettes with super-plump oysters. Some stalls will have long queues or lengthy wait times, but don't be deterred as that's part of the fun. Beer is available from the drinks stall, and often a server will come to your table. Most stalls won't provide napkins, so it's a good idea to carry a packet of tissues with you – you can also use it to *chope* (save) your seat. If you make a right mess of yourself, there are handwashing basins outside the bathrooms. Cash is preferred; most places won't take cards. You'll find ATMs to the left of the main entrance.

Hunt for Thrift Treasure

Grab secondhand bargains at 2nd STREET

Thrifting has never been so stylish – or so organised – thanks to the arrival of Japan's popular **2nd STREET** *(2ndstreet-sg.com)* at 313@somerset. Step inside and discover over 23,000 carefully curated pre-loved treasures flown in from Japan, including vintage streetwear, cult-label gems, luxury bags and accessories. Thoughtfully arranged in spacious, easy-to-browse zones (forget messy bargain bins), the store makes hunting for hidden gems a breeze. Prices range from just S$5 to designer showstoppers at S$5000, with new stock added daily to keep things fresh and exciting.

EATING IN ORCHARD ROAD: FINE DINING

FYSH: Chic Australian grill by chef Josh Niland, dishing up sustainable seafood and prime steaks. *noon-2.30pm & 6-10pm Mon-Thu, to 10.30pm Fri-Sun* $$$

Kakushin: The dishes at this sleek Japanese *omakase* (chef-curated dishes) are so exquisite it almost feels wrong to eat them (of course, we do). *11.30am-3pm & 6-10pm* $$$

Imperial Treasure Super Peking Duck: Must-try crisp-skinned Peking duck expertly carved table-side – pre-order or risk missing out. *hours vary* $$$

Les Amis: French fine-dining spot famed for tasting menus, seasonal dishes and an award-winning wine list. *noon-1.30pm last order & 7-8.30pm last order* $$$

RUSLANKPHOTO/SHUTTERSTOCK

Hawker fare at Newton Food Centre

Partake in the Nation's Favourite Pastime

Sing your heart out at KTV

As you trawl the shopping malls, you'll come across numerous entertainment venues offering KTV – that's karaoke television, for the uninitiated. Here, singing enthusiasts showcase their vocal talents in thematic rooms, complete with state-of-the-art audiovisual systems and (thankfully) soundproofing. You can purchase food and drinks inside, and you pay by the hour. It's always good to check the song lists before heading inside. Orchard Central (p107), **Orchardgateway** and 313@somerset (p107) malls are hubs for this popular Singaporean hobby.

BEST NIGHTSPOTS

Brix: This slightly gritty club in the Grand Hyatt's basement draws late-night revellers with its pumping dance floor and live music acts.

K Bowling Club: Neon-lit, retro-chic spot at 313@somerset, where bowling, arcade games, karaoke and cocktails create the perfect late-night vibe.

Christmas on a Great Street: Orchard Rd's epic Christmas display lights up every November, shining bright through New Year with rides, games and photo fun.

Night at Orchard: Spanning ION Orchard to Ngee Ann City, this open-air night market *(nao.sg)* showcases some of Singapore's top local artisans.

Cow Play Cow Moo: Set in 313@somerset, it's a neon arcade paradise bursting with claw machines and ticket games.

EATING & DRINKING IN ORCHARD ROAD: CAFFEINE HITS

Alchemist The Heeren: Coffee enthusiasts love this sip-and-go spot hugging the outside of the Heeren. The pastries are worth the calories. *9am-9pm*

CMCR On The Go @ Ion Orchard: For a quick refuel, stop by for a speciality brew from this small but mighty caffeine powerhouse. *9.30am-9.30pm*

Puzzle Coffee: Originating from coffee-crazed Melbourne, the brand's Singaporean outpost brews away in the depths of ION Orchard. *9am-8pm*

Piccolo by Hei Kim: A cosy, fuss-free cafe hidden in Far East Plaza, pouring smooth brews with beautifully balanced flavours. *8.30am-5pm Tue-Sun*

Researched by Ria de Jong

HOLLAND VILLAGE, BOTANIC GARDENS & DEMPSEY HILL

THEMED GARDENS AND UPSCALE NEIGHBOURHOODS

Just steps away from the bustling glamour of Orchard Rd, it's almost surreal to discover a serene pocket of greenery, indie boutiques and gourmet hideaways.

As Orchard Rd's towering malls gradually give way to soaring rain trees and peaceful greenery, the Singapore Botanic Gardens – the city's green heart and a UNESCO World Heritage Site – steals the spotlight. This lush oasis invites visitors to stroll among tropical plants, tranquil lakes and fragrant blooms. Nearby, leafy Dempsey Hill, once a British Army barracks, now buzzes with stylish art galleries, chic boutiques, gourmet grocers and upscale dining spots perfect for foodies and culture lovers alike. Further west along Holland Rd, vibrant Holland Village offers a glimpse into local and expat life with its cosy cafes, trendy shops and lively bars. As night falls, unwind with craft beers or cocktails in a relaxed, friendly atmosphere.

TOP TIP

Join local exercise enthusiasts for a lap around the Singapore Botanic Gardens. Early morning is best, when the air is still cool, or else just before sunset.

Singapore Botanic Gardens (p118)

See p207 for places to stay in Holland Village, the Botanic Gardens and Dempsey Hill.

FROM LEFT: MAREK POPLAWSKI/SHUTTERSTOCK, JAHNVIK/SHUTTERSTOCK

Binjai Park
Swiss Club Rd
Eng Neo Ave
Sime Rd
Lornie Rd
2 Bukit Brown Cemetery
Andrew Rd
Clementi Rd
Bukit Timah Rd
Dunearn Rd
Hillcrest Rd
Pan-Island Expwy (PIE)
Adam Rd
Sixth Ave
Rochor Canal
Bukit Timah Rd
Dunearn Rd
Ulu Pandan Rd
Coronation Rd W
Coronation Rd
King's Rd
Farrer Rd
Cluny Park Rd
Evans Rd
1 Singapore Botanic Gardens
Symphony Lake
Holland Rd
Holland Village
Pangium 5
Dalvey Rd
Balmoral Rd
Stevens Rd
Commonwealth Ave W
4
Holland Ave
Tyersall Ave
Cluny Rd
Swan Lake
Nassim Rd
Scotts Rd
Holland Rd
Napier Rd
Dover Rd
North Buona Vista Rd
Queensway
5 Candlenut
Dempsey Hill 3
Orchard Rd
Orchard Blvd
Commonwealth Ave
Ridley Park
Tanglin Rd
Ayer Rajah Expwy (AYE)
Margaret Rd
Grange Rd
Ayer Rajah Ave
National University of Singapore
QUEENSTOWN
River Valley Rd
Alexandra Canal
N
0 1 km
0 0.5 miles

Highlights

❶ Singapore Botanic Gardens ▶

Enjoy a picnic or wander the ancient rainforest and themed gardens. **p118**

❷ Bukit Brown Cemetery

Take a walk through history at this overgrown and wild heritage cemetery. **p122**

❸ Dempsey Hill

Explore the rambling hill station's leafy cafes, sought-after restaurants and art galleries. **p121**

❹ Holland Village

Discover an eclectic mix of heritage hangouts and fresh, new-school shopping spots and eateries. **p124**

❺ Peranakan Cuisine

Savour some of the island's best Straits Chinese cuisine at Malcolm Lee's Candlenut and Pangium. **p121 & p124**

Getting Around

MRT

Holland Village is easily accessible via the Holland Village station, as is the Botanic Gardens – alight at Napier station for the Orchard Rd end and the Botanic Gardens station for the Bukit Timah end.

Bus

Catch bus 7, 75, 77, 105, 106, 123 or 174 from behind Orchard MRT on Orchard Blvd to get close to Dempsey Hill, then walk up the hill to reach it.

Shuttle

A free shuttle service is available to Dempsey Hill; check the website (*dempseyhill .com/shuttlebusschedule .html)* for timings and pickup locations.

HIGHLIGHTS
1 Singapore Botanic Gardens

SIGHTS
2 Botanical Art Gallery
3 Chip Bee Gardens
4 COMO Adventure Grove
5 Dempsey Hill
6 Ethnobotany Garden
7 Forest Discovery Centre @ OCBC Arboretum
8 Fragrant Garden
9 Gallery26
10 Gallop Extension
11 Ginger Garden
12 Healing Garden
13 Heritage Museum
14 Jacob Ballas Children's Garden
15 Learning Forest
16 Lorian Liput
17 Lorong Mambong
18 Museum of Ice Cream
19 National Orchid Garden
20 OK Sculpture Park
21 Palm Valley
22 Ridley Park
23 Symphony Lake

SLEEPING
24 Quincy House Singapore

EATING
25 2am: dessertbar
26 Adam Road Food Centre
27 Bee's Knees
28 Burnt Ends Bakery
29 Candlenut
30 Cluny Court
31 Frankie & Fern's

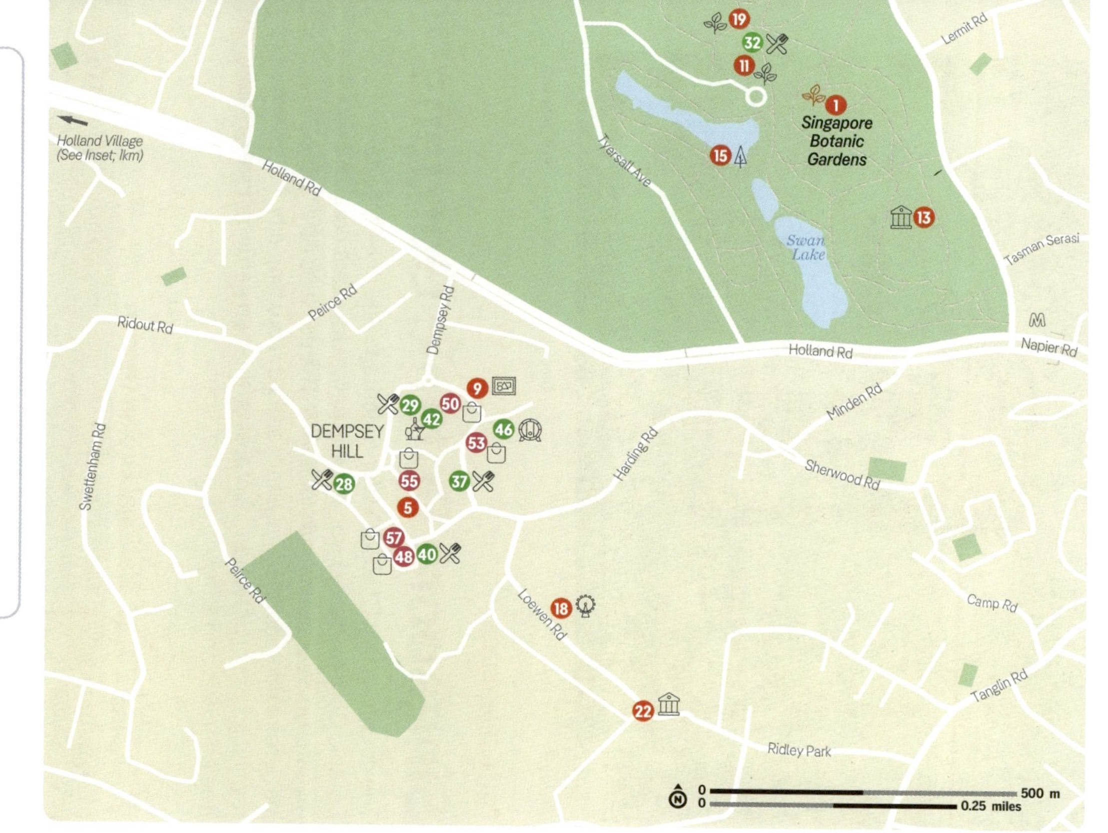

32 Halia
33 Holland Village Food Centre
34 MICRO | bakery
35 Original Sin
36 Pangium
37 PS Cafe
38 Sprouts Food Place
39 Tai Cheong Bakery
40 Tinto

DRINKING & NIGHTLIFE

41 Craftsmen Coffee
42 Dempsey Cookhouse & Bar
43 Le Bon Funk
44 MAVRX
45 Small Batch
46 Tanglin Gin
47 Wala Wala Cafe Bar

SHOPPING

48 ARTitude Galería
49 Atelier Ong Shunmugam
50 Dover Street Market
51 Holland Road Shopping Centre
52 Independent Market
53 Kids 21 Dempsey
54 Lim's Holland Village
55 Mr Bucket Chocolaterie
56 Raffles Holland V
57 REDSEA Gallery
see 30 rue Madame
58 TAKSU

TANG YAN SONG/SHUTTERSTOCK

Clock tower at the National Orchid Garden

TOP EXPERIENCE

Singapore Botanic Gardens

The country's first UNESCO World Heritage Site, the Singapore Botanic Gardens have been a major centre for plant conservation and research in Southeast Asia since 1875. The gardens offer more than just a refreshing burst of greenery amid the bustling city – they're a ravishing sprawl of ancient rainforests, themed gardens, rare orchids, free concerts and alfresco gourmet spots.

DON'T MISS

- National Orchid Garden
- Ginger Garden
- Symphony Lake
- Heritage Museum
- Walk of Giants
- COMO Adventure Grove
- Jacob Ballas Children's Garden

National Orchid Garden

Orchids have been bred and cultivated in the **National Orchid Garden** since 1928. The 3-hectare space is a showcase of over 1000 species and 2000 hybrids, with around 600 on display at any given time. Descend into the futuristic glass-walled **Tropical Montane Orchidetum**, which simulates the climate in a mountainous forest, before ducking inside the **Tan Hoon Siang Mist House**, a palaeotropical garden with highlands conditions. The **VIP Orchid Garden** offers a glimpse into Singapore's unique tradition of orchid diplomacy, showcasing hybrids named after royalty, world leaders and

PRACTICALITIES

- nparks.gov.sg/sbg
- National Orchid Garden adult/child S$15/free
- 5am-midnight daily, hours vary for specific gardens/venues

celebrities. The informational plaques along the trails reveal fascinating details about orchid breeding, including Singapore's iconic national flower, the Vanda Miss Joaquim. First cultivated in 1893 by Agnes Joaquim, this resilient hybrid embodies the nation's spirit of strength and perseverance.

Pick a Theme

Embark on an adventure through the world of botany in the themed gardens that showcase rich plant life. Delve into the aromatic wonders of the **Ginger Garden**, housing over 250 *Zingiberaceae* species, complete with a hidden waterfall cave and the ginger-centric restaurant **Halia** *(thehalia.com)*. Dive into the world of medicinal plants at the **Healing Garden** *(closed Tue)* and learn about their historic remedies. Smell the flowers at the **Fragrant Garden**; the plants' scents are strongest in the evenings. The **Ethnobotany Garden** explores the relationship between plants and people, particularly those traditionally used by indigenous communities in this region.

Perfect Picnicking

More than 200 species of palm trees dot the sweeping, manicured slopes of **Palm Valley**, creating a picture-perfect setting for an alfresco picnic. At its heart, a stage appears to float on **Symphony Lake**, hosting free concerts such as the Singapore Symphony Orchestra's monthly **SSO in the Park** *(sso.org.sg)*. Occasional free movie screenings also take place on the slopes of Palm Valley.

Head for the Trees

Hit the elevated walkways of the **Learning Forest** to explore environments ranging from a freshwater forest wetland to a lowland rainforest. Walk in the shadow of some of the tallest trees in Asia at the **Walk of Giants**, sprawl out on the spider-mesh net of the 8m-high **Canopy Web**, or stroll along the boardwalks alongside the marsh at the **Keppel Discovery Wetlands**.

The **HPL Canopy Link**, a 200m barrier-free pedestrian bridge, connects the Learning Forest to the Gallop Extension, offering panoramic views of the bambusetum and a transition into a recreated lowland deciduous forest habitat. A self-guided audio tour is available at various points along the trail, providing informative commentary on the area's flora and ecological significance.

Heritage Museum

If the heat is too overwhelming, head indoors to the 240-sq-metre **Heritage Museum**, located in Holttum Hall, and browse multimedia exhibits that detail the gardens' rich heritage. The old photographs, artefacts, plant specimens and rare botanical books dating back to the early 19th century give a fascinating look into the past. The museum is closed on the last Monday of each month.

GETTING THERE & AROUND

The Botanic Gardens MRT station (Circle Line) is close to the Bukit Timah Gate, near the Children's Garden. For the National Orchid Garden, enter through the Tanglin Gate from Napier MRT station (Thomson-East Coast Line). It's an eight-minute walk from Farrer Rd MRT (Circle Line) to the Woollerton Gate, near COMO Adventure Grove. Download a map of the gardens at *nparks.gov.sg/sbg*.

PACK A PICNIC

Making a picnic out of your visit can be fun, especially if you have kids in tow. Stock up on picnic goodies at the gourmet delis in upmarket Holland Village or leafy Dempsey Hill. You'll also find plenty of nosh spots within the gardens themselves. And if you're near the Bukit Timah Gate, there's the charming shopping and lifestyle hub **Cluny Court**, or the nearby hawker favourite **Adam Road Food Centre**.

TOP TIPS

- The best time to visit the Botanic Gardens is early in the morning, when the temperature is mild.
- There's shade in most parts of the gardens – but it's still wise to bring a sunhat, sunscreen and plenty of water.
- Watch out for wildlife, especially monitor lizards and otters. Keep a distance and do not feed them.
- Check the gardens website for a schedule of upcoming concerts, which are staged for free by the Symphony Lake.
- The gardens run free guided tours every Saturday (except for the fifth Saturday of the month). Register at the service desk.

Gallop Extension

Offering a blend of history, art and nature, the relatively new **Gallop Extension** is a must-visit. Discover two beautifully restored colonial-era black-and-white houses: **Forest Discovery Centre @ OCBC Arboretum** and **Botanical Art Gallery**. Visitors can delve into Singapore's rainforest heritage, learn about conservation efforts or admire intricate botanical artworks. Beyond the galleries, expansive meadows and themed trails like the **Mingxin Foundation Rambler's Ridge** and the **OCBC Arboretum** showcase native tree species and rare rainforest giants, inviting leisurely walks with panoramic views. Families will appreciate the **COMO Adventure Grove**, centred around a 10m banyan-tree-like structure with climbing ropes, hammocks and a lookout point. There are two swings, a mini obstacle course and climbing structure shaped like a jackfruit.

A Children's World

Those with little ones shouldn't miss the **Jacob Ballas Children's Garden** in the northern end of the gardens (closed on Mondays). This kid-friendly haven features nature-themed interactive zones, including a sensory garden to explore textures and scents up close. Adventurous kids will love the suspension bridge, treehouse and floating platform, while budding green thumbs can discover edible plants in the orchard and farm areas. There's even a gentle stream perfect for dipping tiny toes. After all that play, children can cool off in the colourful water-play area. Adults must be accompanied by a child aged 12 or under to enter. **Small Batch** cafe sits conveniently beside the sand play zone, serving light bites, pastries and kid-friendly treats.

INSPIRED BY MAPS/SHUTTERSTOCK

Hill Station Turned Trendy Enclave

Get to know Dempsey Hill

Once a colonial-era hill station, **Dempsey Hill** *(dempseyhill.com)* now hides amid lush tropical foliage, dotted with chic brunch spots, beautifully curated art galleries and stylish restaurants that draw in expats and well-heeled locals alike. Compared to neighbouring Holland Village, it feels quieter, more upmarket and delightfully tucked away. Previously known as Tanglin Barracks, Dempsey Hill was one of the first British Army barracks constructed in Singapore, built in 1861. The barracks served as the headquarters of the Ministry of Defence between 1972 and 1989, before its current reinvention as an upscale brunch and dining area. The best way to explore? Wander the shaded walkways, linger over artisanal coffee or a decadent brunch, browse designer and artsy finds, then round off your visit with dinner under the canopy of towering trees.

Monochrome Beauties

Stroll around Ridley Park's heritage homes

At the end of Dempsey Hill's Loewen Rd, you'll come to **Ridley Park**, an estate named in honour of Henry Ridley, the inaugural director of the Singapore Botanic Gardens. A walk down Ridley Park Rd unveils a picturesque ring road, offering glimpses of Singapore's famous black-and-white bungalows. These residences once accommodated British officers overseeing the adjacent barracks, but they are now leased out to the highest bidder. The expansive gardens that often accompany these homes are highly sought after.

BRITISH COLONIAL HOUSES

If you enjoyed Ridley Park, make time for **Seletar Aerospace Park** (p159), another area studded with black-and-white bungalows built by the British and now converted into beautiful restaurants and brunch spots.

BEAUTIFUL BLACK & WHITES

Singapore's bungalows, named after Bangalore-style houses, are usually two storeys high, with large verandahs on the upper floor. Most were built in the style now known as 'black and whites', after the mock-Tudor, exposed-beam look adopted between the late 19th century and WWII. The design itself was greatly influenced by the Arts and Crafts movement, which originated in England in the 1860s and placed renewed value on craftsmanship, a reaction to England's rapid industrialisation. By the 1930s, the mock-Tudor style made way for the so-called 'tropical art deco', which favoured flat roofs, curved corners and a streamlined horizontal design.

EATING IN DEMPSEY HILL: OUR PICKS

Burnt Ends Bakery: Irresistible brioche doughnuts filled with decadence. Arrive early to secure the flavour of your choice. *8am-4pm Thu-Sun* $$

Candlenut: Michelin-starred spot where Singaporeans bring out-of-towners for a decadent meal of refined Peranakan cuisine. *noon-3pm & 6-10pm* $$$

PS Cafe: Much-loved all-day dining venue ensconced in tropical foliage. Don't miss the truffle fries. *noon-2.30pm Thu-Sat & 6-11pm Tue-Sat* $$

Tinto: Rustic Spanish eatery serving Basque-inspired tapas, smoky octopus and wood-fired dishes. *noon-2.30pm Fri-Sun & 6-10.30pm Tue-Sun* $$

TOP EXPERIENCE

Bukit Brown Cemetery

Hidden amid lush greenery, Bukit Brown Cemetery is Singapore's largest Chinese burial ground, dating back to 1922 and home to over 100,000 graves. Beyond its atmospheric, overgrown paths lie elaborately carved tombs that tell stories of pioneers and early migrants. Visitors come for guided heritage walks, rich history, wildlife-spotting and an evocative glimpse into Singapore's past.

CHERRY-HAI/SHUTTERSTOCK

Silent Singapore Stories

Step into Singapore's layered past, where moss-covered tombs and twisting roots reveal stories of pioneers and philanthropists. Wander the overgrown trails to find the grand tomb of Ong Sam Leong, one of the largest in Southeast Asia, and the richly adorned grave of Chew Geok Leong, guarded by stone Sikh sentinels. Don't miss Tan Kheam Hock's tomb, which artfully blends Asian and European influences. Wander alone or join a volunteer-led heritage walk (book online), which truly brings these stories to life.

Enter a Sci-Fi World

Look up as you reach the heart of the cemetery to behold towering ancient rain trees draped in moss and vines, creating an otherworldly, '*Avatar*-like' canopy. Increasingly popular with photographers and nature enthusiasts, these giants add a haunting beauty to Bukit Brown's historic landscape.

Making Way for the Living

At the **Sounds of the Earth** installation, visitors can wander among 80 unclaimed tombstones exhumed to build the adjacent Lornie Hwy, arranged in elliptical rings that echo footsteps and voices. This quiet memorial prompts reflection on Singapore's balancing act between relentless development and heritage preservation.

TOP TIPS

- Download a self-guided tour from *singaporeheritage.org*.
- The easiest way to get there is by taxi, or take one of the buses along Adam Rd (Botanic Garden MRT) that stop near the entrance.
- Bring sunscreen, water and mosquito repellant. Good shoes are a must.

PRACTICALITIES

- bukitbrown.com ● free
- 24hr

Unleash Your Inner Child

Go gaga at the Museum of Ice Cream

In vivid contrast to Dempsey Hill's black-and-white aesthetics is the psychedelic-pink **Museum of Ice Cream** *(museumoficecream.com/singapore; S$43)*. This dessert-themed wonderland offers a multisensory journey for photo-hungry travellers. A visit is like entering Willy Wonka's chocolate factory – you get to play with fun, interactive displays, dive into the largest sprinkle pool in Asia, and scoff unlimited ice cream! The flavours are truly unique and constantly rotating – try the more unusual ones like the chendol and lemon yuzu. This outpost – the museum first popped up in New York in 2016 – pays tribute to Singaporean culture through installations such as the Unicorn Playground, an homage to the classic dragon playgrounds that dotted housing estates in the 1970s. It's a celebration of unbridled playtime for both grown-ups and little ones.

Get Lost in a Gin Jungle

Discover distillation at Tanglin Gin

For a positively Singaporean experience (for those 18 years old and above), venture to **Tanglin Gin** *(tanglin-gin.com; tours from S$49)*, a hidden distillery and bar in leafy Dempsey Hill. Here, gin enthusiasts converge to savour unforgettable flavours. You can embark on a distillery tour or indulge in a cocktail masterclass. Don't miss out on signature tipples like the Orchid Gin, infused with Vanilla planifolia orchid, or the bold Black Powder Gin, tailor-made for the adventurous palate.

Singapore's Sweetest Secret

Inside Mr Bucket's chocolate lab

Enter a chocolate lover's dream at **Mr Bucket Chocolaterie** *(mrbucket.com.sg; tour & tasting S$15, workshop S$60)*, where visitors embark on a captivating bean-to-bar journey inside a spacious, glass-fronted chocolate factory. Stroll through the earthy Cacao Garden, watch beans being roasted and tempered, then head to the Creation Station to craft your own chocolate slab using oat milk or dark bases topped with nougat, nuts or petals. Don't miss the Bean-to-Bar Tasting Set, which showcases cacao's journey from farm to plate and is filled with plenty of treats – all made on-site.

SHOPPING IN THE 'HOOD

Dover Street Market: High-fashion concept store stocked with luxury brands and streetwear labels.

Kids 21 Dempsey: Kit your kids from head to toe in designer duds and accessories at this emporium for the under-12 cool crowd.

Atelier Ong Shunmugam: The shop of Priscilla Shunmugam is as stunning as her modern interpretations on Asian dresses.

rue Madame: Parisienne chic meets Singapore heat at this boutique filled with European brands at shopping hub Cluny Court.

Independent Market: Quirky and well-designed Singaporean themed gifts and homewares.

Lim's Holland Village: Well-priced Asian-inspired homewares and furniture pieces.

EATING IN HOLLAND VILLAGE: OUR PICKS

Holland Village Food Centre: Beloved open-air hawker hub dishing out satay, laksa and *char kway teow* (noodles, clams and eggs). *10am-10pm* $

Frankie & Fern's: Artisanal coffee, fresh pastries and wholesome brunch fare in a rooftop location. *9.30am-9.30pm Fri-Sun, to 5.30pm Mon-Thu* $$

Original Sin: Popular vegetarian spot that offers Mediterranean-inspired dishes bursting with fresh, vibrant flavours. *noon-2.30pm & 6-10pm* $$

Tai Cheong Bakery: This bakery may have started in Hong Kong, but its egg tarts are much loved on the Little Red Dot. *10am-10pm* $

FROM KAMPONG TO CULTURAL HUB

Once a sleepy *kampong* (village) surrounded by rubber plantations, Holland Village blossomed in the 1930s and '40s as the go-to hangout for British servicemen stationed nearby. Locals called it *hue hng au,* meaning 'behind the flower garden' in Hokkien – a nod to its leafy location near the Botanic Gardens.

Just across Holland Ave, along Jln Merah Saga, **Chip Bee Gardens** came to life in the 1960s as married quarters for British forces. When the troops departed in the '70s, the neighbourhood transformed: stylish cafes, artisan boutiques and creative studios moved in, turning it into the artsy, bohemian enclave beloved by Singaporeans today. Take a leisurely stroll along its peaceful streets and admire the elegant rows of black-and-white terrace houses that lend the area its unique charm.

Racing Through History

Get revved up at Gallery26's F1 Exhibition

Step into the world of speed at **Gallery26** *(instagram.com/gallery26.dempsey; free),* an immersive F1 exhibition located in Dempsey Hill. Get up close to legendary Ferrari F1 cars – including Kimi Räikkönen's SF16-H – alongside race memorabilia and real parts of the Marina Bay Street Circuit, like 2023 safety barriers. Trace the evolution of the night race, discover race-day engineering secrets, and relive unforgettable moments from 1961 to today. Perfect for a quick stop or an F1 fan's pilgrimage, the exhibition takes about an hour to explore. The gallery is closed on Mondays and Tuesdays.

A Night Out on the Lorongs

Neighbourhood nightlife in Lorong Mambong

As dusk descends over **Lorong Mambong**, the artery that cuts through Holland Village, it transforms into a pedestrian-friendly haven. The after-work crowds flock to the bars and eateries, spilling onto the street as they savour the happy-hour specials. A hot favourite, **Wala Wala Cafe Bar** *(walawala.sg)* is perennially packed thanks to its beer towers and large sports screens. For those after a sugar high, **2am: dessertbar** *(2amdessertbar.com),* tucked away at the end of **Lorong Liput**, will have sweet tooths crying for joy into their posh dessert. The sexy, atmospheric space impresses with an entourage of sweet showstoppers. The mastermind behind this creative joint is the lauded Singaporean chef Janice Wong.

Shop Around the Village 'Hood

Treats and treasure in Holland Road Shopping Centre

Holland Village blends laid-back indie charm with modern retail. Bypass the shiny new, pet-friendly mall One Holland Village and head instead to the ageing **Holland Road Shopping Centre**, where upstairs you'll find art, handicrafts, homewares, nail spas, hair salons and massage joints. Across the road at **Raffles Holland V**, there's a handful of fashion boutiques among the eateries. Just behind, **Chip Bee Gardens** hides indie boutiques, designer homeware stores and artisanal bakeries – perfect for a leisurely wander. Most shops open from around lunchtime to 9pm.

EATING IN BOTANIC GARDENS: OUR PICKS

Pangium: Embark on a delicious journey of Michelin-starred Straits cuisine in a heritage setting. *noon-1.30pm Thu-Sat & 6.30-7.30pm Wed-Sat* **$$$**

Bee's Knees: Delights with casual all-day dining, hearty brunch fare, fresh bakes and artisanal coffee – perfect for a refuel. *8am-10pm* **$$**

Sprouts Food Place: If you have many tastes to satisfy, this small food court tucked away near the Healing Garden is just the trick. *7am-9pm* **$**

MICRO | bakery: Just outside the gardens at Serene Centre, this hole-in-the-wall bakery is heaven for bread and coffee lovers. *8am-4pm Wed-Sun* **$$**

DR DAVID SING/SHUTTERSTOCK

Holland Road Shopping Centre

When Art Meets Outbreak

Artful safety reminders at OK Sculpture Park

Singapore's **OK Sculpture Park** in Holland Village is a post-SARS tribute built in 2003, and once again became timely during the COVID-19 pandemic. It's part art exhibit, part public service announcement – wander around the bronze statues and be reminded of hygiene actions like hand-washing, temperature-taking and mask-wearing that keep Singapore safe. Quirky and oddly charming, it turns pandemic reminders into whimsical sculpture therapy.

WHERE TO SEE & BUY ART

REDSEA Gallery: Leading contemporary art gallery in Dempsey Hill, showcasing both emerging and established international artists.

ARTitude Galería: Independent Dempsey Hill gallery that champions emerging contemporary artists from Southeast Asia and beyond.

TAKSU: This heavy-hitter in Chip Bee Gardens features Southeast Asian contemporary works with a bold urban edge.

Pop Art Gallery: This public art gallery in the void deck of Holland Ave Block 8 has reproductions of iconic pop art with a Singaporean twist.

DRINKING IN DEMPSEY & HOLLAND VILLAGE: OUR PICKS

Dempsey Cookhouse & Bar: Delectable cocktails in a buzzy atmosphere. Mondays are martini night. *6-11.30pm Sun-Thu, to midnight Fri & Sat*

Le Bon Funk: Funky wine bar where a curated selection of drops pair perfectly with inventive small plates. *5-10pm Mon-Fri, from noon Sat & Sun*

Craftsmen Coffee: Great brews from single-origin beans sourced from across the globe. *8.30am-9pm Mon-Thu, to 10pm Fri & Sat, to 8pm Sun*

MAVRX: Trendy micro-coffee bar serving speciality brews and cold brew on tap in a sleek, minimalist setting. *8am-5.30pm*

Researched by Morgan Awyong

EASTERN SINGAPORE

RELIGION, EATS AND PERANAKAN TREATS

East side, best side: the eastern neighbourhoods adjust the city's rhythm to one suited for coastal cycling, colourful culture and cherished cuisine.

Singapore's eastern coastline was once characterised by its *kampongs* (villages), mangrove swamps, coconut plantations and holiday bungalows, but that all changed when the East Coast land reclamation scheme began in 1962, adding 1525 hectares of land.

These days, the eastern neighbourhoods offer faceted peeks into Singaporean culture. Closest to the city, Geylang is a notorious red-light district, yet spiritually rich with temples and mosques. Further east, Joo Chiat (part of the Katong neighbourhood) is a photogenic enclave of multicoloured shophouses, championed by the Peranakan community. Stretching along the seafront, East Coast Park lures visitors with waterside activities and cycling. Most far-flung is Changi, with the Changi Museum and the jetty for riding bumboats to Pulau Ubin island.

INCLUDES

Peranakan terrace houses (p128)

See p207 for places to stay in eastern Singapore.

Highlights

❶ Intan

Experience Peranakan culture over tea with a resident custodian as he shares candid stories in his stunning shophouse. **p133**

❷ Geylang

Explore Singapore's (fairly tame) red-light district, juxtaposed with temples, mosques and some of the island's best food. **p142**

❸ Loyang Tua Pek Kong Temple

Admire a multireligious temple with three different faiths under one roof. **p140**

❹ East Coast Park

Roam this breezy coastline park, beloved by locals and filled with fun and food for all the family. **p134**

◀ ❺ Changi Chapel & Museum

A moving tribute to those interned in the Japanese occupation. **p137**

Getting Around

MRT

New stations make exploring the east easier and faster. The East-West Line is key, travelling from the city to Changi Airport while hitting all the sights apart from Coney Island.

Walking

You'll find shade under a motley collection of shophouses or large trees, but some of Changi's more rustic spots are unsheltered, so bring a hat or umbrella.

Bus

If you love watching the city scenery go by, bus 2 is perfect for getting to Geylang, Katong and Changi. Save some time on the latter by hopping on at Tanah Merah MRT.

Katong

An intermingling of old-world charm and Peranakan flair is showcased through some of the island's most beautiful shophouses. You'll be kept fuelled while exploring the chic cafes and local treats dotting the area.

BEST KATONG BUYS

RetroCrates: Independent store specialising in new and pre-owned vinyl. Head to sister store Goodvibes for merch.

Sojao: The organic-cotton bed linen and loungewear are buttery soft and come in chic sophisticated colours that make bedtime a luxurious indulgence.

Tiger & Lotus: Dreamy shop curating a selection of designer homeware – some whimsical, others luxurious, and all begging to come home with you.

npcc: This is no place to be indecisive: there's only one thing for sale at this concept boutique. Check its social media for the current featured product, inspired by our senses.

Echo Vintage: Like hunting at a flea market – pick up some finished pieces or create your own jewellery with their charms.

Peranakan Perfection

Snap photos of Koon Seng Rd shophouses

If you venture off Joo Chiat Rd midway, you'll discover what is arguably Singapore's most colourful and photographed street: Koon Seng Rd, lined on both sides with extraordinary **Peranakan terrace houses**. These joyously painted beauties are captivating on their own, each flaunting contrasting accent colours for a striking effect – as if chosen like a colouring book by an unbridled child. Together, they're a kaleidoscope that has social media on fire.

Apart from their hues, they may look similar to the casual eye. However, notice that one set has brilliantly glazed tiles about its windows, while the other prefers an assortment of stucco dragons, birds and crabs – each symbolising a different blessing to the family within. What makes them quintessentially Peranakan is their fusion of design influences: bat-shaped vents from the Chinese, timber roof eaves and balustrades from the Malays, and European tiles. Another distinctive feature are the *pintu pagar* (swinging doors) at the dwellings' front entrances, which allow for refreshing cross-breezes while ensuring privacy.

Nowadays most of the terrace houses serve as private homes, which is worth keeping in mind when you visit. Though the occupants seem reconciled to the constant presence of photographers intent on capturing the charm of the neighbourhood, it might try their patience at times, especially if you're blocking their gates. Many sightseers also stroll repeatedly across the street to get that perfect shot, but technically it's jaywalking, so remember to wait for vehicles to pass.

Glorious Dedication to Ganesha

Wander around the Sri Senpaga Vinayagar Temple

One of the most beautiful Hindu temples in Singapore, **Sri Senpaga Vinayagar Temple** *(ssvt.org.sg)* comes across a little differently to its other colourful counterparts on the island with its yellow-and-clay-coloured entrance tower. From humble beginnings as a palm-frond shed with a wooden roof, the site became a place of worship after the local Sri Lankan community discovered a stone statue of the elephant god Vinayagar washed up on a pond here.

SORBIS/SHUTTERSTOCK

Sri Senpaga Vinayagar Temple

After multiple upgrades and surviving WWII damage, the temple has become a symbol of resilience and ardour for Sri Lankan Hindus. After admiring the sculpted pastel panels around the exterior, step past the heavy wooden doors and be greeted by the perfume of incense, essential oils and flowers. Your eyes will automatically dart to either the beautifully painted ceiling frescos with scenes of Hindu mythology or the showstopping 4.5m golden centrepiece. The latter was built at a cost of S$200,000 and is Southeast Asia's first musical pillar, producing different melodic notes when tapped – though the waist-high barriers around it suggest it's for special occasions and certain officials.

No matter. You can still wander about the compound of halls, classrooms and a wedding dais, spotting colourful devotional art with accompanying labels in various languages. Adding to the building's grandeur is the inner sanctum, its lavish roof adorned with a resplendent layer of gold.

If visiting in August or September, you might coincide with the **Vinayaka Chaturthi** festival. The birthday celebration sees the temple grounds heavy with garlands from roof to walls, with trumpet song and drum beats punctuating the festive air.

KATONG'S HIDDEN CHARMS

A heritage and urban development content creator, **Wee Liang** *(@takenodes)* points out some of Katong's quieter gems, adding to approach the residences with respect.

Conserved Terrace Houses: Parallel to Sea Ave is a tiny lane with technicoloured low-rise terrace houses. The side mural has sea turtles from which Katong got its name.

Chip Guan Heng: Major distributor for the street carts serving the popularised ice-cream sandwiches. Purchase a classic *potong* (cut) popsicle for just S$1.

Ng Eng Teng House & Zubir Said Apartment: Former homes of notable figures in Singapore's history. Ng Eng Teng was an acclaimed sculptor; a bronze statue can be seen from outside. Zubir Said composed the national anthem and scored local films in his apartment.

EATING IN KATONG: HERITAGE HAUNTS

Chin Mee Chin Confectionery: Century-old bakery pumping out old-style coffee and bakes. Try the house-made *kaya* (coconut and egg jam). *8am-4pm Tue-Sun* $

Sin Heng Claypot Bak Koot Teh: Peppery or herbal? Both versions bathe tender pork ribs in rich broth made smoky with claypots. *10am-11.30pm Tue-Sun* $

Janggut Laksa: That other original laksa maker; the version here is just as unctuous and aromatic, if a tad sweeter. *10.30am-4.30pm* $

Kway Guan Huat Joo Chiat Popiah: This 1938 institution adds a fried-fish crisp twist to its turnip rolls, wrapped in chewy skin. *9am-2pm Tue-Sun* $

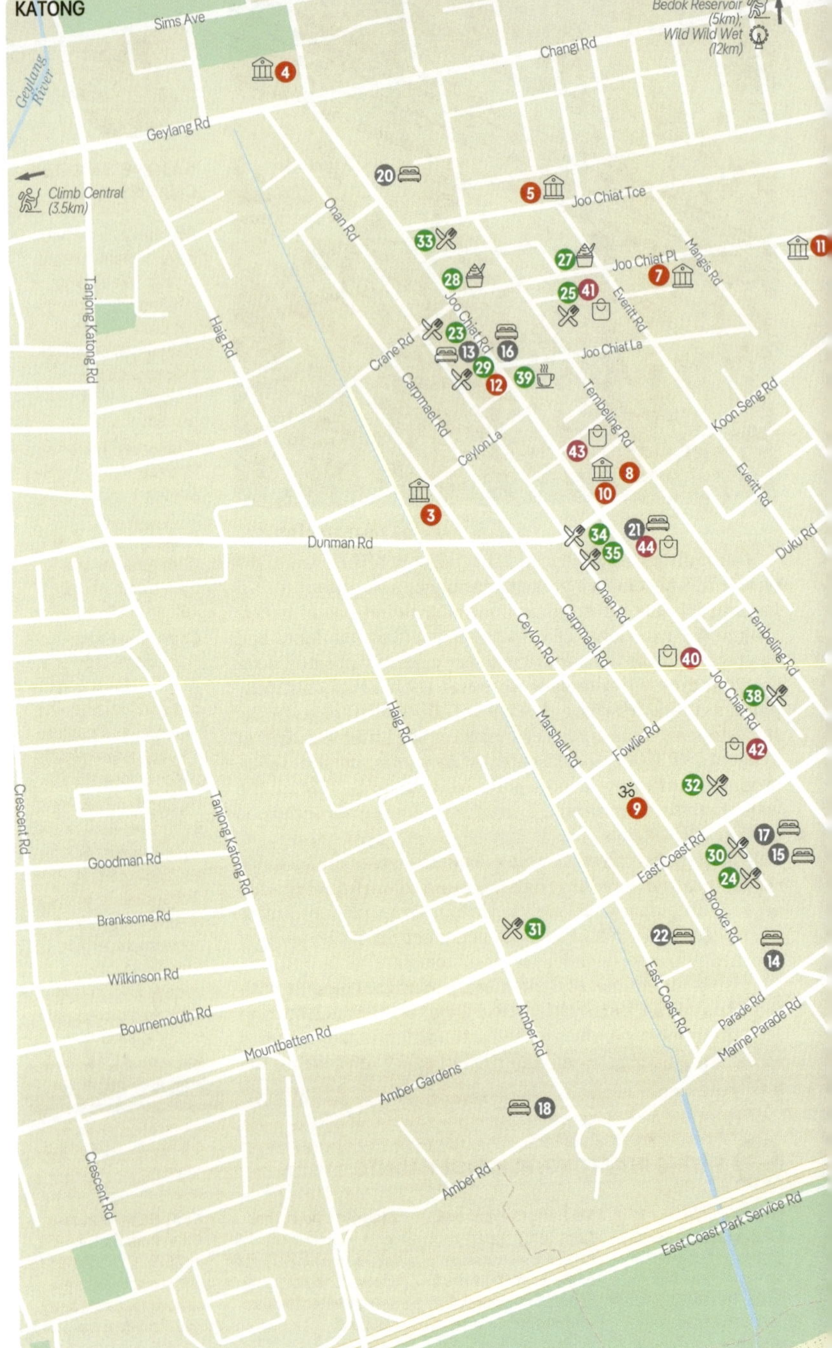
KATONG
Sims Ave
Changi Rd
Bedok Reservoir (5km); Wild Wild Wet (12km)
Geylang River
Geylang Rd
Climb Central (3.5km)
Joo Chiat Tce
Onan Rd
Joo Chiat Pl
Mangis Rd
Everitt Rd
Joo Chiat Rd
Joo Chiat La
Crane Rd
Carpmael Rd
Tanjong Katong Rd
Haig Rd
Tembeling Rd
Koon Seng Rd
Ceylon La
Everitt Rd
Dunman Rd
Duku Rd
Ceylon Rd
Carpmael Rd
Onan Rd
Tembeling Rd
Joo Chiat Rd
Haig Rd
Marshall Rd
Fowlie Rd
Crescent Rd
Goodman Rd
Tanjong Katong Rd
East Coast Rd
Branksome Rd
Brooke Rd
Wilkinson Rd
East Coast Rd
Bournemouth Rd
Amber Rd
Parade Rd
Marine Parade Rd
Mountbatten Rd
Amber Gardens
Crescent Rd
Amber Rd
East Coast Park Service Rd

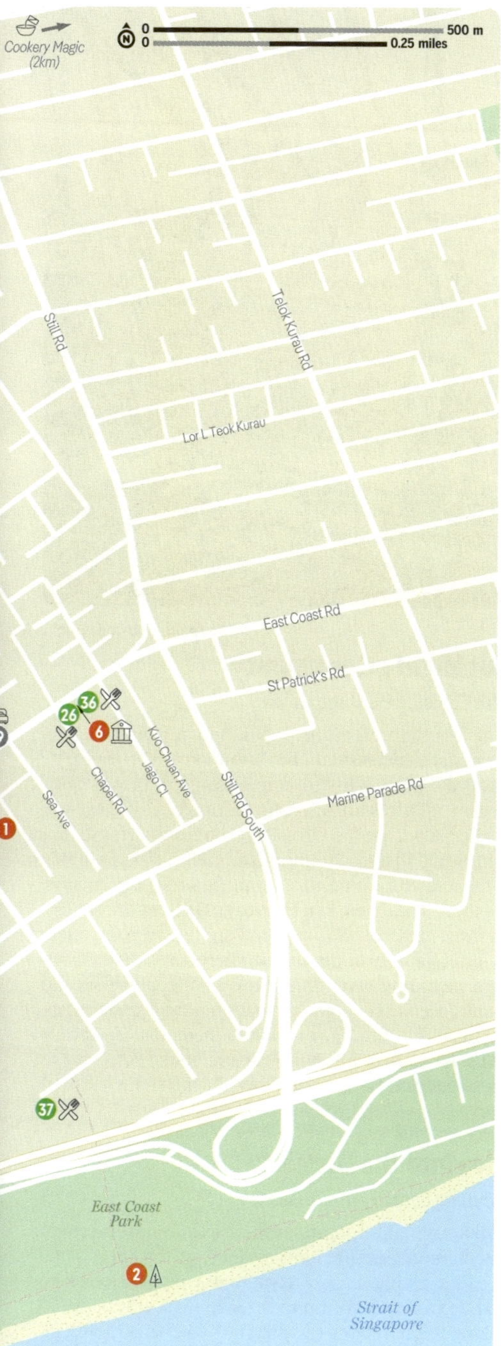

SIGHTS
1 Conserved Terrace Houses
2 East Coast Park
3 Eurasian Heritage Gallery
4 Geylang Serai Heritage Gallery
5 Intan
6 Katong Antique House
7 Ng Eng Teng House
8 Peranakan Terrace Houses
9 Sri Senpaga Vinayagar Temple
10 Straits Enclave
11 Zubir Said Apartment

ACTIVITIES
12 Betel Box Tours

SLEEPING
13 Betel Box
14 Grand Mercure Roxy
15 Holiday Inn Express Katong
16 Hotel 81 Sakura
17 Hotel Indigo
18 ISA Hotel
19 Santa Grand Hotel East Coast
20 STORIES Joo Chiat, a Hotel by Cove
21 Venue Hotel
22 Village Hotel Katong

EATING
23 174Bingo
24 Bei-Ing Wanton Noodles
25 Cata Coffee
26 Chin Mee Chin Confectionery
27 Chip Guan Heng
28 Ecstatic Desserts
29 Guan Hoe Soon
30 Janggut Laksa
31 Katong Mei Wei
32 Kim Choo Kueh Chang
33 Kway Guan Huat Joo Chiat Popiah
34 Mr & Mrs Mohgan Super Crispy Roti Prata
35 Old Bibik's Peranakan Kitchen
36 Peranakan Inn & Lounge
37 Roland Restaurant
38 Sin Heng Claypot Bak Koot Teh

DRINKING & NIGHTLIFE
39 Common Man

SHOPPING
40 Echo Vintage
41 npcc
42 RetroCrates
43 Sojao
44 Tiger & Lotus

BEST EASTERN SINGAPORE TOURS

Betel Box Tours: Legendary food walks, particularly the Friday-evening Sins and Salvation through Geylang's *lorongs* (alleyways).

Cookery Magic: Cooking classes in chef Ruqxana's home. Whip up dishes from regional cuisines including Peranakan and Eurasian classics.

Singapore Sidecars: Take in Joo Chiat from the sidecar of a vintage Vespa – super-fun and great for photos!

Supernatural Confessions: Explore the dark side of Changi on this resident-led walk filled with creepy stories at Singapore's most haunted spots; see p139.

Let's Go Tours: The East Coast Bicycle Tour will have you pedalling past coastal scenery, charming residential estates and local food haunts.

YVETTE CARDOZO/ALAMY

Intan residence-museum

Small but Mighty Community

Discover the Eurasian Heritage Gallery

Constituting less than 1% of the population, Singapore's Eurasian community may be small, but it embodies the country's multicultural dynamic. This unique ethnic group was born from the fusion of European and Asian heritage. As you explore the three galleries within the Eurasian Community House, you can delve into this diverse community's rich history, notable achievements and vibrant culture, spanning religion, cuisine, music and sports. The **Eurasian Heritage Gallery** *(eurasians.sg/our-heritage-gallery; S$5)*, situated on the 3rd floor, offers an enlightening journey of discovery. There's a section on notable figures, including Benjamin Sheares, Singapore's second president, and Joseph Schooling, the national swimming champion and Singapore's first Olympic gold medallist. To savour the delightful flavours of Eurasian cuisine, make your way to **Quentin's**, located on the ground floor. The museum is closed on Monday.

Deep Dive into the District

Tour the Geylang Serai Heritage Gallery

This small but well-laid-out **museum** gives a wonderful snapshot of the communities that have called Geylang Serai home over the decades, giving context to your later explorations. The free open-style gallery is split into three main sections. 'Making of Geylang Serai' relates the district's history, tracing its origins as a lemongrass and citronella plantation through its transformation into an outlying settler community and then a modern residential estate. There are pictures of how it used to look with trams running through plantations. The 'Living in Geylang Serai' section focuses on the area's present-day incarnation, and 'Our Geylang Serai: Community and Heritage' shares the local community's experiences and memories through photographs, recordings, books and other exhibits. Artefacts like the *gubahan,* a bouquet made of currency, along with classical musical instruments and toys bring things to life. The faux record player broadcasting famous hits from the past is a nice touch.

Dive into Joo Chiat's Peranakan Culture

Private museums worth booking

Two of these private museums are open by appointment only, but they're well worth the advance planning for their intimate setting filled with personal stories. They all offer an enriching deep dive into all things Peranakan.

A private residence-museum on Joo Chiat Tce, the **Intan** *(the-intan.com; adult/child S$64.20/32.10)* offers a range of classes and experiences. The owner and curator Alvin Yapp – former air steward with Singapore Airlines – warmly welcomes visitors and shares the captivating stories behind the extensive collection of Peranakan antiques, artefacts and textiles he has been amassing over three decades. He first shares stories about the museum and his ethnic heritage, before bringing guests up to the 2nd-floor no-photo zone where his prized collections are kept. Yapp invites questions and answers all effusively, ensuring every narrative addresses both queries and curiosity. Treat yourself to the Tea Experience, where you can savour delightful Nonya *kuehs* (bite-sized snacks) while being regaled by the polyglot (at our session, he spoke five languages!). Outside the regular programmes, Yapp also welcomes private tours.

The lifelong passion of late Mr Peter Wee, founder and fourth-generation Peranakan, **Katong Antique House** *(instagram.com/katongantiquehouse; S$15)* on East Coast Rd is filled with painstakingly curated antiques, artefacts, furniture, pictures and jewellery. The museum is now lovingly maintained by its new guardians, Eric Ang and Angeline Kong, who passionately strive to preserve Mr Wee's dream and heritage. Sessions require a minimum of two to begin.

WHO ARE THE PERANAKANS?

In Singapore, Peranakan (locally born) people are descendants of immigrants who married local women mainly of Malay origin. Hundreds of years of immersion and the meeting of foreign and local customs have resulted in an intriguing hybrid culture.

It's acknowledged that the Peranakan fall into three broad categories. The Chitty Melaka and Jawi Peranakan are descended from Indian migrants, while the Straits Chinese Peranakan, Singapore's largest group, are of mainland Chinese origin.

The rich mixture of heritage, culture, customs and traditions comes to life in a captivating display, either retold by its keepers at the private museums in Katong, or the official Peranakan Museum (p67) on Armenian St.

EATING IN KATONG: BEST PERANAKAN EATS

Guan Hoe Soon: Singapore's oldest Peranakan restaurant, since 1953. Try the *ayam buah keluak* (chicken stewed with dark nuts). *11am-3pm & 5.30-9pm* $$

Old Bibik's Peranakan Kitchen: Time-honoured recipes ensure faithful customers. The beef rendang melts in your mouth. *11.30am-9.30pm* $$

Peranakan Inn & Lounge: Classics like Nonya *chap chye* (mixed veggies) and *kueh pie tee* (turnip and shrimp in a pastry) are tops. *11am-3pm & 6-10pm* $$

Kim Choo Kueh Chang: Traditional Nonya *kueh* and rice dumplings since 1945. The ondeh ondeh (sweet pandan rice-cake ball) is the top pick. *9am-9pm* $

WHAT AM I LOOKING AT?

With their colourful glazes and romantic designs, Peranakan tiles are quintessential home accent pieces for any self-respecting Nonya or Baba (Peranakan women or men). Originating from Europe and later Japan, the objects allude to the blessings the owners wish to invite to their home. See if you can spot peapods, pomegranates or aubergines – symbols of fertility with their plentiful seeds – or popular flowers like roses and peonies for beauty and status. Cranes and deer bring hopes of longevity, as do fruits like peaches. Phoenixes and dragons are commonly featured, representing the female and male energies at their highest form, often seen on wedding items. But what of bats? While a pest in some cultures, the critters are lucky harbingers in Chinese tradition – their name a homophone for 'fortune'.

For walk-ins, **Straits Enclave** *(singaporeperanakanmuseum.com; S$12)* takes over a former co-working space along Joo Chiat Rd and delivers a full Peranakan experience with a museum, costume rental and retail offering. Discover Baba-Nonya culture while feasting your eyes on an incredible collection of colourful antiques and artefacts. Don't miss the 150-year-old bed, perfectly prepared and laid out for a traditional Peranakan wedding. The sparkling beaded sash above the frame took approximately six years to complete. Professional photoshoots can be arranged, complete with authentic clothing styles, hair and makeup. It helps that the museum is right beside the famous terrace-houses stretch of Koon Seng Rd. Workshops are available, offering hands-on experiences in Peranakan pastimes such as intricate beadwork and batik fabric painting, or you can book teatime and dinner experiences with home-cooked dishes.

Get Active in the East

Break a sweat in East Coast Park

Eastern Singapore covers a vast swathe of land from Geylang to Changi, so there's abundant space to stretch your legs and get your heart pumping.

Known as East Coasters' communal backyard, the 15km stretch of seafront in **East Coast Park** *(nparks.gov.sg)* is where Singaporeans come to swim, windsurf, wakeboard, kayak, picnic, bicycle, skateboard and in-line skate. You'll find swaying coconut palms, patches of bushland, a lagoon, sea-sports clubs and some excellent eating options. Kid-friendly playgrounds abound, and bike rentals are scattered along the shoreline. Take the MRT to Marine Parade station and dodge into the Marine Parade Underpass to start your beach break.

Over at Bedok Reservoir, the action-packed treetop **Forest Adventure** *(forestadventure.com.sg; from S$31.90)* is an exhilarating aerial escapade catering to various age groups with its three distinct courses (minimum height requirement of 110cm and recommended minimum age of five). Thrill-seekers will revel in wobbly crossings, adrenaline-pumping zip lines, and even a free-fall moment. Older children and adults will squeal as they conquer the awe-inspiring Big Zip spanning 300m over water from a 14m-high platform. For more heart-racing activities, the **HomeTeamNS Clubhouse Bedok Reservoir** *(hometeamns.sg/bedok-reservoir)* offers **Double Trouble** *(S$35),* Singapore's largest indoor water slide; or thrilling

EATING & DRINKING IN KATONG: BEST CAFES

174Bingo: Bakes are the highlight here, with the pistachio tart and cherry pie often selling out. *8.30am-4.30pm Wed-Sun* $

Cata Coffee: Sip a darn good brew under a rainbow at this balmy joint. Standing tables are perfect for those on the go. *8am-4pm* $

Ecstatic Desserts: Soft mochi and ice-cold dessert soups are a natural response to the hot weather, especially when this good. *11am-9pm Wed-Mon* $

Common Man: All-day brunch at its finest. It has a coffee academy and a roastery – good coffee is a given. *7.30am-9.30pm Tue-Sun, to 5pm Mon* $

A WALK OF DISCOVERY THROUGH JOO CHIAT

Joo Chiat is best seen on foot so that you can admire the architecture and duck into the area's boutiques and cafes.

START	END	LENGTH
Geylang Serai Market & Food Centre	328 Katong Laksa	3km; 2.5hr

Start your adventure at 1 **Geylang Serai Market & Food Centre**. Explore the wet market before grabbing some eats at the hawker centre. Head south across Changi Rd before taking a left onto Joo Chiat Tce. Check out the 2 **Intan** (p133), a private museum (tour bookings are required).

Turn right at Everitt Rd and continue south to Joo Chiat Pl. Pop into the radical retail space 3 **npcc** (p128), where only one conceptual product is sold per season. Continue west and head left down Tembeling Rd to the ornate 4 **Kuan Im Tng Temple** before turning right to get to Joo Chiat Rd.

Grab a caffeine boost at 5 **Common Man**, before heading down Koon Seng Rd for snaps of the colourful 6 **Peranakan terrace houses** (p128). Once you're photo-ed out, continue down Joo Chiat Rd, popping in and out of contrasting shops, such as old rattan haven 7 **Teong Theng Co** and funky boutiques like 8 **Cat Socrates**. Turn right when you reach East Coast Rd to find Peranakan boutique 9 **Rumah Bebe** and snack purveyor 10 **Kim Choo Kueh Chang** (p133). Finally, pop by Ceylon Rd to visit the stunning 11 **Sri Senpaga Vinayagar Temple** (p128), then double back to cult-status 12 **328 Katong Laksa** for a bowl of lip-smacking goodness.

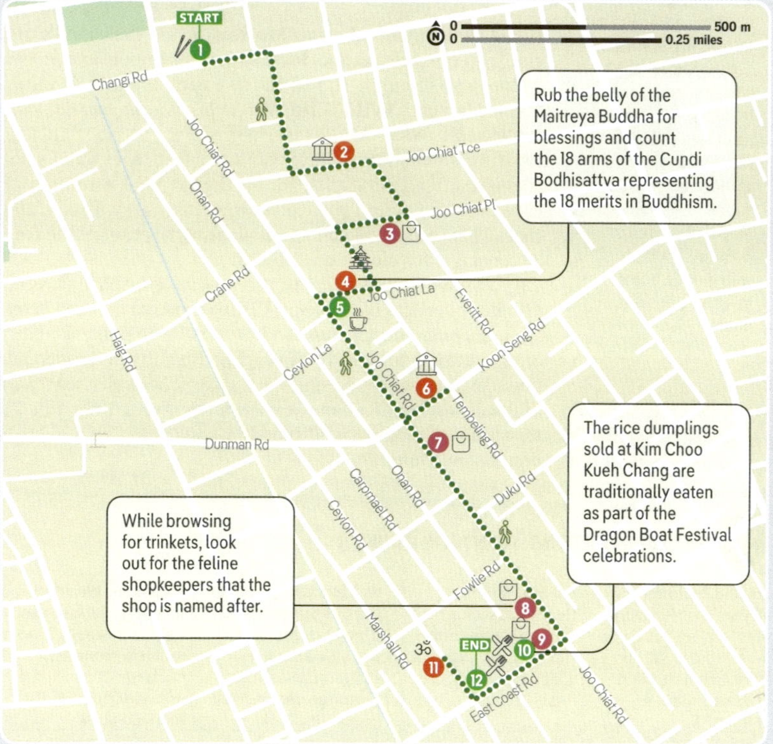

START
END
0 500 m
0 0.25 miles
Changi Rd
Joo Chiat Rd
Joo Chiat Tce
Joo Chiat Pl
Joo Chiat La
Onan Rd
Crane Rd
Haig Rd
Ceylon La
Everitt Rd
Koon Seng Rd
Tembeling Rd
Dunman Rd
Carpmael Rd
Ceylon Rd
Duku Rd
Fowlie Rd
Marshall Rd
East Coast Rd

Rub the belly of the Maitreya Buddha for blessings and count the 18 arms of the Cundi Bodhisattva representing the 18 merits in Buddhism.

The rice dumplings sold at Kim Choo Kueh Chang are traditionally eaten as part of the Dragon Boat Festival celebrations.

While browsing for trinkets, look out for the feline shopkeepers that the shop is named after.

BOUGIE & BUDGET

The notable Swan and Maclaren produced many of Singapore's landmark structures, including the renowned Raffles Hotel, Goodwood Park Hotel, Victoria Theatre and Concert Hall, and now-defunct Tanjong Pagar Railway Station. Other projects were much more humble, such as Joo Chiat's **Hotel 81 Sakura**, sporting a pink and white facade across its modern shophouse structure, with details like the red-brick upper walls and narrow windows adding to its throwback charm. The hotel operators have added some Japanese touches to the spaces – but less so in its rooms. Consider a stay at these conserved shophouses, but also note that the brand is known to offer wink-nudge hourly rates for transient guests.

ZHAFIRAHTRI/SHUTTERSTOCK

Cyclists, East Coast Park (p134)

timed challenges at **Action Motion** *(S$35)*, the island's first gamified obstacle course. It's a lot harder than it looks!

More splash-happy fun in the sun can be found at water-themed fun park **Wild Wild Wet** *(wildwildwet.com; day pass adult/child from S$29/21)* in Pasir Ris. Its 16 'rides' include twisting water slides, a wave pool and a mat-racer water slide. If you're after a serious thrill, hit the Torpedo, an 18m-high capsule for a free fall you won't forget in a hurry. Thankfully, there's also a Jacuzzi and a tube-floating river to soothe frazzled nerves. It's closed on Tuesday.

If your fingers are twitching, ascend to awe-inspiring heights at indoor vertical playground **Climb Central** *(climbcentral.sg; entry pass adult/youth S$27.25/21.80)*. The Kallang facility offers multiple high walls of varying difficulty and welcomes newbies and seasoned climbers alike. The walls soar past multiple levels in Kallang Wave Mall to give a different spin to window-shopping, and there's a bouldering area to truly engage your muscles.

EATING IN KATONG: HERITAGE HAUNTS

Roland Restaurant: According to Roland, it was his mum, Mrs Lim, who invented Singapore's chilli crab in the 1950s. *11.30am-2.30pm & 6-10pm* $$

Bei-Ing Wanton Noodles: Saucy al dente thin egg noodles with slippery dumplings that glide down your throat. *noon-4.30pm* $

Mr & Mrs Mohgan Super Crispy Roti Prata: Flaky dough pancakes served with savoury curry; add your choice of egg, cheese or onion. *6.30am-1.30pm Thu-Tue* $

Katong Mei Wei: This shopping-mall basement stall has a steady following for its silky boneless chicken and fragrant rice. *10.45am-7.15pm Tue, 11am-7pm Wed-Sun* $

Changi

Time slows down when you visit Singapore's eastern tip. Apart from the glamorous airport, the area is subdued, keeping its stories close. For the intrepid, it can be uncovered in its memorials and empty mansions.

Sea Breezes & Village Feel

Enjoy a beachside city break

On the far northeast coast, Changi Village is a welcome respite from the commotion of the city. Exploring this area provides a glimpse of a more laid-back side to Singapore, where locals embrace the quintessential heartlander uniform of sleeveless T-shirts, board shorts and flip-flops. While the low-slung buildings are modern, the atmosphere exudes a village-like charm, with the lively **Changi Village Hawker Centre** the focal point. Foodies flock here for the three nasi lemak (coconut rice) stalls, sparking endless debates about which serves the best version.

Crossing the footbridge to **Changi Beach**, you'll come to a place where thousands of Singaporean civilians were executed during WWII. It's hard to believe such violence took place in this picturesque spot. You can stroll and sunbathe here, but the beach isn't ideal for swimming.

Adjacent to the hawker centre and a short distance from Changi Beach is the ferry terminal, where you can catch **bumboats** (motorised sampans) to Pulau Ubin island or to Malaysia's Desaru Coast. Just beyond the terminal is the starting point for the **Changi Point Coastal Walk**, a breezy 2.2km-long boardwalk that takes you past mangroves, a sandy beach and the verdant grounds of government holiday villas.

The walk leads to the private Changi Sailing Club, whose public **Georges@Changi** *(georges.com.sg)* restaurant-bar is a beautiful spot to polish off a couple of beers while gazing out at bobbing yachts and Pulau Ubin. Alternatively, head back to Changi Village and take a seat at **Little Island Brewing Co** *(libc.co)*, a microbrewery and smokehouse, for sundowners and live music.

JOURNEY TO THE FAR EAST

Getting to Changi Village is an adventure in itself. The first option is to catch the East-West MRT to Tanah Merah station, from where bus 2 will whisk you right into the heart of the village. The second option is to grab a bike from one of the rental kiosks in East Coast Park and pedal the flat 15km route to the village. You'll go east through tranquil coastal parkland, north along Changi Coast Rd (it's heaven for plane-spotters) and finally west along Changi Beach. Make sure you order some sugarcane juice when you arrive – you're welcome.

Stories from the Inside

Explore Changi Chapel & Museum

The revamped **Changi Chapel & Museum** *(heritage.sg/changichapelmuseum; adult/student/child under 6yr S$9/7/free)* stands as a tribute to the resilience and courage of the civilian internees and prisoners of war (POWs) who were held here during the Japanese occupation. In eight zones,

SIGHTS
1 Changi Beach
2 Changi Chapel & Museum
3 Johore Battery
4 Loyang Tua Pek Kong Temple
5 Old Changi Hospital

ACTIVITIES
6 Changi Point Coastal Walk

EATING
see 7 Changi Famous Nasi Lemak
7 Changi Village Hawker Centre
8 Cosford Container Park
9 Georges@Changi
see 7 International Muslim Food Stall Nasi Lemak
see 7 Mizzy Corner

DRINKING & NIGHTLIFE
10 Little Island Brewing Co

SHOPPING
11 Jewel Changi Airport

TRANSPORT
12 Pulau Ubin Bumboat

the museum chronicles the internees' harrowing experiences through personal artefacts, interactive displays, photographs and gripping accounts. A poignant highlight is the replica Changi Prison cell, complete with an authentic door; built for one, cells like this were used for up to four prisoners. Visitors can hear historical recordings of conversations between internees through speakers strategically placed within the cell. Resourcefulness and determination are showcased in the tiny Morse code transmitter hidden in a matchbox and the replica British and Australian patchwork quilts created by women internees – these quilts sometimes carried secret

EATING IN CHANGI: BEST COCONUT RICE

Mizzy Corner: Generous portions and an all-round favourite for its balanced flavours and airy basmati rice (stall 01-26 in Changi Village Hawker Centre). *24hr* $

International Muslim Food Stall Nasi Lemak: For smokier flavours, opt for sambal chilli, seasoned chicken and aromatic rice (stall 01-03). *7am-2pm & 6pm-midnight Tue-Sat* $

Changi Famous Nasi Lemak: Those who love their saucy add-ons in terms of beef or chicken rendang or *sambal sotong* (chilli-paste squid) head here. *hours vary* $

codes embedded in the motifs, with messages only loved ones could decode.

The museum is also home to remarkable full-size replicas of the famous **Changi Murals** painted by POW Stanley Warren in the old POW hospital. The original murals, located in Block 151 of the nearby Changi Army Camp, are inaccessible to the public. The museum's centrepiece is a replica of the **Changi Chapel** built by inmates as a focus for worship and a sign of solidarity; here, visitors can find the **Changi Cross**, crafted in 1942 using the casing of a 4.5in howitzer shell and brass strips sourced from camp workshops. Interactive robot Temi offers tours through the eyes of an interned soldier. It's free and lasts 50 minutes. The museum is closed on Monday.

THE HOSPITAL'S STORY

Built in 1935 by the British as a military hospital, the infamous Old Changi Hospital was taken over by WWII Japanese troops to be used as a holding compound for POWs. It was this period, with rumours of torture in locked cells, that left a dark stain in its history. After the Japanese surrender, the hospital regained its function serving military personnel before it was opened to the public as Changi Hospital. When it closed in 1997, its chequered past and whispered lore of ghost sightings drew the curious to explore – that is, until officials barricaded the grounds, citing public safety as the reason.

Singapore's Most Famous Haunt

Tour the notorious Old Changi Hospital

Without a doubt, nine in 10 Singaporeans will point to this **abandoned complex** as the island's most notorious haunt. Stand before the dilapidated structure – gated to prevent intruders – and you'll be convinced, seeing the grimy building with only night creatures rustling the dark forest around you. Come face-to-gate by travelling up Hendon Rd near the Coastal Settlement. The 15-minute uphill walk passes multiple abandoned mansions adding to the spooky tension, especially at night. Once at the top, a small path leads down past a raised platform for offerings to the back gates of the hospital. Peer in and take your time; just don't think about entering, with the tight security system in place.

Those with less nerves can come by during the day, or join the three-hour tour by **Supernatural Confessions** *(supernaturalconfessions.com; S$98)*. Having spent decades growing up in Changi, co-founder Eugene Tay enthralls with his retelling of local superstitions and mysterious tales as he guides you from tragic site to morbid spot – but always respectfully.

Naval Guns & Plane-Spotting

Visit the Johore Battery

Military buffs should make their way to the **Johore Battery**, which lies just north along Cosford Rd. Part of the British coastal artillery defence network, the battery was armed with three monstrous 15in naval guns, which were engaged during the Battle of Singapore in 1942. The original guns are long gone, but there's a replica in position for visitors to see. A small hut provides photos and information, though it was locked when we went by. Just a few steps further down the road is **Cosford Container Park** *(cosfordcontainerpark.com)*. The cluster of eateries offer international menus, with most guests opting for the seats facing the airport runway – happy plane-spotters with a beer or slushie in hand.

MORE MEMORIES & MONUMENTS

For a deeper understanding of Singapore's military history, you can visit a number of poignant sites, including the **Battlebox** (p64) museum in Fort Canning Park, Bukit Timah's **Former Ford Factory** (p151), and **Kranji War Memorial** (p173).

CHANGI AIRPORT'S BEST HERITAGE FOOD GIFTS

Rich & Cake Shop: These Swiss rolls keep it simple with quality ingredients, including slow-cooked *kaya* (coconut and egg jam).

Bee Cheng Hiang: Glistening sheets of barbecued pork jerky or cotton-candy-like pork floss? The only answer: get both!

Kwong Cheong Thye: Keep your meals saucy the Singaporean way with these moreish chilli and soy sauces.

Eu Yan Sang: Founded in 1879; its curative supplements and tonics based on traditional Chinese medicine are trusted by all.

Irvins Salted Egg: Dusted with the savoury, creamy flavours of cured egg yolk, the potato and salmon skin chips are cracklingly good.

SQUARE BOX PHOTOS/SHUTTERSTOCK

Jewel Rain Vortex

Airport Mall Like No Other

Check out an indoor waterfall

If you're travelling through Changi Airport, save some time for the architecturally awe-inspiring **Jewel** *(jewelchangi airport.com),* accessible only on the land side. Looking like the set of *Jurassic Park* thanks to its cascading gardens, this multidimensional lifestyle destination was designed by Moshe Safdie of Marina Bay Sands fame. The levels are filled with everything you could dream of finding at an airport: top-notch restaurants, local and global retailers, a cinema, spas, a hotel – the list goes on. Head to the topmost level for a hedge maze, play nets, sculptural viewpoint – all in a canopy park. But the true marvel is the 40m-high waterfall descending from the glass-dome ceiling. The world's largest indoor waterfall, the **Jewel Rain Vortex** will take your breath away (note it only operates from 10am to 10pm). A public light-and-music showcase heightens its beauty at 8pm and 9pm Mondays to Thursdays, with an additional 10pm show on weekends.

A Religious Melting Pot

The three religions of Loyang Tua Pek Kong Temple

Loyang Tua Pek Kong Temple *(lytpk.org.sg)* has its origins in the 1980s, when a simple hut was constructed to house statues of Taoist, Buddhist and Hindu deities discovered near the Loyang coastline. A fire in 1996 devastated the shrine, leading to the construction of a temple at Loyang Way before the institution moved to its current location in 2007. Today, this contemporary temple showcases impressive wooden carvings, intricate designs of swirling dragons, and hundreds of colourful effigies depicting deities, gods and saints. It represents the inclusive Singaporean approach to spirituality, bringing together three religions – Hinduism, Buddhism and Taoism – under one vast roof. There's even a shrine dedicated to Datuk Kung, a revered figure in Malay mysticism and Chinese Taoist traditions.

To participate beyond praying, you can sit before the '4D Oracle Stone' to scry for winning lottery numbers amid the rising smoke of your incense. At the rear, you can make a wish after doing a round on the golden abacus, starting and ending with your Chinese horoscope sign. For a peek into the future, draw a divination after praying to the main god, Tua Pek Kong, and retrieve the associated ticket from the corresponding lot drawer.

Ride Through a Wildlife Haven

Cycling around Coney Island

Accessible to the public via two pedestrian roads, the wild nature reserve of **Coney Island** *(nparks.gov.sg)* makes for a perfect escape from the city. With a diverse range of flora and fauna, it's a paradise for birdwatchers, who will love the bird hides. The reserve encompasses a variety of habitats, including mangroves and coastal forests, connected by two main parallel trails that span the island.

Take the MRT to Punggol Coast and enter via the west entrance, about 500m from the Punggol Settlement. While you're here, be sure to use the bathrooms (note there's only one Portaloo on the island!) and stock up on water. Long pants or insect repellent are advised for the sandflies. Hiring a bike is recommended as it provides the ideal pace to explore. The nearest option is **Jomando Adventure & Recreations** *(facebook.com/JomandoAdventureNRecreation)* at the Punggol Settlement. With a sprawling adventure camp being developed on the eastern side of the island, you'll want to double back after reaching the east entrance.

For the best wildlife sightings, arrive early; a family of otters loves to bask on the beaches here. Just keep an eye out for monkeys, who will quickly relieve you of your food, especially if it's in plastic bags. And as the signs suggest, be prepared for crocodiles that have appeared in recent years.

Cycle along the wide dirt path to enjoy more scenes of tall, dreamy casuarina trees. Choose the route nearer to the coast for more shade and access to the beaches. When the wind passes above, the falling needles sound like rain. **Beaches A** and **B** are more popular for their proximity to the entrance, and are also cleaner. Gates close for the day at 7pm sharp.

THE LEISURELY ROUTE

To encourage green commuting, Singapore has been steadily expanding its network of park connectors. One scenic route goes from the airport's Terminal 4 to Marina Bay Sands. Pick up your rental at the airport's **Hub & Spoke** *(hubnspokecafe.com)*, then head south down the Changi Airport Connector. The **Jurassic Mile** is fun, with prehistoric reptiles poised for attack. Heading south, the East Coast is around the 3km mark, adding refreshing sea breezes to the ride. The next 9km are dotted with jetties, a bougainvillea garden, playgrounds and food stops like the **East Coast Lagoon Food Village**. The route moves away from the coast at the 12km mark, approaching Bay East Garden. The area is under development so stick to the path until you reach **Marina Barrage**. Wending through the **Gardens by the Bay**, finish your ride at the iconic hotel and mall.

Geylang

There's no denying Geylang's infamy and vice-riddled lanes, but its gritty presence and thriving supper scene is a breath of fresh air – a counterweight that locals have grown to love and not judge.

KING OF FRUITS

Durians get a bad rap in Singapore. They're banned from nearly all public transport (most notably the MRT); few hotels will allow one through their doors; and many shopping malls enforce a 'no durians' policy. Why? Well, they're really, really pungent. However, people in Southeast Asia – including many Singaporeans – adore them, so you should at least try one. You'll find several streetside stalls with tables for feasting at the city end of Sims Ave. The sellers will happily advise what to pick and how to eat the fruit. Tip: do use the offered gloves, or your hands will stink for days.

The Sacred & the Secular

Discover Geylang's hidden charms

All those rumours about Geylang being peppered with brothels, girly bars, dubious hotels and alley after alley lined with sex workers are absolutely accurate. The district is a long way from Bangkok's Patpong, but a nocturnal stroll along its streets reveals a pretty risqué ambience – well, by Singaporean standards. And only at night.

Yet Geylang is also one of the Lion City's spiritual hubs, with huge temples and mosques, and picturesque alleys dotted with religious schools, shrines and smaller temples. **Masjid Khadijah** *(khadijahmosque.org)*, named after a generous female donor, offers prebooked tours; its minarets are unmissable along the main stretch. A daytime stroll through the *lorongs* (alleys) that run north to south between Sims Ave and Geylang Rd unravels little-seen charm for those who take the time to look. These include **Lorong 27** and **Lorong 29**, where decorated Buddhist, Taoist and Hindu temples sit side by side.

Geylang's other blessing is its food scene. Geylang Rd and Sims Ave teem with cheap, tasty, unceremonious local eateries. If you're feeling adventurous, treat yourself to a bowl of frog porridge, for which the area is famous. Try it at **Geylang Lor 9 Fresh Frog Porridge** *(geylanglor9.com)*. Late-night revellers can head to never-closed **126 Dim Sum Wen Dao Shi** *(facebook.com/126wendaoshi)* for a delicious dumpling pick-me-up, or **Yong He Eating House** *(yonghetoast.com)* for silky beancurd, fried fritters and savoury oyster vermicelli. The infamous durian takes centre stage with streetside sampling at **Durian Culture** *(facebook.com/durianculture)*.

A Master of Memories

The crafts of Eng Tiang Huat Chinese Cultural Shop

Cross the threshold of this enchanting Geylang **shophouse** *(facebook.com/ChineseCulturalShop)* to behold a treasure trove of Chinese antiques, textiles, opera props, costumes and traditional instruments, and an abundance of vibrant red banners with hand-sewn details. However, it's the unassuming old Singer sewing machine that steals the spotlight, for it's here that third-generation owner Jeffery Eng preserves his memories as a master of embroidery crafts. Jeffery's grandfather

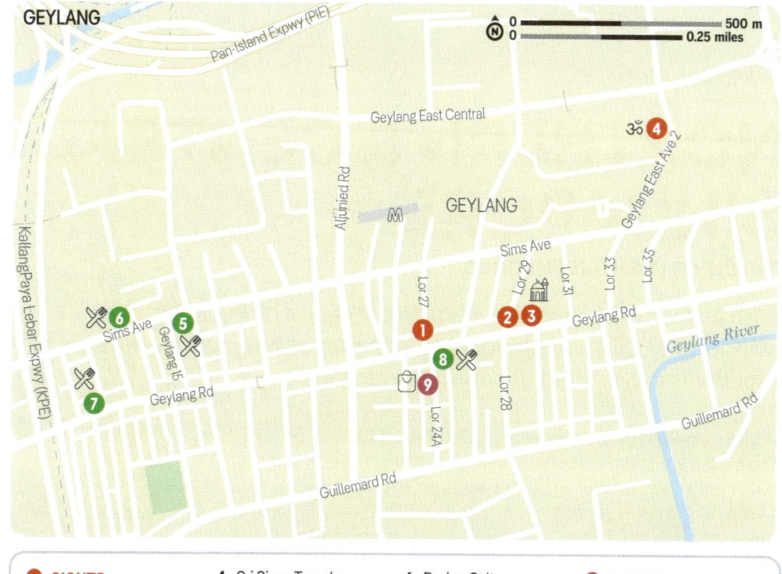

SIGHTS
1 Lorong 27
2 Lorong 29
3 Masjid Khadijah
4 Sri Sivan Temple

EATING
5 126 Dim Sum Wen Dao Shi
6 Durian Culture
7 Geylang Lor 9 Fresh Frog Porridge
8 Yong He Eating House

SHOPPING
9 Eng Tiang Huat Chinese Cultural Shop

established a tailoring business at the site in the 1930s (and the store still bears his name). Due to stiff competition, the business began importing Chinese-made goods and then slowly morphed into a purveyor of traditional Chinese cultural products. Jeffery's children are opting for other careers, so it's likely he will be the last in the line. Today, Jeffery is only too happy to guide visitors through his store, sharing his craft, his stories and perhaps his most recent commission.

Travelling Temple Tales

Visit the Sri Sivan Temple

This is the story of the travelling temple. Constructed on Orchard Rd in the 1850s, the **Sri Sivan Temple** *(sst.org.sg)* honours the deity Shiva. In the 1980s the land on which it was built was acquired for development, and the temple was uprooted and temporarily relocated to Serangoon Rd, before finally settling in its present Geylang location in 1993. What sets the temple apart is its whimsical and intricate design, combining elements from North and South Indian architectural styles. This fusion is beautifully showcased in the grand octagonal structure made from thousands of hand-carved marble and limestone pieces. Visitors are welcome to explore inside; wear respectful attire and remove your shoes at the door.

ROAD TO VICE

Did Geylang's activities stem from geomancy? As far-fetched as that may sound, those in the triads leaned into it. In Chinese lore, there were five major poisons, with one of them coming from the centipede (and the other four being the snake, toad, scorpion and spider). If you look at a map of the neighbourhood with the main thoroughfare, Geylang Rd, resembling the 'body', you can see how the many small *lorongs* (alleyways) represent the centipede's legs! While not as auspicious for others, this was a boon for vice-related trade, and sex work found a home.

Researched by Jaclynn Seah

NORTHERN & CENTRAL SINGAPORE

THE CITY'S LUSH GREEN LUNGS

With its medley of nature reserves, parks and hiking trails, this wonderfully wild and gloriously green part of Singapore offers an excellent respite from the concrete jungle.

While over 90% of Singapore's original forests have been decimated since the British arrived in the 19th century, the last remaining swathes of wilderness can still be found in its north and central region. The 24km Rail Corridor trail slices through the island's central forests, with plenty of access points leading to hidden quarries, heritage bridges and even Singapore's highest peak.

This area blends natural wonders with nostalgic traces of a slower, rural past. Spend a day at Mandai Wildlife Reserve with its conglomeration of five wildlife parks, all dedicated to conservation education. Or go off the beaten track to find Singapore's last village, its only natural hot spring and other curiosities outside the downtown area.

TOP TIP

Singapore's heat and humidity can be overwhelming. Pack plenty of water, douse in mosquito repellent and cover liberally with sun protection before you hit the trails.

TreeTop Walk (p158), MacRitchie Reservoir

See p208 for places to stay in northern and central Singapore.

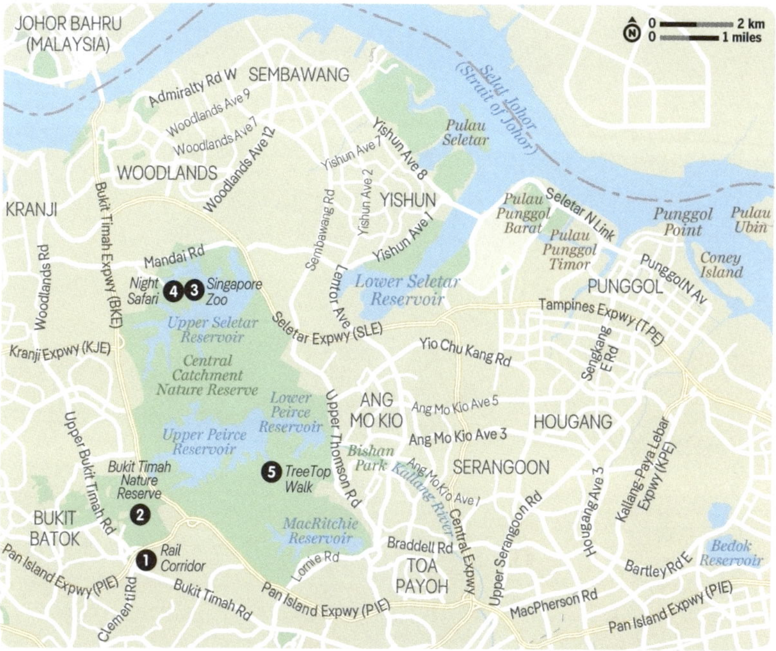

Highlights

❶ Rail Corridor
Hike the 24km passageway spanning the island from Kranji in the north to Tanjong Pagar in the south. **p148**

❷ Bukit Timah Nature Reserve
Visit one of Singapore's largest surviving tracts of primary rainforest. **p150**

❸ Singapore Zoo ▼
Get up close to a diverse range of animals in open enclosures at this award-winning zoo. **p154**

❹ Night Safari
Sign up for a rare chance to encounter nocturnal animals at the world's first night zoo. **p155**

❺ TreeTop Walk
See the jungle from new heights on the 25m-high TreeTop Walk at MacRitchie Reservoir. **p158**

Getting Around

MRT
The North-South Line links northern Singapore to the Orchard Road and Downtown Stations. Rail Corridor is best accessed on the Downtown Line. Northeast and Circle Lines get you closer to MacRitchie Reservoir, Seletar and Buangkok.

Bus
Public buses serve the areas not on the MRT network like Mandai Wildlife Reserve, Seletar Aerospace Park and Sembawang Hot Spring Park.

Walking
Bukit Timah Nature Reserve and Central Catchment Nature Reserve are linked by forest paths, providing lots of hiking opportunities.

FROM LEFT: NATE HOVEE/SHUTTERSTOCK, LEV LEVIN/SHUTTERSTOCK

NORTHERN & CENTRAL SINGAPORE
Johor Bahru
JOHOR BAHRU (MALAYSIA)
Selat Johor (Strait of Johor)
SEMBAWANG
Sungei Simpong
Admiralty Rd W
Woodlands Ave 10
Admiralty Park
Riverside Rd
Woodlands Ave 9
WOODLANDS
Woodlands Ave 7
Marsiling Park
Woodlands Ave 3
Woodlands Ave 5
Woodlands Ave 12
Yishun Ave 8
Yishun Ave 7
KRANJI
Seletar Expwy (SLE)
Sembawang Rd
Yishun Ave 2
Yishun Ct
Yishun Ring Rd
YISHUN
Orchid Country Club
Mandai Ave
Yishun Ave 1
Mandai Rd
Mandai Wildlife Reserve
Upper Seletar Reservoir
Lower Seletar Reservoir
Mandai Lake Rd
See Mandai Wildlife Reserve Enlargement
Woodlands Rd
Lentor Ave
Bukit Timah Expwy (BKE)
Kranji Expwy (KJE)
Upper Thomson Rd
Central Catchment Nature Reserve
ANG MO KIO
Ang Mo Kio Ave 4
Upper Peirce Reservoir
Lower Peirce Reservoir
Dairy Farm Rd
Ang Mo Kio Ave 1
Sin Ming Ave
Bishan Park
Bukit Batok Town Park
See Bukit Timah Nature Reserve Enlargement
Kallang River
Bukit Timah Nature Reserve
Upper Bukit Timah Rd
BUKIT BATOK
Singapore Island Country Club (Bukit Location)
MacRitchie Reservoir
Braddell Rd
Lornie Rd
Marymount Rd
TOA PAYOH
Pan Island Expwy
Pan Island Expwy (PIE)
Bukit Timah Rd
Thomson Rd
Balestier Rd
Adam Rd
Clementi Rd
Sixth Ave
Commonwealth Ave
Ulu Pandan Rd
Rochel Canal
Dunearn Rd
Ayer Rajah Expwy (AYE)
Farrer Rd
Singapore Botanic Gardens
Stevens Rd
Holland Rd
Alexandra Village Food Centre (3km)
43
54
52
33
44
18
40
24
3
1
57
9
16
48
11
34
4
15
32
21
41
46
19
35
37
39
10
45

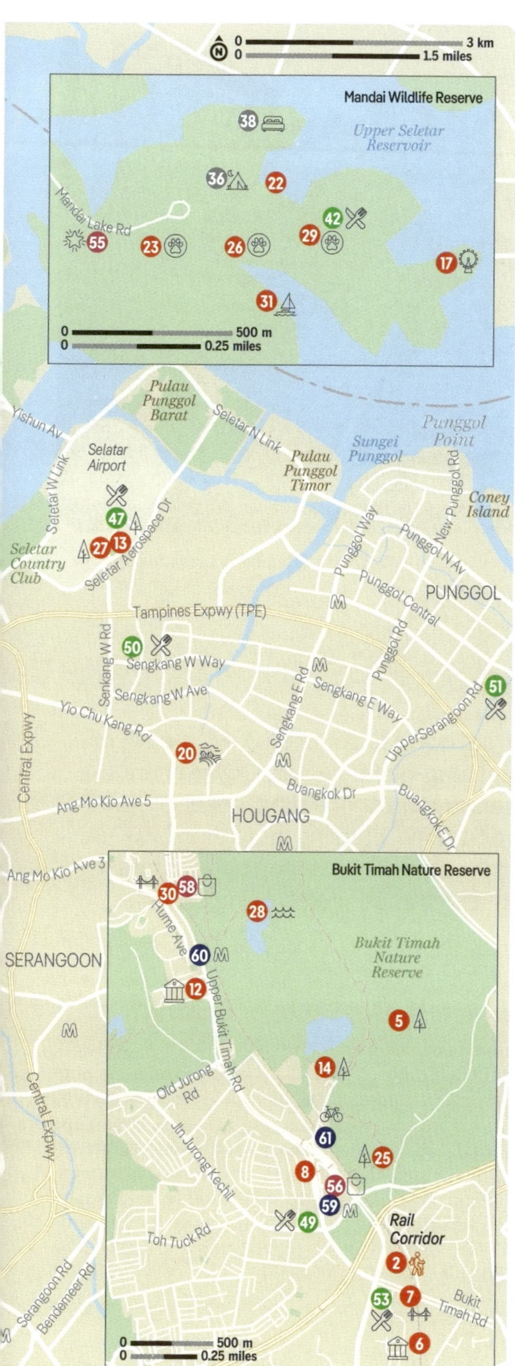

HIGHLIGHTS
1 Mandai Wildlife Reserve
2 Rail Corridor

SIGHTS
3 Bird Paradise
4 Bukit Batok Town Park
5 Bukit Timah Nature Reserve
6 Bukit Timah Railway Station
7 Bukit Timah Truss Bridge
8 Cheong Chin Nam Road
9 Chestnut Nature Park
10 Clementi Forest
11 Dairy Farm Nature Park
12 Former Ford Factory
13 Hampstead Wetlands Park
14 Hindhede Nature Park
15 Jelutong Tower
16 Kebun Baru Birdsinging Club
17 KidzWorld
18 Kranji Node
19 LIVINGSPACE
20 Lorong Buangkok
21 MacRitchie Reservoir
22 Mandai Boardwalk
23 Night Safari
24 Rainforest Wild ASIA
25 Rifle Range Nature Park
26 River Wonders
27 Seletar Aerospace Park
28 Singapore Quarry
29 Singapore Zoo
30 Upper Bukit Timah Truss Bridge

ACTIVITIES
31 Amazon River Quest
32 Paddle Lodge
33 Sembawang Hot Spring Park
34 TreeTop Walk

SLEEPING
35 Aloft Singapore Novena
36 Colugo Camp
37 Courtyard Singapore Novena
38 Mandai Rainforest Resort by Banyan Tree
39 Oasia Hotel Novena
40 Orchid Country Club
41 Swiss Club Guesthouse

EATING
see 58 Acqua e Farina
42 Ah Meng Restaurant
43 Beaulieu House
44 Chong Pang Nasi Lemak
45 Chuan Kee Boneless Braised Duck
46 Come Daily Fried Hokkien Prawn Mee
47 Hangar 66 Cafe
48 Mellben Seafood
see 33 Sembawang Eating House Seafood
49 Sin Chew Satay Bee Hoon
50 Thasevi Food Jalan Kayu
51 Uncle Leong Seafood
see 27 Wheeler's Estate
52 White Restaurant
see 27 Wildseed Café
53 Yeast Side

DRINKING & NIGHTLIFE
54 Nelson Bar
see 27 Youngs Bar & Restaurant

ENTERTAINMENT
55 Creatures of the Night

SHOPPING
56 Beauty World Centre
57 Junction 10
58 Rail Mall

TRANSPORT
59 Beauty World MRT
60 Hume MRT
61 Unsprung

Walking to Upper Bukit Timah Truss Bridge

TOP EXPERIENCE

Rail Corridor

Set to span the entire island from north to south by 2026, the 24km Rail Corridor is Singapore's first long-distance trail. Government agency NParks has turned a railway line connecting Singapore and Malaysia into a contiguous green spine, planting more than 52,000 native trees and shrubs along the corridor, restoring belts of forest and rebuilding the natural habitat for endangered animal species.

DON'T MISS

- Bukit Timah Railway Station
- Hinhede Nature Park
- Singapore Quarry
- Bukit Timah Truss Bridge
- Clementi Forest
- Kranji Node

Rail Corridor: North, South or Central?

The long-distance hiking trail is divided into three sections. The **central trail** (4km) near Bukit Timah is the most popular tract, packing in interesting historical features such as steel bridges and restored stations. South of Bukit Timah, the **southern trail** (10km) is less scenic and still undergoing restoration; its main appeal is the Clementi Forest. The **northern trail** (10km), north of Hillview station, takes you through the real countryside of Singapore. Visitors with limited time are best advised to focus on the central trail and explore the offshoot nature reserves in the vicinity.

PRACTICALITIES

- railcorridor.nparks.gov.sg

Kranji Node

To experience the northern trail, begin your trek at the newly opened **Kranji Node**, across the road from Kranji MRT station. It's an easy, shaded walk on flat ground. As Kranji is located along the coast, several native trees and coastal plants such as *geronggang* (known for its timber) have been planted by NParks. As you trudge through the corridor towards the Hillview stretch, you'll traverse an elevated ridgeline to reach a 6m-high lookout deck offering views of the Singapore Quarry and Bukit Timah Nature Reserve.

Singapore Quarry

Once used to mine granite, **Singapore Quarry** has long been filled with water and is now a jade-green lake backdropped by craggy cliffs and thick forest. Linger awhile and you might spot rare birds, fish, turtles or monitor lizards. There's a spacious viewing deck at the side of the lake to take in the outlook and observe dragonflies flitting over the water.

Hindhede Nature Park

Just south of the quarry, **Hindhede Nature Park** is crisscrossed with easy hiking trails and well-marked footpaths. This scenic place is excellent for birdwatching – try to spot the resident banded woodpecker. Little ones will enjoy the several adventure play areas that are dotted around the park.

Bukit Timah Railway Station

Take a break at the central trail's midway point, marked by the **Bukit Timah Railway Station**. After a two-year restoration, the station and the former staff quarters have been given a facelift and repurposed as a heritage gallery. The track-switching levers, station signs and ticketing booth have remained untouched. Just a short walk from the railway station is the emblematic 1932 **Bukit Timah Truss Bridge**, complete with its sturdy black steel frames.

Clementi Forest

The most scenic stretch of the southern trail is an 85-hectare pocket of wilderness in the bustling Clementi residential area. **Clementi Forest** is the most important and largest unprotected patch of forest along the Rail Corridor, home to 98 species of vascular plants, including the rare *Dienia ophrydis* orchid. The hiking trail is as wild as it gets in Singapore, with tall trees looming over you, two rivers running beneath the trail, and certain sections of the path covered in mud. If you're lucky, you might just spot an oriental pied hornbill soaring over your head.

WHERE TO START YOUR HIKE

The two endpoints of the Rail Corridor can be accessed from Kranji MRT station and (by 2026) Tanjong Pagar Railway Station. To walk the entire 24km, begin at the Kranji Node (northern end) or Spooner Rd (southern end), a short walk from Outram Park MRT. For a shorter, 7.5km hike along the route's most historic parts, start at Buona Vista station and end at Hillview station.

TOP TIPS

- Visit early to make the most of mild morning temperatures.
- Wear proper hiking shoes, as the trail can get muddy.
- A sunhat, sunscreen and plenty of water are essential.
- There are several places to refuel; the **Rail Mall** (p151; *railmall.com.sg*) has a range of cafes and restaurants.
- You'll see long-tailed macaques and monitor lizards along the trail; observe from a distance and don't feed them.
- The Rail Corridor is not lit at night, so bring your torch (flashlight) with you and avoid hiking alone. Extra care is needed at night because of active wildlife.

A RAIL LEGACY

The Rail Corridor (p148) traces the historic railway track that facilitated the transport of passengers and cargo between Singapore and the Malay peninsula. Launched in 1903, the railway was operational for over 100 years and saw many tweaks, including the deviation of its original tracks for its southern leg, and a failed branch line to the western Jurong industrial area.

The land where the railway tracks – run by the former Malayan Railway (Keretapi Tanah Melayu Berhad or KTM) – were laid and its surroundings officially belonged to Malaysia. It was only after the railway closed in 2011 that land parcels were exchanged and Singapore started to develop the Rail Corridor as we know it today – a continuous green artery through the island.

GOWILDGONATURE PICTURES/SHUTTERSTOCK

Long-tailed macaque at Bukit Timah Nature Reserve

Singapore's Highest Point

Hike to Bukit Timah Nature Reserve

Topped by Singapore's tallest hill, **Bukit Timah Nature Reserve** *(nparks.gov.sg)* is a swathe of primary rainforest embellished with hiking trails and bike paths. Once teeming with tigers, this is the only reserve that has been protected under the management of the Singapore Botanic Gardens since the 1930s (the other reserves were all worked for timber). The last tiger was shot in the 1920s, but you'll still find plenty of long-tailed macaques and dozens of bird species.

The 163-hectare sprawl is crisscrossed by five well-established walking trails that range in length and difficulty (return trips take 35 minutes to two hours), plus a popular 6km mountain-bike trail. You can rent bikes, helmets and other gear from **Unsprung** *(unsprung.com.sg; bike rental from S$50)* along Hindhede Rd – book in advance if you can.

For those who prefer to explore on foot, the quickest, most popular hike is the one leading to the **summit of Bukit Timah** (163m), Singapore's highest peak.

EATING IN NORTHERN SINGAPORE: BEST LOCAL EATS

Thasevi Food Jalan Kayu: This place has been tossing up Singapore's best *roti prata* (Indian flatbread) and fish curry since the 1960s. *24hr* $

Come Daily Fried Hokkien Prawn Mee: Awarded a Michelin Plate, this stall in Toa Payoh West Food Centre has a huge following. *8.30am-2pm Wed-Sun* $

Uncle Leong Seafood: Feast on the island's most-loved chilli crabs. The riverside outlet in Punggol East Container Park has great vibes. *hours vary* $$

Mellben Seafood: Contender for the best crabs in town. Its signature claypot *crab bee hoon* (rice vermicelli noodles) is soul food. *5-10pm* $$

To get to the reserve, take the MRT to **Beauty World station** (Exit A) and walk towards Hindhede Dr, where you'll find the reserve's official entrance. It has a visitors centre with restrooms, water fountains and an exhibition on the forest's flora and fauna. Take plenty of water, smother yourself in mosquito repellent – and don't feed the monkeys, no matter how cute they are!

Echoes of WWII

Tour the Former Ford Factory

In the midst of the nature reserves stands the former Ford Motors assembly plant, a landmark of significant importance in Singapore's history. The **Former Ford Factory** *(corporate.nas.gov.sg; admission S$7.13)* was where the British surrendered Singapore to the Japanese on 15 February 1942 during WWII.

The factory is now a museum with exhibitions that chart Singapore's descent into war, the three dark years of Japanese occupation and the island's path to independence. This sombre story is told through audio interviews, newsreels and harrowing personal accounts. A highlight of the exhibition is the **Surrender Room** – the boardroom where the surrender took place. Learn more through free English guided tours on Saturdays and Sundays at 11am and 3.30pm.

Take the MRT to Hume station and walk five minutes down Upper Bukit Timah Rd. The museum is closed on Mondays.

Boardwalks & Wetlands

Hike the Rifle Range Nature Park

Established in 2022 as a buffer for Bukit Timah Nature Reserve, the 66-hectare **Rifle Range Nature Park** *(nparks.gov.sg)* occupies the site of the Sin Seng Quarry. NParks occasionally runs walks exploring its rich biodiversity.

The main entrance is near Beauty World MRT station. Learn about conservation at the Visitor Pavilion before traversing the elevated Gliders Boardwalk to the **Quarry Wetland**, a freshwater ecosystem backed by cliffs. Hike the **Colugo Trail** for a panorama of the quarry; choose between the 30m steep trail or the moderate 50m stepped route. Look out for animal-crossing features such as rope bridges and colugo poles along the way.

REST STOPS ALONG THE RAIL CORRIDOR

Junction 10: Modern shopping centre named for its 10-mile (16km) distance from the Fullerton Hotel. At Choa Chu Kang Rd.

Rail Mall: Stretch of eateries housed in former plantation workers' quarters. Near Upper Bukit Timah Truss Bridge.

Beauty World Centre: Slightly dated-looking mall named after its early days as an amusement park. At Beauty World MRT station.

Cheong Chin Nam Road: Row of shophouses opposite Beauty World Centre with lots of eateries.

Alexandra Village Food Centre: Heartland hawker centre tucked in a light-industry area. Located near Gillman Flyover.

EATING ALONG THE RAIL CORRIDOR: OUR PICKS

Acqua e Farina: Italian chefs serve authentic pizzas and pastas in a cosy restaurant at the Rail Mall. *11.30am-2.30pm & 5.30-10pm Tue-Sun* $$

Sin Chew Satay Bee Hoon: Famously tasty bowls of rice vermicelli doused in thick peanut gravy. *1am-2.30pm & 5-8.30pm Wed & Thu, Sat & Sun* $

Yeast Side: Wide range of craft beers on tap to pair with its pizzas and foccacia sandwiches. Located at King Albert Park. *9am-11pm Wed-Sun* $$

Chuan Kee Boneless Braised Duck: Tender braised duck meat atop savoury rice. Long-time stalwart at Ghim Moh Food Centre. *9.30am-8pm Mon-Sat* $

QUARRY VIEWS & HISTORICAL SIGHTS

Explore the natural and historical sights off the Central Rail Corridor on foot or by MRT.

START	END	LENGTH
Hume MRT Station	Beauty World Centre	8km; 4-5hr

Emerging from 1 **Hume MRT station** (DT4), it's a five-minute walk south along Upper Bukit Timah Rd to the 2 **Former Ford Factory** (p151) to learn about Singapore's WWII history. Later, walk back up Upper Bukit Timah Rd for 15 minutes till you see the black beams of 3 **Upper Bukit Timah Truss Bridge**. Cross the bridge to the 4 **Rail Mall** (p151), a row of single-storey shophouses with arches above their signs, for some food.

This entrance to the Rail Corridor is marked by the old 9-Mile Platform. A five-minute walk southwards reveals the 5 **Singapore Quarry Bridge** overhead. Take the staircase to the right, cross the bridge and join the paved road to the picturesque 6 **Singapore Quarry** (p149) five minutes away.

Double back to the Rail Corridor and keep walking south till 7 **Hindhede Crossing**. Go down the stairs on the left and follow Hindhede Dr to the 8 **Bukit Timah Nature Reserve stone marker** past the car park. A five-minute stroll on the boardwalk leads to the scenic 9 **Hindhede Quarry Lookout Point**. If you're still raring to go, make the 1.2km climb up the Main Rd to 10 **Bukit Timah Summit** (p150), 163m high. Otherwise, continue down the Rail Corridor and take the exit and overhead bridge that leads to 11 **Beauty World Centre** (p151) to end your walk.

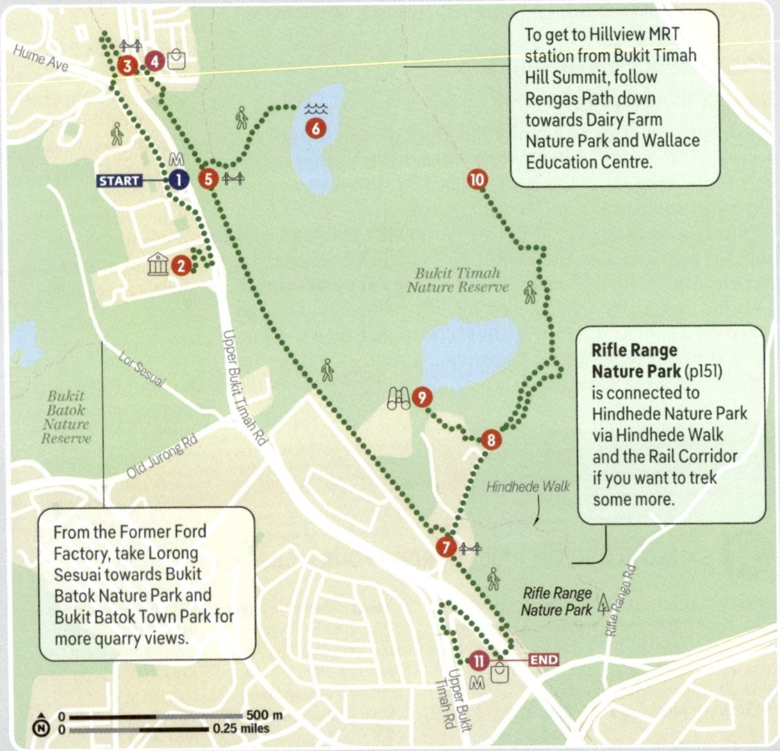

To get to Hillview MRT station from Bukit Timah Hill Summit, follow Rengas Path down towards Dairy Farm Nature Park and Wallace Education Centre.

Rifle Range Nature Park (p151) is connected to Hindhede Nature Park via Hindhede Walk and the Rail Corridor if you want to trek some more.

From the Former Ford Factory, take Lorong Sesuai towards Bukit Batok Nature Park and Bukit Batok Town Park for more quarry views.

DLENG/SHUTTERSTOCK

Chestnut Observation Tower

Two-Wheeled Adventures

Mountain biking in Chestnut Nature Park

Mountain bikers, take note! **Chestnut Nature Park** *(nparks.gov.sg)* is the first park in Singapore with dedicated mountain-biking trails, from beginner to crazy advanced. Novices can practise in the two skill parks, while daredevils can execute drop-offs and jumps at the pump track.

Set across 81 hectares of dense jungle, this is also Singapore's largest nature park, woven with hiking trails that run adjacent to the bike paths, separated by a barrier. The flat, easy **Northern Trail** (1.5km) leads to the spiralling **Chestnut Observation Tower**. It's a good spot for wildlife-watching – more than 25 species of birds have been sighted in this park. If you're lucky, you might even see a sunda colugo (an arboreal gliding mammal). The 2.1km **Southern Trail** is rockier and steeper, but also more scenic and interesting. Restrooms, water fountains and bike rentals *(from S$15 per hr)* are available at **Chestnut Point**.

To get here, take the Bukit Panjang LRT to Pending LRT station, then walk 20 minutes southeast along Bukit Panjang Rd and Chestnut Ave. A taxi from the city is about S$20 each way.

FROM GRANITE QUARRIES TO SCENIC PARKS

The demand for public housing and roads in Singapore during the 1980s and '90s led to a spike in demand for granite, which was mined from several quarries in the hills around Bukit Timah and Bukit Batok. By 2000, encroaching residential areas and the dangers of quarry mining led to the quarries being shut down, filled in and transformed into picturesque neighbourhood parks teeming with wildlife.

Bukit Batok Town Park is home to Singapore's second-tallest hill and a quarry that's nicknamed 'Little Guilin' for its resemblance to China's Guilin Mountains. While most quarries are filled with water to form deep quarry pools, Dairy Farm Quarry at **Dairy Farm Nature Park** is unusual because it was filled in with earth instead.

BOULE/SHUTTERSTOCK

Above: Orangutans, Singapore Zoo; Right: Malayan tiger enclosure, Rainforest Wild ASIA (p157)

TOP EXPERIENCE

Mandai Wildlife Reserve

Surrounded by the lush jungles of Singapore's Central Catchment Region, the open-concept Singapore Zoo has evolved from humble beginnings into Mandai Wildlife Reserve, a world-class conservation hub with a collection of five distinctive wildlife parks, including the pioneering nocturnal zoo, a luxurious eco-resort and a growing number of nature-based experiences to engage visitors of all ages.

DON'T MISS

- Singapore Zoo
- Night Safari
- River Wonders
- Amazon River Quest
- Bird Paradise
- Rainforest Wild ASIA
- Mandai Boardwalk

Singapore Zoo

Sprawled across 26 lush hectares on a peninsula jutting into the Seletar Reservoir, 50-year-old **Singapore Zoo** *(mandai.com/singapore-zoo; adult/child S$49/34; 8.30am-6pm)* is a tropical wonderland with over 4200 animals in spacious natural enclosures and many roaming across wide open spaces. It's been lauded as one of the best zoos in the world for its conservation and educational efforts.

PRACTICALITIES

- mandai.com
- single-park admission adult S$49-58, child S$33-41
- hours vary

DANNY YE/SHUTTERSTOCK

There are keeper talks and animal feedings throughout the day to learn more about the animals. The orangutans are the stars of the show in the park's centre – watch as they swing overhead from tree to tree. The **Fragile Forest** enclosure lets you encounter free-roaming creatures in an enclosed forest. Take the tram to save some energy navigating the park.

Kids can run free at the colourful **KidzWorld**, with slides, swings and a carousel. Little ones can also ride ponies, feed farmyard animals and get wet in the water-play area. (Don't forget to pack swimwear, sandals and a change of clothes.)

There's a rotating cast of animal ambassadors like orangutans, sea lions and penguins that you can have breakfast with at the zoo's **Ah Meng Restaurant**.

Night Safari

Singapore's acclaimed **Night Safari** *(mandai.com/night-safari; adult/child S$58/41; 6.30pm-midnight)* just west of the zoo offers a completely different type of nightlife. As its barriers melt away in the darkness, the park gives you the feeling of travelling through a jungle filled with lions, leopards and elephants. It's home to more than 130 species.

Popular open-sided shuttle trams take visitors on a 45-minute tour (with commentary) of the park's animals and habitats, but some parts of the park can only be explored on foot via the atmospheric walking trails. On the **Leopard Trail** you can get up close to wild spotted felines, porcupines and badgers. The **Eastern Lodge Trail** leads you to highly endangered species such as sloth bears, aardvarks and hyenas, while the **Tasmanian Devil Trail** takes you through an owl aviary and enclosures where the Tasmanian devil and other animals from Australia, New Zealand and New Guinea live.

A QUICK TIMELINE OF MANDAI WILDLIFE RESERVE

Inaugurated in 1973 as the Singapore Zoological Gardens, the open enclosures were a radical idea. The Night Safari opened in 1994 as the world's first nocturnal zoo, and River Safari (now River Wonders) launched in 2012. Bird Paradise predates the zoo, opening as the Jurong Bird Park in 1971; it was relocated to Mandai and renamed in 2023. Rainforest Wild ASIA opened in 2025.

WHICH PARK TO VISIT?

Singapore Zoo If you only have time for one park, make it this one.

Night Safari For those who hate the sun. Stars as the world's first night zoo.

River Wonders Smallest park but also the most sheltered. Best wet-weather option.

Bird Paradise For lovers of open aviaries and up-close animal encounters.

Rainforest Wild ASIA Best for those willing to pay for extra adventure activities.

TOP TIPS

- If you plan to visit more than one park, save money with a multi-park pass. Tickets are valid for five days from the first park visit and one-time entry to each park.
- To catch the last MRT train home after the Night Safari, leave the park by 10.45pm. Otherwise, the taxis out front can set you back about S$30 to S$50 for a ride downtown.
- Fee shuttle buses connect two main areas: Mandai Wildlife West (Bird Paradise and Rainforest Wild) and Mandai Wildlife East (Singapore Zoo, Night Safari, River Wonders).

Kids will enjoy **Creatures of the Night**, an interactive 20-minute show featuring the otter, raccoon dog and bearded pig. Book seats online two hours before the presentations (7.30pm, 8.30pm and 9.30pm).

River Wonders

Tucked between Singapore Zoo and the Night Safari, this compact river-themed wildlife park is a refuge for more than 11,000 land and aquatic animals. **River Wonders** *(mandai .com/river-wonders; adult/child S$45/33; 10am-7pm)* shines a spotlight on the underwater habitats of world-famous rivers, including the Nile, Yangtze and Congo. The **Mekong River** section particularly impresses with an aquarium rippling with giant catfish and freshwater stingrays. But the highlight of them all is the massive **Amazon Flooded Forest**, where manatees and gigantic arapaimas swim in a colossal corral. The **Giant Panda Forest** also draws quite the crowd with the park's celebrity panda couple, KaiKai and JiaJia.

You can't leave the park without going on the **Amazon River Quest** *(additional S$5 per person)* boat ride, which swooshes gently past roaming jaguars, tapirs and giant anteaters. Young kids must be at least 1.06cm tall to take the ride (note that it's suspended in the event of rain). Don't miss the **Once Upon a River** presentation (at 11.30am, 2.30pm and 4.30pm; online seat reservation essential), headlined by the green iguana, capybara and agouti.

MOLPIX/SHUTTERSTOCK

Giant Panda, River Wonders

Bird Paradise

Over at Mandai Wildlife West is a sanctuary to more than 3500 feathery residents across 400 species. **Bird Paradise** *(mandai.com/bird-paradise; adult/child S$45/34; 9am-6pm)* is divided into eight walk-through aviaries that replicate habitats from across the world. The largest is **Heart of Africa**, modelled on the forested valleys of continental Africa, while **Penguin Cove** has one of the world's biggest sub-Antarctic, cold salt-water habitats.

In the Sky Amphitheatre, birds of prey flaunt their skills at **Predators on Wings** *(10.30am & 2.30pm)*, while pelicans and flamingos feature at **Wings of the World** *(12.30pm & 5pm)*. Next to the Sky Amphitheatre are restaurants, a treetop playground and a kids' water-play area.

Rainforest Wild ASIA

Rainforest Wild ASIA *(mandai.com/rainforest-wild-asia; adult/child S$45/33; 9am-6pm)*, located next to Bird Paradise, is Mandai's first wildlife adventure park.

The natural landscapes of the park have been recreated admirably, from craggy karst mountains jutting out from the ground to the dank cool caves inspired by Sarawak's Mulu Caves. The elevated boardwalk around the park is wide and accessible, but those keen on a little adventure can take the 'wilder' treks on the forest floor with dirt paths and log bridges to cross streams.

The adventure activities alongside the animal enclosures are novel experiences, but the top-up charges for each activity can add up quickly. **Wild Apex Adventure** *(S$56; 9am-4.30pm)* lets you climb across the karst mountains as curious François' langur monkeys judge you from adjacent rocks. **Wild Cavern Adventure** *(S$66; 9.30am-2.30pm)* is a three-hour caving course through tight tunnels with just your headlamp; sessions start every hour. Adrenaline seekers can try the **Canopy Jump** *(13m/20m S$20/26; 10am-6pm)*, a short freefall from a tower 13m or 20m high.

Mandai Boardwalk

A free way to experience Mandai Wildlife Reserve is to take a stroll along the **Mandai Boardwalk** *(7am-7pm)*. This paved path traces the perimeter of the Singapore Zoo and River Wonders, along the shore of Upper Seletar Reservoir.

The boardwalk is about 3.9km in total, and takes about an hour or so to complete. There are two access points: **Kingfisher Entrance A** near Curiosity Cove, and **Tree Frog Entrance B** next to the River Wonders entrance.

Morning or late afternoon is best as there isn't much shelter along the boardwalk. You can enjoy views of the wild flora and fauna around the reservoir, and mostly hear and smell the animals in the zoo. Around the second pavilion from Tree Frog Entrance B is where you can spot the tall giraffes walking around. There's an additional extension to the nest-like **Iora Lookout** to the right of Tree Frog Entrance B.

GETTING TO MANDAI WILDLIFE RESERVE

Taking a rideshare or taxi is the fastest way to get here as it's quite out of the way compared to other attractions downtown.

Mandai City Express *(mandaicityexpress.com; one-way transfer S$8)* is the most convenient, with direct transfers for stops along Orchard Rd and Basah Rd to the Coach Bays in Mandai Wildlife Reserve.

There's also a Mandai Khatib Bus that runs every 15 to 20 minutes between the park and Khatib MRT station (NS14) from 8.30am until midnight.

You can also take public bus 138 from Ang Mo Kio station (NS16) and Springleaf station (TE4), or bus 928 from Choa Chu Kang station (NS4).

KEBUN BARU BIRDSINGING CLUB

An unusual sight sits at the foot of **Ang Mo Kio Town Garden West**: a small field crowded with nearly 400 tall metal poles rising from the ground. Visit on a weekend morning and you'll see colourful songbirds in ornate cages hoisted high atop the poles, while their proud owners gather below, chatting, comparing notes and listening closely to the chorus above.

This is the **Kebun Baru Birdsinging Club**, one of Singapore's last pockets of a once-widespread pastime. For decades, enthusiasts have met here to train and showcase their prized birds, believing that height, fresh air and the company of other birds help them sing at their best. Regular singing competitions keep the tradition lively. For visitors, it's a rare window into old-school Singaporean life and local culture.

RAY'S IMAGES/SHUTTERSTOCK

Kayaker, MacRitchie Reservoir

Rise & Shine at MacRitchie Reservoir

Stroll above the tree canopy

Right in the centre of Singapore, **MacRitchie Reservoir** *(nparks.gov.sg)* is a lush green space carved around the massive Central Catchment Area. The nature reserve has six trails ranging from 3km to 11km, with the 11km loop around the reservoir the most popular route. The trails skirt the water's edge and snake through the mature secondary rainforest, home to long-tailed macaques, colugos and huge monitor lizards. This is one of the best places in Singapore for wildlife-spotting. A word of warning, though: the macaques here can be aggressive – do not feed or antagonise them.

MacRitchie's biggest appeal is the **TreeTop Walk** (closed on Mondays), a free-standing, 250m-long suspension bridge that connects the two highest points in the reserve – Bukit Kalang and Bukit Peirce – giving an aerial view of the forest canopy from 25m above the ground.

Entry is at the ranger station, reached via the **Peirce Track**. The trailhead at **Windsor Nature Park** offers a slightly shorter trek that saves about an hour's walk. You can also trek over from **Rifle Range Nature Park**. Rifle Range Link connects to **Sime Track**.

A kilometre south of the TreeTop Walk, the thick foliage parts to unveil the **Jelutong Tower**, an eight-storey panoramic structure with spiralling stairs that lead to equally impressive canopy views.

To paddle in the glassy waters of the reservoir, you can rent kayaks at the **Paddle Lodge** *(scf.org.sg; from S$18 per hr)*. There's a designated area close to shore for novice paddlers. Only kids aged seven and up can kayak with adults, but kids aged 10 to 12 can sign up for the **Kid-in-a-Kayak** programme organised by the Singapore Canoe Foundation.

Several buses stop right in front of MacRitchie Reservoir, while Caldecott MRT station on the Circle Line/Thomson-East Coast Line is a 15-minute walk away.

Aviation-Themed Fun

Veer off the beaten path at Seletar Aerospace Park

East of Mandai Wildlife Reserve, the little-visited **Seletar Aerospace Park** *(seletarairport.com)* is something of a local secret. But this cloister of colonial-era buildings, boardwalk and wide green space with an aviation-themed playground is a great area for a family day out or a low-key date night.

On the fringes of Seletar Aerospace Park is a **wooden boardwalk** (near Hyde Park Gate) that runs parallel to the airport. Dotted with little wooden benches shaped like origami paper planes, this manicured walkway is a lovely spot to watch private jets take off, particularly at sunset.

Strolling eastwards will lead you to the recently opened **Hampstead Wetlands Park** *(nparks.gov.sg)*, an inviting marshland area studded with observation decks for birdwatching. The boardwalk takes you along the rim of the water-lily lake, where you can often spot kingfishers and barbets.

It's not the easiest place to get to. Either take a taxi or catch bus 103 from the bus interchange at Serangoon MRT station.

CHANGI AIRPORT

Aviation geeks who enjoyed watching the planes take off at Seletar should make time to linger at **Changi Airport** (p140). Besides a dizzying array of shops and restaurants, the airport also has the world's tallest indoor waterfall, the Jewel Rain Vortex.

SELETAR'S PAST FLIGHTS

During the colonial days, the British developed the Seletar area to build a Royal Air Force station that served Singapore from 1928 to 1971. To house officers and their families, they also erected a cluster of black-and-white bungalows, with the help of Samsui women (female Chinese immigrants who took on construction jobs).

Today, the area is mostly dominated by the tiny Seletar Airport, which serves chartered flights and provides training sessions. Thirty-two of the former colonial-era houses have been given a facelift and transformed into an assembly of restaurants, spas and shops called the Oval.

Bubbling Goodness

Soak in Sembawang Hot Spring

It comes as a surprise to many that a hot spring exists in Singapore, an island famously sheltered from tectonic activity. The rather remote **Sembawang Hot Spring Park** *(nparks.gov.sg)* features a cascading pool where sizzling 70°C hot water is drawn up directly from the ground, and naturally cools down to a balmy 40°C in the lower tier where you can

EATING & DRINKING AT SELETAR AEROSPACE PARK: OUR PICKS

Wheeler's Estate: A stunning green lawn for alfresco brunch, dinner and cocktails with live music by local bands every evening. *hours vary Tue-Sun* $$

Wildseed Café: Slinging freshly roasted coffee, tempting cakes and pastries, and hearty weekend brunches. Dog-friendly. *8am-4.30pm & 5-11pm* $$

Youngs Bar & Restaurant: Idyllic spot for modern European dishes on a Sunday afternoon. *11.30am-midnight Mon-Thu, 8.30am-1am Fri & Sat, to midnight Sun* $$

Hangar 66 Cafe: Relaxing aviation-themed cafe located within WingsOverAsia hangar (entrance along Seletar Aerospace View). *11.30am-10pm Wed-Sun* $$

SEMBAWANG HOT SPRING'S HIDDEN PAST

Discovered in 1909, the Sembawang hot spring became popular with locals, who believed the water was curative and therapeutic. In 1922 soft-drink giant Fraser & Neave took over the spring and bottled its water. During WWII the Japanese converted the site into thermal onsen baths, but a bomb fell on the area and caused the spring to fall into disuse. It was eventually restored in the early 1960s. Following appeals from the public to preserve the spring, the government kept it open – it existed as a mere tap in the ground for a long time – transforming it into Sembawang Hot Spring Park, which opened in January 2020.

sit and soak your feet. Leave your swimsuit at home – you're only allowed to dip your feet in! Bring your own pail to enjoy your footbath in quieter corners around the landscaped park. Note that the pool is closed regularly for cleaning (11am to 2pm Monday and Thursday).

A special feature is the egg station. Place your eggs in a small container and let the steaming hot-spring water work its magic. You will need to bring your own eggs, containers and cutlery. The on-site **Sembawang Eating House Seafood** *(sehseafood.com),* set in a glasshouse, serves good home-cooked dishes such as buttercream chicken.

There's no drop-off area along the park's entrance at Gambas Ave – the closest bus stop and parking lot is a 10-minute walk away at Blk 114 along Sembawang Rd. Canberra MRT station (NS12) is twice as far a walk.

Learn How the Locals Live

See the evolution of public housing at LIVINGSPACE

Toa Payoh is Singapore's oldest public housing town and an important milestone in the nation-building story. Developed by the Housing & Development Board (HDB), it was the first 'new town' planned with integrated amenities, and HDB's main office still sits right in the heart of Toa Payoh Central.

In the basement of Toa Payoh Hub, you'll find **LIVINGSPACE** *(hdb.gov.sg; free),* a small but engaging gallery that traces the evolution of Singapore's public housing. Through detailed models, archival photos and hands-on displays, it explains how town planning, community spaces and building technology have changed over the decades, and what future HDB estates might look like.

For tourists, it's an eye-opening look at how Singapore houses most of its population and creates liveable neighbourhoods despite scarce land. After exploring the gallery, take a stroll around Toa Payoh to see real-life examples of the ideas showcased inside.

Singapore's Last Remaining Kampong

Explore Lorong Buangkok

Singapore has developed so quickly that the island's once-ubiquitous *kampongs* (villages) have all but disappeared. Just one remains on the main island as a blip of resistance against the tide of modernisation. Visiting wonderfully rustic **Lorong Buangkok** is an evocative way to experience what life was like in Singapore before independence. Elders sit out on the

EATING & DRINKING AROUND SEMBAWANG: OUR PICKS

Nelson Bar: Opened in the 1930s, this venerable bar has retained its history through sailors' old pictures and scribbles on its walls. *2pm-midnight* $$

White Restaurant: Famous for its traditional rice vermicelli doused in luscious seafood gravy. Opposite Sembawang Shopping Centre. *10am-9.30pm* $

Chong Pang Nasi Lemak: A household name serving nasi lemak, aromatic rice doused in spicy sambal and served with a crispy chicken wing. *5pm-6am* $

Beaulieu House: Home-style seafood dishes in a colonial-era bungalow on the coast of Sembawang Park. *hours vary* $$

DEREKTEO/SHUTTERSTOCK

Lorong Buangkok

verandahs of their crumbling wooden houses, stray cats snooze on corrugated-tin roofs, and the crowing of roosters drowns out the noise of traffic. The 26 remaining families who live here seem carefree and oblivious to the breakneck pace of life happening outside their rural oasis (the S$6 to S$30 monthly rent probably helps).

The area is slated for redevelopment, with plans for a major road, two schools and a neighbourhood park, but the Urban Redevelopment Authority has confirmed that this will not happen for a few decades. The 1.22-hectare area is small, so expect to spend just 30 minutes or so here. You can catch a taxi (best ask the driver to wait for you), or take the MRT to Ang Mo Kio station (North-South Line), then bus 88 in the direction of Pasir Ris.

This is a private neighbourhood, so take care not to disturb the residents. Those keen to go deeper could join **Lets Go Tour Singapore** *(letsgotoursingapore.com)* on a guided wander through the *kampong*, listening to stories about provincial life and learning about the traditional village spirit. Take a stroll around the neighbourhood with your local guide and get the chance to step inside one of the *kampong* houses and chat with local residents. Tours run from 9am to 11am and cost S$250 to S$300 for a group of up to five people.

PULAU UBIN'S KAMPONG

The only other remaining *kampong* in Singapore is on the offshore island of **Pulau Ubin** (p194), where around 30 residents live simple, relaxed lives. Pulau Ubin offers an even deeper time-travel experience and is worth the day trip from mainland Singapore.

PUBLIC HOUSING IN SINGAPORE

Did you know that about 80% of Singaporeans live in public housing? These high-rise, government-subsidised Housing & Development Board (HDB) flats are central to how the city manages limited land and how it tackled a post-independence housing crisis in the 1960s. Early blocks were simple slab buildings built for speed and affordability, but today's estates feature distinctive architecture and colourful facades – lively, self-contained neighbourhoods where people from all walks of life live side by side.

Venture into the heartlands for a taste of everyday Singapore: sip a *kopi* at the local *kopitiam* (coffeeshop), pick up a warm waffle slathered with *kaya* (coconut and egg jam) from the bakery, stroll through park connectors and playgrounds, or simply people-watch as daily life unfolds around you.

Researched by Ria de Jong

WEST & SOUTHWEST SINGAPORE

WILD WONDERS AND OFF-RADAR ATTRACTIONS

This region, witness to intense WWII battles, now hosts some of the country's finest nature reserves, offering underrated opportunities for hiking and wildlife enthusiasts.

Despite Singapore's global image as a sleek, meticulously planned Garden City, the island's west and southwest conceal surprising pockets of rugged, untamed greenery and scattered farmlands. Historically, this region remained largely rural and apart from the downtown's rapid urbanisation. Beginning in the 1970s, Singapore's drive for economic growth dramatically transformed the west: forests were cleared, coastlines reclaimed and offshore islands converted into hubs for petrochemical and heavy industry. Today, the western district is the nation's manufacturing powerhouse, continually modernising with new infrastructure and transport networks. Yet those who venture beyond the city centre will find an enticing blend of wild nature, farmland charm and industrial heritage.

TOP TIP

Singapore's west and southwest is a fairly large area. Not all sights are conveniently reached by public transport, so plan by location to minimise travel time.

Henderson Waves pedestrian bridge (p176), Southern Ridges

See p208 for places to stay in west and southwest Singapore.

FROM LEFT: BELOVA IRINA/SHUTTERSTOCK, DANNY YE/SHUTTERSTOCK

Highlights

❶ Southern Ridges
Hike the 10km trail from Kent Ridge to Harbourfront for spectacular nature and city views. **p176**

❷ Sungei Buloh Wetland Reserve ▶
Explore Singapore's first ASEAN Heritage Park, a haven for mangrove biodiversity and migrating birds. **p175**

❸ Haw Par Villa
Enjoy an offbeat park with quirky sculptures and dioramas about Chinese ethics and stories. **p166**

❹ Jurong Lake Gardens
Roam through a family-friendly urban oasis featuring themed gardens and playgrounds. **p172**

❺ Gillman Barracks
Immerse yourself in culture, art and food while wandering around this rambling art outpost. **p171**

Getting Around

MRT
This vast area is served fairly well by the MRT; there are a number of new stations under construction which will add to the area's accessibility.

Taxi
For more out-of-the-way places, hop in a taxi or rideshare car from the MRT station.

Bus
Extensive bus routes connect to MRT stations, but relying solely on buses for your entire journey from the city can be quite time-consuming.

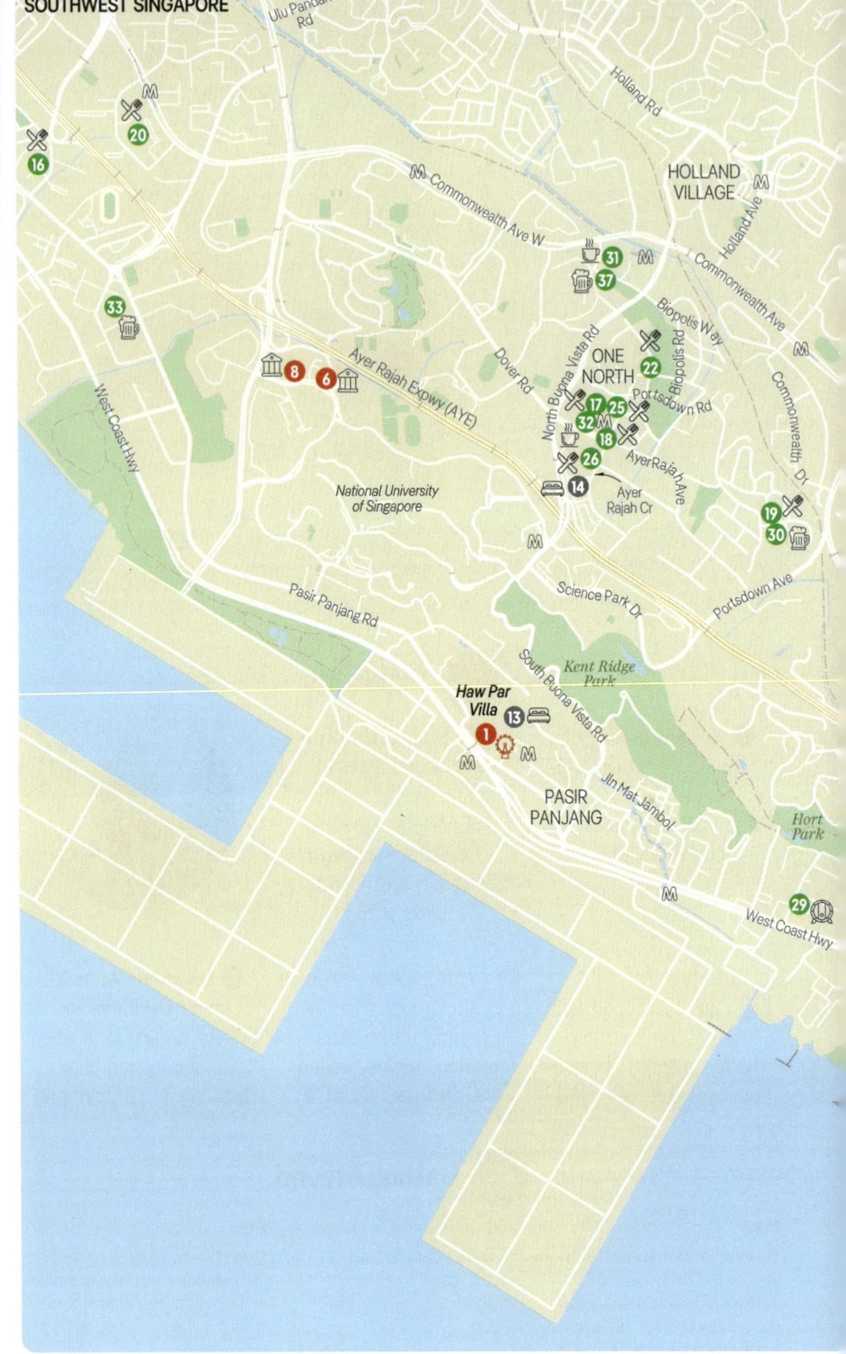
SOUTHWEST SINGAPORE
Ulu Pandan Rd
Holland Rd
HOLLAND VILLAGE
Holland Ave
Commonwealth Ave W
Commonwealth Ave
Biopolis Way
Biopolis Rd
ONE NORTH
North Buona Vista Rd
Portsdown Rd
Commonwealth Dr
Dover Rd
Ayer Rajah Expwy (AYE)
Ayer Rajah Ave
Ayer Rajah Cr
West Coast Hwy
National University of Singapore
Science Park Dr
Portsdown Ave
Pasir Panjang Rd
Kent Ridge Park
South Buona Vista Rd
Haw Par Villa
Jln Mat Jambol
PASIR PANJANG
Hort Park
West Coast Hwy
1
6
8
13
14
16
17
18
19
20
22
25
26
29
30
31
32
33
37

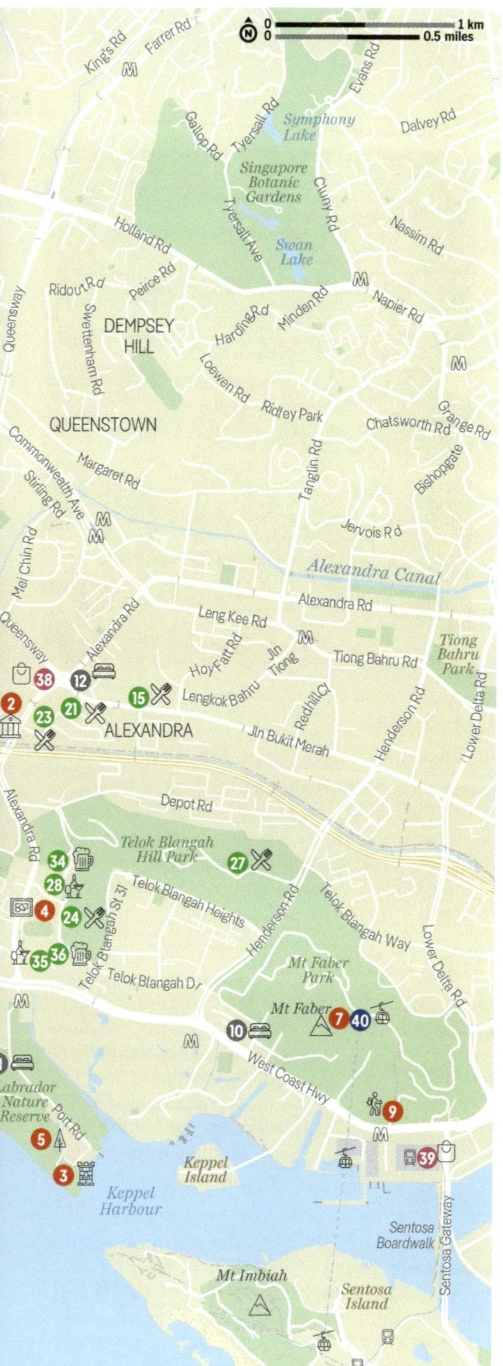

HIGHLIGHTS

1 Haw Par Villa

SIGHTS

2 Alexandra Hospital
3 Fort Pasir Panjang
4 Gillman Barracks
5 Labrador Nature Reserve
6 Lee Kong Chian Natural History Museum
7 Mt Faber
8 NUS Museum

ACTIVITIES

9 Marang Trail

SLEEPING

10 Hotel Faber Park Singapore – Handwritten Collection
11 Labrador Villa
12 Momentus Hotel Alexandra
13 Shipping Container Hotel @ Haw Par Villa
14 Train Pod @ one-north

EATING

15 ABC Brickworks Food Centre
16 Ayer Rajah Food Centre
17 Bread Yard
18 Casa Pietrasanta
19 Ce Soir
20 Clementi 448 Food Centre
21 Depot Road Zhen Shan Mei Claypot Laksa
22 Jimmy Monkey Café
23 Keng Eng Kee (KEK) Seafood
24 Naked Finn
25 One Fattened Calf Burgers
26 Timbre+ One North
27 Una
see 27 Wildseed Café

DRINKING & NIGHTLIFE

28 Blackbird
29 Brass Lion Distillery
30 Colbar
31 Dewgather
32 Dutch Colony Coffee Co.
33 Get Some
34 Handlebar
35 Hopscotch
36 Little Island Brewing Co @ Gillman Barracks
37 Picotin Brewhaus

SHOPPING

38 Queensway
39 VivoCity

TRANSPORT

40 Mt Faber Cable Car Station

TOP EXPERIENCE

Haw Par Villa

Step into a technicolour fever dream at Haw Par Villa, the brainchild of Aw Boon Haw and Aw Boon Par, sons of the man behind the famous Tiger balm. This eccentric park reflects the family's passion for Chinese culture, depicting classic myths, legends and moral tales in fanciful dioramas. Quirky, kitschy and gloriously over-the-top, it's an unforgettable, slightly bizarre journey through Asia's storytelling traditions.

DEREKTEO/SHUTTERSTOCK

TOP TIPS

- Haw Par Villa MRT station is just a short walk away.
- Go early or late to avoid the midday heat and enjoy softer light for photos.
- Free online guides help uncover hidden stories and local legends behind each quirky scene.

PRACTICALITIES

- Map p164
- hawparvilla.sg ● park free, museum adult/child S$20/10, parental guidance advised for children under 9yr ● park 10am-8pm daily, museum to 6pm Tue-Sun

Mythical Mayhem

Step into Haw Par Villa's riotous maze of dioramas and keep your eyes peeled for the Monkey King's wild antics from *Journey to the West,* the tragic romance of Madam White Snake, and timeless scenes from Chinese legends. Don't miss the giant Laughing Buddha, heroic generals astride tigers, and cheeky animal-human hybrids – each tableau brimming with quirky details and storytelling magic.

Descend into Hell

Step into the dimly lit tunnel of the Ten Courts of Hell at the **Hell's Museum**, where each chilling tableau invites uneasy reflection on life's choices. Locals recall childhood visits that sparked equal parts fear and fascination. Wander slowly, letting each gruesome scene reveal its moral lesson. The horror is both cautionary and captivating, prompting visitors to weigh right and wrong long after leaving this surreal museum.

After-Dark Thrills

For a different kind of nightlife, join the Journey to Hell by **Journeys Heritage Tours** *(journeys.com.sg; adult/child S$40/20)* every Friday at 6.30pm. This two-hour walk through Haw Par Villa and the eerie Hell's Museum blends history, humour and ghost stories into a spine-tingling adventure – perfect for anyone craving something memorably macabre.

Diplodocid sauropod, Lee Kong Chian Natural History Museum

Go Back to School

MAP P164

Hidden-gem museums on NUS campus

The National University of Singapore campus is home to two underrated museums. The grassy, boulder-like building that houses the **Lee Kong Chian Natural History Museum** *(lkcnhm.nus.edu.sg; adult/child S$24/15)* displays over a million specimens showcasing the biodiversity of Southeast Asia and Singapore, and has a historical collection dating back to the 19th century. It's a high-tech, family-friendly museum with lots of interactive elements. Be sure to say hi to Prince, Apollonia and Twinky, the three giant diplodocid sauropod skeletons right in its centre.

Next door, the **NUS Museum** *(museum.nus.edu.sg; free)* is a cultural delight, encompassing more than 8000 artefacts ranging from ancient Chinese ceramics and classical Indian sculptures to contemporary Southeast Asian art pieces. Don't miss the gallery dedicated to the works of celebrated Singaporean sculptor Ng Eng Teng – it offers an inspiring glimpse into the bold forms and humanistic spirit of the 'Grandfather of Singapore Sculpture'.

THE BATTLE OF OPIUM HILL

Opium Hill (Bukit Chandu in Malay) stands on Pasir Panjang Ridge (now Kent Ridge) and was named after the opium-processing factory that was once located at its foot. The Battle of Pasir Panjang unfolded on 13 February 1942 during the defence of Singapore when the Japanese invaded in WWII. Japanese forces sought to breach the Allied defences along the island's west coast. The 1st and 2nd Battalions of the Malay Regiment, made up primarily of local soldiers, heroically attempted to defend the ridge, but the Japanese prevailed. The battle marked a crucial stage in the fall of Singapore, highlighting the determination of Allied forces and their ultimate defeat.

DRINKING IN THE WEST: BEER BREWS

MAP P164

Little Island Brewing Co @ Gillman Barracks: Perfecting its brews on the island for nearly a decade. *noon-11pm Tue-Sat, to 10pm Sun*

Picotin Brewhaus: Traditional German brewing techniques and state-of-the-art cooling systems ensure fresh and perfectly chilled brews. *11am-11pm*

Get Some: With local craft beers on tap, this neon-signed watering hole is a beacon for brew lovers. *5pm-midnight Mon, from 10.30am Tue-Sun*

Handlebar: As the sun dips, motorcycles rumble into this biker-themed bar for ice-cold beers. *4-11pm Mon, noon-midnight Tue-Fri, from 10am Sat, 10am-11pm Sun*

WHY I LOVE SINGAPORE'S WEST

Ria de Jong, Lonely Planet writer

My first introduction to this part of the island was the Southern Ridges trail, a three-hour wander that carried me through nature, art, history and architecture in one seamless sweep. Along the way I stumbled upon the rambling Gillman Barracks, which quickly became a weekend favourite. I can lose hours of my weekend drifting between galleries or kicking back with a few afternoon beers before dancing into the night to live bands. What keeps drawing me back are the lived-in neighbourhood corners, quiet green pockets and unexpected coastal views. And then there are the quirky discoveries, from the colour-saturated Haw Par Villa to Thow Kwang Pottery Jungle.

HUNTERGOL HP/SHUTTERSTOCK

Maritime History & Mangrove Boardwalks

MAP P164

Uncover the secrets of Labrador Nature Reserve

The smallest of Singapore's four nature reserves at just 10 hectares, **Labrador Nature Reserve** *(nparks.gov.sg)* offers its visitors more than a quick walk in the park. Wildlife lovers will appreciate Singapore's only rocky sea cliff found on the mainland and the three boardwalks that meander through mangroves and forests. History buffs can explore the artillery remains of **Fort Pasir Panjang**, which once defended Keppel Harbour. Enjoy panoramic sea views, spot coastal birds or unwind at waterfront picnic spots.

Sweeping Views of Southern Singapore

MAP P164

Ride the cable car at Mt Faber

Formerly a signal hill and defence fort, **Mt Faber** *(nparks.gov.sg)* is one of the best places for a lofty view of Singapore's southern coastline – its highest point is about 100m above

EATING IN THE WEST: HAWKER CENTRES

MAPS P164 & P170

ABC Brickworks Food Centre: A great place to fuel up before or after taking on the Southern Ridges trail. *8am-11pm* $

Clementi 448 Food Centre: You'll find all your beloved hawker favourites here, but go early or expect long queues. *7am-9pm* $

Yuhua Village Food Centre: This hidden food gem near Jurong Lake Gardens is filled with Michelin Bib Gourmand–awarded stalls. *7am-11pm* $

Ayer Rajah Food Centre: Known for its large number of stalls serving Malay and Indian fare, it's perfect for spice lovers. *6am-midnight* $

Labrador Nature Reserve

sea level. The peak is located at one end of the Southern Ridges walk (p176), but most people visit Mt Faber to ride the **cable car** *(mountfaberleisure.com; adult/child from S$35/25)* that links to HarbourFront and Sentosa Island. Look down as the cable car moves off – several colonial-style black-and-white bungalows can be spotted amid the forested hillside, a stark contrast to the sleek architecture of the luxurious condominium complexes along the waterfront. For an extra thrill, hop into a SkyOrb Cabin – the world's first chrome-finished spherical cable-car cabin with transparent glass floors.

There are some restaurants at Mt Faber peak if you want to dine with a view – sunset is a popular time to come. The restroom here proclaims to be the most scenic one in Singapore and has floor-to-ceiling glass panels for a stunning skyline view as you wash your hands. You can drive or take a taxi to the peak if you'd rather not take the cable car, or hike up **Marang Trail**.

MORE CABLE-CAR ACTION

If you love the cable-car ride to Sentosa Island, there's good news: the island has its own **cable car** (p191), offering beach and treetop views from Imbiah Lookout to Siloso Point, as well as the 79m-tall **SkyHelix Sentosa** (p191) gondola.

EATING IN THE WEST: CULT CLASSICS

MAPS P164 & P170

Keng Eng Kee (KEK) Seafood: Family-run restaurant serving hearty Chinese *zi char* (family-style) dishes in a casual setting. *11.30am-2pm & 5-10pm* $

Depot Road Zhen Shan Mei Claypot Laksa: There's always a queue for this stall's much-lauded bowls of laksa. *9am-3.30pm Mon, Tue & Thu-Sat* $

Laifabai: Cult-favourite *won ton mee* (won ton noodles) and wood-fired meats joint in Bukit Batok. *11.30am-3pm & 6-9pm Tue-Fri, from 11am & 5.30pm Sat & Sun* $$

One Fattened Calf Burgers: Juicy, no-nonsense smashburgers in fluffy potato buns, paired with fries and lime slushies. *11am-3pm & 5-8pm Mon-Sat* $$

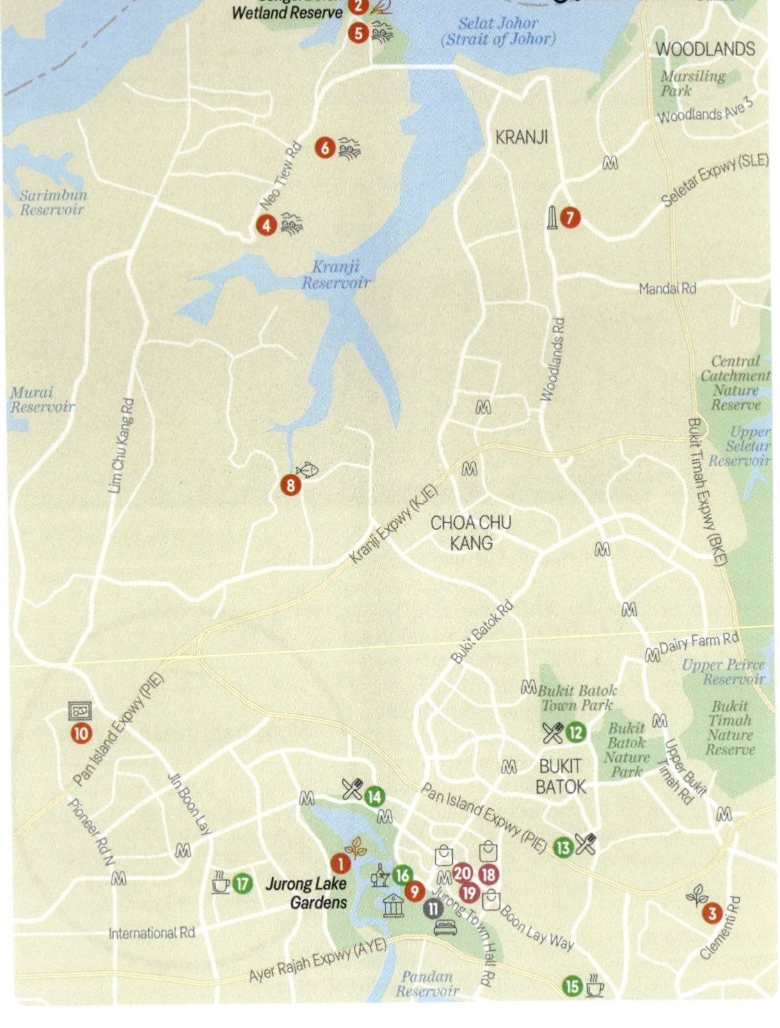

HIGHLIGHTS
1 Jurong Lake Gardens
2 Sungei Buloh Wetland Reserve

SIGHTS
3 Bee Amazed Garden
4 Bollywood Farms
5 Hay Dairies Goat Farm
6 Kranji Countryside
7 Kranji War Memorial
8 Qianhu Fish Farm
9 Science Centre Singapore
10 Thow Kwang Pottery Jungle

SLEEPING
11 Genting Hotel Jurong

EATING
12 Coexist Coffee Co.
13 Laifabai
14 Yuhua Village Food Centre

DRINKING & NIGHTLIFE
15 Glass Roasters
16 Pavilion Live House
17 Suzuki Gourmet Coffee

SHOPPING
18 IMM
19 Jem
20 Westgate

World of Wonder for Young Minds

MAP P170

Learn and play at the Science Centre Singapore

The **Science Centre Singapore** *(science.edu.sg; adult/child S$12/8)* is fun no matter how old you are, promising hours of discovery and laughter. Wander through more than 20 hands-on galleries covering everything from ecosystems and human anatomy to dazzling optical illusions. Catch lively science shows and jaw-dropping demos that make learning feel like magic.

Don't miss the **Omni-Theatre** *(S$14)*, where an enormous IMAX screen brings nature documentaries and space adventures to thrilling life. Beat Singapore's heat at **Snow City** *(snowcity.com.sg; adult/child S$31/24)*, where you can whoosh down an icy slope or build your own snowman or woman. For the youngest explorers, **KidsSTOP** *(adult/child peak S$13/23)* has colourful zones designed for little hands and curious minds. Round out your visit by tackling brain-teasing puzzles, experimenting at discovery zones or peering at the fiery Tesla coil. Whether you're geeking out over galaxies or giggling through optical illusions, it's a day packed with wonder, play and science made spectacular.

Where History Meets Art

MAP P164

Enjoy an afternoon at Gillman Barracks

Where soldiers once marched, art lovers now wander. Built in 1936 as a British military encampment, **Gillman Barracks** has transformed into a leafy creative enclave dotted with restaurants, cafes and contemporary art galleries. Exhibitions range from avant-garde installations and Southeast Asian works to striking photography and sculpture by globally renowned artists. Notable stops include **Sundaram Tagore Gallery** *(sundaramtagore.com)*, showcasing names like Edward Burtynsky and Annie Leibovitz, and **FOST Gallery** *(fostgallery.com)*, known for championing Singapore's emerging talent. With free, rotating exhibitions year-round, every visit brings something fresh.

For motorheads, the **Southern Depot** *(thesoutherndepot.com; free)* has a fascinating collection of motorcycles and bicycles. Feeling hands-on? Join a flower-arranging workshop at **Charlotte Puxley Flowers** *(charlottepuxleyflowers.com; from S$245)*, one of Singapore's most stylish floral studios.

To get here, take the MRT to Labrador Park station and walk about 800m north along Alexandra Rd; the entrance to Gillman Barracks is on your right. A taxi from the CBD costs around S$12 one way.

BEST MALLS FOR RETAIL THERAPY

VivoCity (Map p164): Singapore's largest shopping centre has over 300 stores (mainly midrange), waterfront dining options and a kids' playground.

Westgate (Map p170): Family-friendly Westgate ticks all the boxes. The Wonderland adventure playground has dry and wet areas and a 10m-tall treehouse.

Jem (Map p170): Large lifestyle mall directly linked to Jurong East MRT, with an IMAX cinema.

IMM (Map p170): With over 90 outlet stores and touting discounts of up to 80% off retail prices, this is the place to hit if you're after a bargain.

Queensway (Map p164): Singapore's iconic 'Sports Mall' is filled to the brim with sports, optical, electronic and thrift stores.

EATING IN THE WEST: COVETED CAFES & BAKES

MAPS P164 & P170

Jimmy Monkey Café: Get a taste of Melbourne cafe culture at this spot known for its all-day brunch options and popular coffee blends. *8am-4pm* $$

Bread Yard: Artisanal bakery for out-of-the-oven sourdough and flaky matcha cruffins. *8am-5.30pm Mon-Wed, to 8.30pm Thu & Fri, to 3pm Sat & Sun* $

Coexist Coffee Co.: Perched on the top floor of an industrial building, this hidden cafe serves hearty brunches and tasty lunches. *9am-6pm* $$

Wildseed Café: Picturesque floral cafe in the Alkaff Mansion, along the Southern Ridges. *8am-5pm Mon, to 9pm Tue-Thu & Sun, to 11pm Fri & Sat* $$

TOP EXPERIENCE

Jurong Lake Gardens

Set aside a few hours to explore Jurong Lake Gardens, Singapore's newest national garden, easily accessible via Chinese Garden and Lakeside MRT stations. The expansive Lakeside Garden on the west shore features winding boardwalks, engaging play areas for children and carefully preserved natural habitats including mangrove swamps, streams and open grasslands showcasing the region's rich biodiversity.

JOHANNESS/SHUTTERSTOCK

Cloud Pagoda, Chinese Garden

A Playground Paradise

Dive into nature-inspired fun at **Forest Ramble**'s 13 adventure zones, thoughtfully designed to let kids mimic the movements of animals that live in freshwater swamps, helping them connect with nature through play. Watch them scurry, slither and climb across slides, rope courses, see-saws and swings! Beyond the playground, wander through the inclusive **Therapeutic Garden** designed for children and adults with special needs. Thrill-seekers can tackle Singapore's largest outdoor skate park, complete with sheltered skate pods for all-weather fun, or conquer the 3m-high bouldering wall. Finally, cool off and splash around at **Clusia Cove**'s lively water playground.

Picture-Perfect

A haven for shutterbugs, the **Japanese and Chinese Gardens** showcase traditional architecture, tranquil ponds and lush landscaping. Designed to celebrate Singapore's rich cultural heritage, they provide endless photo ops – from graceful pagodas and elegant bridges to meticulously trimmed bonsai trees.

Cycle into the Wild

Bikes are available for rent at **GoCycling** *(gocycling.sg)*, located in the shops diagonally opposite Chinese Garden MRT station. It's a cool way to explore the gardens at your own pace.

TOP TIPS

- Dress kids in leggings or long shorts for comfort and added protection during play.
- It's best to visit early, as shade is limited and the sun can be intense.
- During the **Mid-Autumn Festival** (check dates), the gardens dazzle with stunning lanterns.

PRACTICALITIES

- Map p170
- juronglakegardens.nparks.gov.sg
- free
- 24hr; hours vary for specific gardens/venues

Time for a Tipple

MAP P164

Sample Singapore gins at Brass Lion Distillery

The iconic Singapore sling is a gin cocktail, but if you're curious about what a made-in-Singapore gin tastes like, check out the **Brass Lion Distillery** *(brassliondistillery.com; tours S$49, tastings S$70)*, one of the island's gin pioneers. Step into this intimate distillery for a guided tour of its gleaming copper still, Nala. Its signature Singapore Dry Gin is an amalgamation of 22 locally sourced botanicals, including Asian flavours such as lemongrass, torch ginger flower and galangal. Learn craft-gin secrets, stroll through the botanical garden, taste a flight of signature gins, then linger for cocktails, canapés and laid-back vibes in the Tasting Room.

BEER WITH A VIEW

The world's highest urban microbrewery is at **Level 33** (p50), where five craft beers are hand-brewed. Down a pint while admiring the fabulous view of Marina Bay.

Potter Through Some Pottery

MAP P170

Hunt for treasures at Thow Kwang Pottery Jungle

If there were ever such a thing as a pottery jungle, then **Thow Kwang Pottery Jungle** *(thowkwang.com.sg; workshops from S$50)* would surely be it. Rooms overflow with teetering stacks of colourful ceramic treasures, creating an irresistible maze for pottery lovers. It's dusty, hot and absolutely worth it – especially to glimpse Singapore's last surviving dragon kiln, still run by the Tan family, who've been crafting ceramics here since 1965. Firing this massive wood-burning kiln is an intense process, so it only comes alive a few times a year – but pottery workshops are held year-round. Though it's tucked away off the beaten path, few can leave empty-handed.

In Memory of the Fallen

MAP P170

Pay respects at Kranji War Memorial

The austere white structures and gently rolling hillside of the **Kranji War Memorial** *(cwgc.org)* honour thousands of Allied servicemen and women from the British Commonwealth who fell during WWII. As you wander the serene grounds, you'll

BEST NIGHTSPOTS IN THE WEST

Hopscotch (Map p164): An impressive cocktail list and a pumping band Friday and Saturday evenings for a chilled night on the town local-style.

Pavilion Live House (Map p170): It's a wonder this live-music venue above Snow City doesn't melt the snow below with the heat radiating from its dance floor!

Blackbird(Map p164): Local rock, blues and jazz acts from Tuesday to Sunday evenings; Fridays and Saturdays kick on late with a DJ.

Timbre+ One North (Map p164): Graffiti-decorated food park with live bands and DJs Monday to Saturday – head for the eats and stay for the beats.

Art After Dark Part of January's Singapore Art Week, lighting up Gillman Barracks (p171) with contemporary art, music and festivities.

DRINKING IN THE WEST: COFFEE SPOTS

MAPS P164 & P170

Suzuki Gourmet Coffee: At Singapore's oldest coffee roaster, baristas meticulously prepare each drop to awaken your senses. *8.30am-5.30pm Tue-Sun*

Dewgather: Using sustainably sourced beans from South America to create an exclusive blend roasted in-house. *8am-10pm Mon-Sat, from 7.30am Sun*

Glass Roasters: This hole-in-the-wall coffee stop offers a rotating selection of beans for an impeccably crafted cup of joe. *9am-5pm Wed-Mon*

Dutch Colony Coffee Co.: Sip on third-wave coffee at this artisanal cafe and treat yourself to hearty breakfast toasts and bagels. *8am-6pm*

GETTING AROUND THE KRANJI COUNTRYSIDE

The best way to get to Singapore's Kranji Countryside is to take the MRT to Kranji station and transfer to bus 925, or hop in a taxi or Grab for a faster and more comfortable ride. For maximum flexibility, the best way to explore the area is to hire a private car driver for a few hours, so you can easily visit multiple farms and attractions at your own pace. Occasionally, special events are organised in the farmlands area, and a dedicated shuttle bus service is provided to make access even easier. Check the website *kranjicountryside.com* for details.

SUNSETMAN/SHUTTERSTOCK

Kranji War Memorial (p173)

notice many headstones simply inscribed with the words 'a soldier of the 1939–1945 war' lined in quiet, dignified rows across manicured lawns. Marble walls bear the names of over 24,000 men and women who lost their lives in Southeast Asia; visitors can consult registers to trace them. Each year, a poignant memorial service takes place on the Sunday nearest 11 November (Remembrance Day).

Surprising Farm Adventures

MAP P170

A taste of Singapore country life

While land-scarce Singapore has little room for agriculture and imports most of its food supplies, there are farms you can visit for a rare chance to see a less metropolitan side of this nation. The **Kranji Countryside** *(kranjicountryside.com)* in the northwestern corner of Lim Chu Kang is the best-known farm cluster. **Hay Dairies** *(haydairies.sg)* is Singapore's only goat farm, where you can drink fresh goat milk, watch the daily milking (9am to 10.30am) and hand-feed goats; it's closed on Tuesdays. Wander around the crops and trails of- organic **Bollywood Farms** *(bollywoodfarms.com)*, open Wednesday to Sunday, and grab a farm-to-fork lunch at **Poison Ivy Bistro**. Admire the many tanks of ornamental fish at **Qianhu Fish Farm** *(qianhudiscover.com)* and have a go at catching small fish with a net, feeding koi or dipping your feet into a fish spa. A free shuttle bus operates from Choa Chu Kang MRT station to the farm; check the website for schedules.

Away from Kranji, check out the **Bee Amazed Garden** *(beeamazed.com.sg)* in Clementi, where you can safely interact with local honeybees, learn basic beekeeping and enjoy some honey tasting.

TOP EXPERIENCE

Sungei Buloh Wetland Reserve

Step into an eco-wonderland where over half of Singapore's bird species find sanctuary alongside seasonal migratory visitors escaping the winter chill. Covering more than 200 hectares of mudflats, mangroves, ponds and forests, this sprawling reserve offers an immersive escape into nature – perfect for discovery walks, wildlife-spotting and connecting with Singapore's natural heritage.

DANNY YE/SHUTTERSTOCK

Milky stork

Walking Trails & Boardwalks

The wetlands are bursting with life, so lace up your hiking shoes and begin your adventure at the **Coastal Trail**, offering sweeping views of the Straits of Johor. Duck into the lush greenery of the **Forest Trail**, where cool, dense canopies provide shade for you and a variety of wildlife – keep an eye out for butterflies, birds and monitor lizards. Finally, meander along the **Mangrove Boardwalk** to marvel at twisted roots and bustling mudflats. Stay alert as you might spot darting mudskippers, smooth-coated otters or even a stealthy estuarine crocodile.

Mangrove Gallery & Nature Gallery

Explore the Visitor Centre's **Mangrove Gallery** to learn about mangroves and the creatures that call the mud home. Then visit the Wetland Centre's **Nature Gallery** to discover local wildlife and their habitats. Take your time with the interactive exhibits and enjoy a hands-on learning experience.

Buloh Tidal Ponds

Head for a walk around this carefully restored freshwater habitat, teeming with diverse plants and wildlife. Visit at low tide for the best views, and use the camouflaged birdwatching huts and tower to quietly observe migratory birds in their natural surroundings.

TOP TIPS

- The migratory-bird season runs from September to March.
- Early morning and early evening are the best times to visit, or during low tide.
- Binoculars are a must for getting an up-close view without disturbing the wildlife.

PRACTICALITIES

- Map p170 ● nparks.gov.sg
- free ● 7am-7pm

HIKE THE SOUTHERN RIDGES

Made up of a series of parks and hills, the Southern Ridges will have you trekking through the jungle without ever really leaving the city.

START	END	LENGTH
Kent Ridge Park	Mt Faber	10km; 3hr

Discover Singapore's green corridor on this hike through the Southern Ridges. Set out from ❶ **Kent Ridge Park**, where an elevated canopy walk offers a bird's-eye view and links to ❷ **Reflections at Bukit Chandu**, a small WWII museum in a restored colonial-era house.

Continue east to ❸ **HortPark**, where themed gardens and prototype glasshouses hint at the design of Gardens by the Bay. For a creative detour, head to ❹ **Gillman Barracks** (pictured right; p171), once a British military camp and now home to contemporary galleries and restaurants.

Near Labrador Park MRT, pick up the ❺ **Berlayer Creek Boardwalk**, winding through mangroves towards the sea. The trail leads into the ❻ **Labrador Nature Reserve** (p168), notable for Singapore's only protected rocky shore, historic beacons and wartime relics.

Retrace your steps to HortPark, cross the leaf-shaped ❼ **Alexandra Arch**, then follow the steel-gridded ❽ **Forest Walk** among treetops to reach ❾ **Telok Blangah Hill Park**. Explore the picturesque Terrace Garden or stop for a meal at the colonial-era ❿ **Alkaff Mansion**. Nearby, discover the towering trees of the Forest of Giants.

Finally, cross the timber-clad ⓫ **Henderson Waves** – Singapore's highest pedestrian bridge – to ⓬ **Mt Faber Park** and end at its historic peak ⓭ **Mt Faber** (p168), where views stretch over the city skyline and southern coastline.

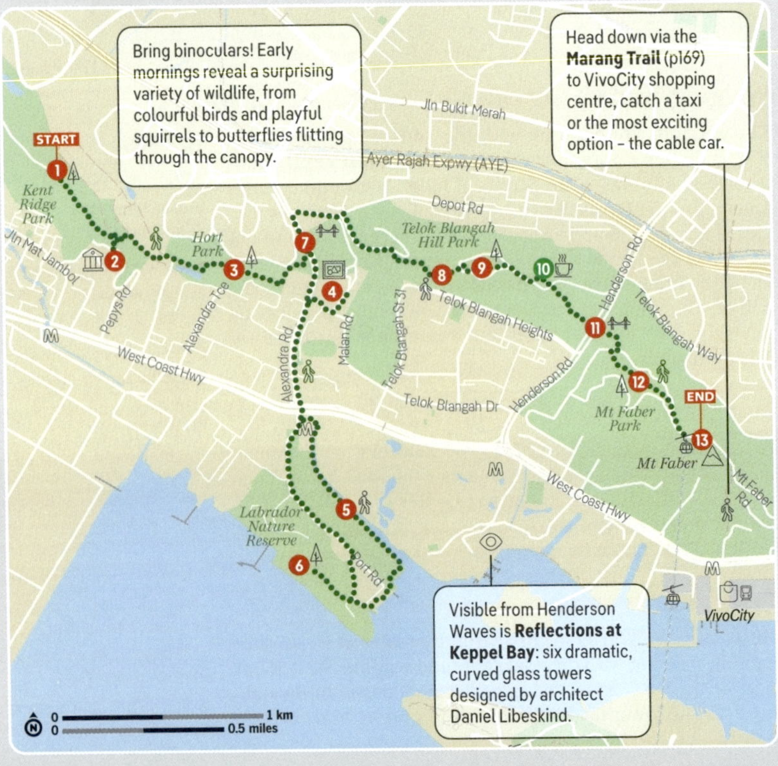

Bring binoculars! Early mornings reveal a surprising variety of wildlife, from colourful birds and playful squirrels to butterflies flitting through the canopy.

Head down via the **Marang Trail** (p169) to VivoCity shopping centre, catch a taxi or the most exciting option – the cable car.

Visible from Henderson Waves is **Reflections at Keppel Bay**: six dramatic, curved glass towers designed by architect Daniel Libeskind.

Gillman Barracks

Heritage Haunt

MAP P164

Check out a former officers' mess

Off Portsdown Rd you'll find Wessex Estate, and within it the raffish **Colbar** (short for 'colonial bar'), once a British officers' mess and now a wonderfully languid drinking spot. It still feels like the 1950s here: cash kept in a drawer, vintage football photos on the walls, and regulars lingering over beers and affordable ciders on the breezy verandah. Meals are simple but satisfying – the chicken curry rice and breaded pork cutlet are standouts. From Buona Vista MRT, hop on bus 191 and alight at the eighth stop; as you enter Whitchurch Rd, Colbar appears on your right. Payment is by cash only.

A WARTIME TRAGEDY

Opened in 1938 as the British Military Hospital, **Alexandra Hospital** (Map p164) played a tragic role during WWII. On 14 February 1942, as Japanese forces advanced on Singapore, the hospital – clearly marked with red crosses – was attacked. In a brutal incident known as the Alexandra Hospital massacre, Japanese troops stormed the wards, killing doctors, nurses, patients and staff over two harrowing days. Despite this dark history, the hospital continued operations after the war, eventually transitioning into a civilian hospital in 1971. Today, its colonial-era buildings and leafy grounds stand as a poignant reminder of the sacrifices and turbulence of Singapore's wartime past.

EATING IN THE WEST: SUBLIME RESTAURANTS

MAP P164

Naked Finn: Natural flavours with minimal seasoning shine through at this contemporary seafood restaurant. *noon-2.30pm & 6-9.30pm Mon-Sat* **$$$**

Ce Soir: Flowers, fantasy and French fine dining come together in a black-and-white bungalow. *noon-3.30pm Thu-Sun & 6.30-11pm Wed-Sun* **$$$**

Casa Pietrasanta: Indulge in freshly made pasta and authentic dishes at this modern Italian joint. *11.30am-2.30pm & 5.30-10pm Mon-Sat* **$$**

Una: Spanish powerhouse located in the Alkaff Mansion, the perfect backdrop for a romantic meal. *noon-2.30pm Tue-Fri & 6-10.30pm Tue-Sun* **$$**

Researched by Morgan Awyong

SENTOSA ISLAND

SINGAPORE'S ISLAND OF FUN

Will you party from sunset to moonrise at the beach clubs, or spend hours staring at drifting jellyfish? Be a forest wanderer, historical wiz or wand-waving witch – it's all possible at Singapore's premier island escape.

Queuing for a ride at Universal Studios, it's hard to imagine that the resort island of Sentosa was once quiet, tree-filled Pulau Blakang Mati, home to an assortment of small fishing villages.

It became a defence outpost for the British in 1878, but in the 1970s the island was renamed Sentosa and became a resort with a rotating slew of attractions. The place only really started to shine after Resorts World Sentosa came along in 2010, and at its peak drew more than 19 million visitors a year.

Today's Sentosa is manicured and acts as Singapore's playground for escapism, blending entertainment, luxury residences and tropical attractions in a 500-hectare haven.

TOP TIP

Sentosa can get oppressively busy on weekends and public holidays. Go earlier in the week and save time by purchasing tickets online. Be prepared for elevated prices.

Palawan Beach (p188)

See p209 for places to stay on Sentosa Island.

Highlights

❶ Singapore Oceanarium
Explore the aquarium's 22 zones of immersive habitats and rich multimedia storytelling. **p184**

❷ Universal Studios
Enjoy the thrilling rides and blockbuster-themed spaces of Sentosa's hugely popular theme park. **p182**

❸ Fort Siloso ▼
Visit Singapore's last remaining preserved coastal fort. **p191**

❹ Palawan
Relax in a family-friendly enclave with indoor racing, mini golf and floating water park. **p189**

❺ Harry Potter: Visions of Magic
Wave wands at this spellbinding interactive experience. **p186**

Getting Around

Monorail
Take the MRT to HarbourFront station and swap to the Sentosa Express, which has three stations (Waterfront, Imbiah and Beach). On the island, the monorail, tram and buses are free.

Bus
Two bus routes (A and B) link the main attractions. Both run a loop from the central Beach station every 15 minutes. The 'beach tram' (an electric bus) shuttles the length of all three beaches.

Cable Car
Reach the island from Mt Faber or the HarbourFront. A separate line takes you deeper into the island with stops at Merlion Station, Imbiah Lookout and Siloso Point.

SENTOSA ISLAND

Sentosa Cove

See Main Map

Serapong Golf Course
Mt Serapong
Selat Sengkir
Mt Imbiah
Siloso Rd
Imbiah Walk
Siloso Beach
Allanbrooke Rd
Bukit Manis Rd
Ocean Dr
Cove Dr
Tanjong Golf Course
SENTOSA COVE
Tanjong Beach
Strait of Singapore

0 — 1 km
0 — 0.5 miles

HIGHLIGHTS
1 Universal Studios

SIGHTS
2 Fort Siloso
3 Harry Potter: Visions of Magic
4 Palawan Beach
5 Quayside Isle
6 Sensoryscape
7 Sentosa Cove
8 Siloso Beach
9 Singapore Oceanarium
10 Southernmost Point of Continental Asia
11 Tanjong Beach
12 Tanjong Rimau

ACTIVITIES
13 Adventure Cove Waterpark
14 AltitudeX
15 Coastal Trail
16 HydroDash
17 HyperDrive
18 Imbiah Nature Trail
19 Mega Adventure
20 Scentopia
21 Siloso Skywalk
22 SkyHelix Sentosa
23 Skyline Luge
24 Skypark Sentosa by AJ Hackett
25 UltraGolf

SLEEPING
26 Amara Sanctuary
27 Barracks Hotel
28 Capella
29 Equarius Villas
30 Hotel Ora
31 Outpost Hotel

32 Raffles Sentosa
33 Siloso Beach Resort
34 Village Hotel Sentosa
35 W Singapore – Sentosa Cove

EATING
36 Blu Kouzina
37 Good Old Days Food Court
38 International Food Street
39 Malaysian Food Street
40 Marrybrown
41 Palawan Food Trucks
42 Splash Tribe

DRINKING & NIGHTLIFE
43 +Twelve
see 31 1-Altitude Coast
see 32 Chairman's Room
44 Coastes
45 Harry's
see 28 Pineapple Room
46 Tanjong Beach Club

ENTERTAINMENT
47 Wings of Time Fireworks Symphony

TRANSPORT
48 Sentosa Cable Car Line
49 Sentosa Cable Car Station
50 Siloso Point

ALSIMONOV/GETTY IMAGES

TOP EXPERIENCE

Universal Studios

Southeast Asia's only Universal Studios is one of Universal's smaller parks but has an array of thrilling rides and interactive shows alongside a slew of restaurants and shops, all themed after Hollywood blockbusters. There's something for everyone, from kid-friendly attractions to adrenaline-pumping rides, but be prepared for long queues in Singapore's sweltering heat during peak season.

DON'T MISS

- Battlestar Galactica: HUMAN vs CYLON
- Revenge of the Mummy
- TRANSFORMERS The Ride: The Ultimate 3D Battle
- Despicable Me Minion Mayhem
- Canopy Flyer

Thrilling Roller-Coasters & Rides

Battlestar Galactica: HUMAN vs CYLON in the Sci-fi zone is the world's tallest duelling roller-coaster and the park's highlight – the red HUMAN track is exciting enough, but for more thrills choose the blue CYLON track, where your legs dangle freely. **Revenge of the Mummy** in the Ancient Egypt section is a bumpy but exhilarating ride navigating tunnels in the dark in search of the *Book of the Living*, while **TRANSFORMERS The Ride: The Ultimate 3D Battle** uses 3D

PRACTICALITIES

● rwsentosa.com/en/attractions/universal-studios-singapore ● adult/child S$85/64 ● 10am-8pm

glasses to immerse you in the action as you zip through the city with the Autobots to fight the Decepticons. The **Jurassic Park Rapids Adventure** – closed at the time of writing – starts off as a leisurely float down a river on a circular raft that rapidly turns into something more exhilarating when the dinosaurs go on a rampage. Bring your own poncho so you don't get wet, or prepare to fork out an exorbitant amount for a flimsy piece of plastic in the queue.

Meet Your Favourite Characters

Indulge your children (or your inner child) by snapping photos with life-size characters around the park that hail from famous film and television franchises, including *Despicable Me, Madagascar, Kung Fu Panda, Shrek, Sesame Street* and *The Mummy. Jurassic Park* fans will love the particularly life-like **raptor encounter** with a surprisingly realistic animatronic dinosaur. The walking, talking **Transformers** that make snarky remarks are also fan favourites and you can take pictures with them if you don't mind being potentially roasted.

Show-Stopping Performances

The theme park's marquee show **WaterWorld**, based on the titular Kevin Costner flick, is a crowd pleaser with the right mix of explosive pyrotechnics, acrobatic stunts and lots of splashes. Unfortunately, it's been 'temporarily unavailable' since COVID-19 restrictions came into effect in 2020, though no updates have been given on the show's future. **Lights, Camera, Action! Hosted by Steven Spielberg** is a fun insight into movie magic and the wonders of special effects coming to life on a soundstage. The **Shrek 4-D Adventure** will make you feel as though you've been dropped into the actual *Shrek* world.

For the Kids

Good news for the faint-hearted or those with kids: not all the rides are gut-wrenchers. For some milder thrills, Far Far Away is a good section to start in, with the junior roller-coasters **Puss in Boots' Giant Journey** and **Enchanted Airways**. Newest to the park is Minionland, and here, the **Despicable Me Minion Mayhem** is a sensory riot as you transform into a minion. The **Treasure Hunters** ride in the Ancient Egypt section is also popular, allowing you to 'drive' through an excavation site. The **Canopy Flyer** allows you to fly above the crowds like a pterodactyl, while **Dino-Soarin'** lets the kids go up, up and away astride their favourite flying dinosaur. The **Sesame Street Spaghetti Space Chase** is another fun ride that the whole family can enjoy – you 'go into space' with Elmo and Grover.

UNIVERSAL EXPRESS

Universal Express is an add-on to your admission ticket that allows you to use the express queues at several popular rides. The quantity available and the price depend on park capacity; Universal Express can cost more than the admission ticket itself. You can pre-purchase or buy in the park after you gauge whether the crowds warrant forking out the extra cash.

TOP TIPS

- Plan ahead for savings – it may be cheaper to bundle the Universal Studios admission ticket with other Sentosa attractions.
- Check whether your e-ticket allows direct entry to the park, or you may have to spend extra time queueing at the park's ticketing counter to exchange it for an admission ticket.
- Download the Universal Studios app to gauge queuing times and check opening hours in case of ride closures.
- Lockers in different areas are free for different durations. Keep a credit card on you in case long queues cause you to exceed the free period.

THE COST OF ENTERING SENTOSA

Sentosa's admission fee depends on how you enter the island.

Walking or cycling across the **Sentosa Boardwalk** bridge from the HarbourFront is completely free. Taking public bus 123 also only requires the standard distance-based bus fare without any additional fee.

The **Sentosa Express** monorail from VivoCity shopping mall to Waterfront, Imbiah and Beach stations costs S$4 per person. If you're in a small group, consider taking a car or taxi, as this adds only S$2 to S$6 per vehicle to the travel fare, depending on the time of day.

The most scenic way to reach Sentosa is via **cable car** from Mt Faber or the HarbourFront. Round-trip tickets start from $32.90 and can go up to S$47.40 depending on the type of cabin you choose.

Part of That Watery World

Explore the state-of-the-art Singapore Oceanarium

One of the world's largest aquariums, the former SEA Aquarium, is now the **Singapore Oceanarium** *(singaporeoceanarium.com; adult/child from S$50/39)*. Three times larger than before, it has 22 zones that feel like a blissful never-ending underwater world. Combining immersive habitats (the **Ancient Waters** hall has gigantic animatronic specimens) with interactive elements and multimedia storytelling, the sub-aquatic exploration becomes an engaging adventure for both kids and adults alike.

The showstopper comes almost immediately after with **Ocean Wonders**. Featuring one of the world's largest sea jelly habitats, your viral social media moment awaits before the staggering 6.8m-diameter kreisel tank filled with countless moon jellies drifting within. Equally dramatic is the **Whale Fall** room. Replicating a gigantic whale carcass on the sea

EATING IN SENTOSA: CHEAPER EATS

Malaysian Food Street: This indoor hawker centre beside Universal Studios dishes up street-food favourites from Singapore's neighbour. *8.30am-8.30pm* $

Good Old Days Food Court: Near Beach Station, this food court has Asian delights; the local offerings on the 2nd level are halal-certified. *hours vary* $

International Food Street: A fun beachside enclave of food-truck-style finger food at the Central Beach Bazaar. *11am-9pm* $

Marrybrown: Halal fried chicken in a bucket, burger or with some coconut-milk rice? It's all possible at this fast-food chain. *11am-10pm* $

MAZUR TRAVEL/SHUTTERSTOCK

Singapore Oceanarium

bed complete with a walkable rib cage 'tunnel', it includes rare glimpses of the secretive creatures that live there. Most haunting is the **Trenches** hall, mesmerising visitors with ghostly deep-sea specimens frozen in midair – courtesy of a clear preservative.

Filled with tunnels and dwarf-sized viewing rooms for kids, the oceanarium invites slow exploration and there are multiple seated zones for you to rest your feet. Apart from the occasional snack kiosk, there's also a full-fledged **Explorer's Nook** cafe at the **Spirit of Exploration** room for when you feel peckish. Themed-attraction food tends to be gimmicky but we found the food here to be good, especially when staring at the massive Omani ship on display.

It wasn't pure gawking either: there's a healthy sprinkle of education included in the experience. There are windows showcasing staff at work in their labs, and touchpools at **Singapore's Coast** feature a chatty crew who dispense instruction and trivia in good measure as guests handle sea critters. Deepen your experience by adding one of the special programmes while booking – the **Insider Experience** includes exclusive back-of-house access and a chance to meet the playful dolphins, while visitors with scuba-diving certification can take a plunge and come face-to-face with the oceanarium's precious manta rays.

THE SOUTHERNMOST POINT?

Past the busy activities happening at Palawan Beach, a long rope bridge extends towards a tiny offshore islet. The lookout tower is reason alone to visit, but it's also proudly billed as the '**Southernmost Point of Continental Asia**'. While the claim is romantic, a quick check on the map will reveal that it's geographically not true. Parts of Sentosa Cove should hold claim to that honour – until you consider the reclaimed land in Singapore's western part of Tuas, which stretches even further south 'continentally'. The southernmost point of Singapore is Pulau Satumu, the small island where the Raffles Lighthouse sits. In any case, the existing label remains one of Sentosa Island's more charming illusions.

THE ISLAND BEHIND DEATH

Sentosa means 'tranquillity' in Malay – it's an apt name for a resort devoted to rest and relaxation. But the island's former name would have been far less enticing to tourists: it was once called Pulau Blakang Mati (The Island Behind Death).

It's not known how this ominous name came about. One theory says it stems from the bloodthirsty acts of piracy that were prevalent in bygone days. Another story goes that the island was used as a burial ground for the losers of grudge-match duels between neighbouring tribes.

A nationwide contest was held to find a suitable name to support the island's tourism aspirations, and in 1969 Pulau Blakang Mati's name was officially changed to Sentosa.

Splish, Splash & Snorkel

Watery fun at Adventure Cove

Stay cool in Singapore's sultry humidity and have a splashing good time. **Adventure Cove Waterpark** *(rwsentosa.com; adult/child S$40/32)* has several twisting, spiralling water slides for thrill-seekers – the **Pipeline Plunge** is particularly exhilarating because you slide in the dark, while the washout rides swirl around and surprise with sudden drops. The bravest can attempt the **Riptide Rocket** for the steepest dips, made extra gravity-defying with the region's first hydro-magnetic coaster. Just don't ask us how it works. Little ones can enjoy the kid-friendly **Big Bucket Treehouse** and **Seahorse Hideaway** water playgrounds – you'll know them by the squeals of delight from afar. Ready to leave but your towel's all damp? Convenient full-body dryer machines will have you spiffy and dry in minutes!

For those who prefer something more sedate, enjoy bobbing around in the giant wave pool at **Bluwater Bay** – weekends are great for a spot of DJ-led music. Or float around the park along the **Adventure River**, passing stirring themed zones of jungle flora and mysterious grotto caves.The **Rainbow Reef** is quite the imaginative addition to a water park. The massive circular tank offers you some leisurely snorkelling with more than 20,000 tropical fish darting about – perfect for beginners to get used to open waters.

Sentosa's Hidden Paths

A naturalist-led beach walk

At certain hours, Sentosa reveals a hidden world not normally seen by visitors. No, it's not magic – just the tides. Join Dennis Chan of **The Untamed Paths** *(theuntamedpaths.com; from S$96)* at Tanjong Rimau Beach for a messily good walk during intertidal hours, and watch the retreating waters reveal the sometimes colourful, sometimes alarming, but always fascinating creatures below your feet (step carefully now). As you spot mud crabs, sea slugs, reef sharks, cuttlefish, stingrays and other lesser-known biodiversity, the naturalist will fill you in with facts about them. The scene will be fleeting but the memories created with fellow shore hunters will last long after.

Ready Those Wands

A Harry Potter–themed amusement park

If you've ever dreamt of ditching your Muggle life and being teleported to a world on a zany bus ride to potion-filled alleys or magical treasuries, it's possible on Sentosa. You can pick up a wand and amble into the multimedia sets of the famed *Harry Potter* fantasy series. Featuring 10 immersive zones with recognisable appearances from the Knight Bus, Ministry of Magic and the Pensieve, **Harry Potter: Visions of Magic** *(harrypottervisionsofmagic.com/sg; adult/child from S$59/49)* includes two surprise Singapore exclusives: The Trap Door and Chamber

RICK SIU/SHUTTERSTOCK

Entrance to Harry Potter: Visions of Magic

of Secrets. The latter is particularly impressive in its recreation, with the massive snake guardians firing their hisses and glowing ominously with your casting.

Multiple interaction points across the rooms often disperse the small groupings, but there will inevitably be bottlenecks where a little patience is needed before it's your turn. If so, just peer about for more sigil-marked spots to trigger before returning. You are allowed to linger for as long as you want but you're not allowed to retrace your steps (the costumed staff have their wands at the ready).

You'll emerge from the 10 rooms to the richly decorated retail store, with a side cafe serving House-aligned desserts and butterbeer. Pick up some enchanted goods in the form of scarves, plushies and keychains, and download your entrance-taken photos and videos digitally with your preferred magical background.

The attraction is located in Resorts World Sentosa's newest lifestyle enclave dubbed WEAVE. The lush biophilic structure with its undulating forms is pleasant to stroll through, and launched in July 2025 with several dining options.

HUNGRY? GET A PASS!

If you're a bona fide foodie or are staying for a couple of days on the island, consider Sentosa's **Food Discovery Pass** *(sentosa.com.sg/en/deals/food-discovery-pass)* to save on your meals, drinks and snacks. Load up on credits to an amount you prefer (S$100 is the minimum) on the pass, and flash the card during ordering to redeem discounts and freebies valued up to S$72. From crème brûlée and rosé wine, to fast-food chicken fillets, your meals are automatically upsized with the pass. Credits last up to 180 days from the day of top-up. As an additional perk, you get two complimentary island admissions, so you can return for more. See the website for pass options and participating restaurants.

DRINKING IN SENTOSA: BEST WATERING HOLES

1-Altitude Coast: The infinity pool might be a little small, but the attitude's big at the tallest bar on the island, perched atop the sexy Outpost Hotel. *hours vary*

Pineapple Room: Celebrate stately elegance from yesteryear at this spot with playful nods to the prickly fruit and enjoy the curated cocktails. *5.30-11pm*

Chairman's Room: A haven in Raffles Sentosa hotel featuring calligraphy and chinoiserie. The tart Sentosa sling here beats the original in our opinion. *9am-11pm*

Harry's: First established in 1992 at Boat Quay; this outlet has the largest selection of drinks on tap locally. Go for its signature craft beers. *11am-11pm*

PICK YOUR VIBE

Each of Sentosa's beaches has its own personality and attracts a different crowd. **Tanjong Beach** is generally more tranquil, though the daybeds and loungers by the beachfront pool at its award-winning club always seem packed. More family-friendly **Palawan Beach** has an assortment of activities, from outdoor mini golf to indoor racing tracks. Sentosa's dazzling marquee show 'Wings of Time Fireworks Symphony' (p190) can be seen at the Central Beach Bazaar leading to **Siloso Beach**, which has the most beach clubs.

Note that most beach clubs require a minimum spend from customers to rent their facilities, especially during peak periods. If you're on a budget, bring your own food, drinks, mat and umbrella. There's plenty of sand to sit on, or find a sheltered spot in the Sapphire and Emerald Pavilions on Siloso Beach.

SENTOSA DEVELOPMENT CORPORATION

Tanjong Beach Club

Beachy Keen

Chill out at a beach club

If you prefer the water of a swimming pool to the sea, skip the salty splashes and sandy toes and dip yourself into the crystal-clear pools of any beach club along the coast of Sentosa.

Tanjong Beach Club *(tanjongbeachclub.com)* is a longstanding institution, recently returned after a glamourous glow-up. Chic coral-coloured sunshades and day beds are pitched next to the pool and on the shore, their warm hues perfectly calculated to complement the turquoise waters. The music playlist is impeccable with coastal-forward beats.

But for the best views, head to **+Twelve** *(thepalawansentosa.com/plustwelve)*. Set in the Palawan lifestyle precinct, the adults-only club has a terraced structure with 12 private cabanas that guarantees unblocked sea views for all. Yes, minimum spending starts at S$300, but if you've been asking around, you'll know the pricing's a steal – especially when you can share it with up to 10 (though four is ideal). The best part? Each cabana gets its own private plunge pool for some cooling relief and sick cocktail-sipping shots. The vibes are amped up by the musical programme curated by the DJ Dispensary, shuttling between deep house and tropical beats to EDM and R&B. You won't feel left out if you're deckside. There's a swim-up bar (the only beach club to have one) for an idyllic soak, and picnic tables are set out on Palawan Beach for those who love the crunch of sand beneath them.

Good Times at the Palawan

Mini golf, go-karts and more

Like a mini version of Sentosa, the Palawan is a lifestyle precinct that offers something for everyone. Situated at Palawan Beach, the integrated hub features four activity zones – including one for the furkids – and five dining outlets.

For family-friendly fun, **UltraGolf** *(thepalawansentosa.com/ultragolf; adult/child S$22/18)* is an 18-hole mini-golf experience that can be crowded with participants. Singapore's only floating aqua park, the inflatable obstacle course **HydroDash** *(thepalawansentosa.com/hydrodash; per hr S$30)* is great for those who enjoy a little competition and a lot of falling into the sea. Nearby is Asia's first indoor gamified electric go-kart arena, **HyperDrive** *(thepalawansentosa.com/hyperdrive; from S$40)*, where real-life racing and virtual gaming come together around a three-level indoor racetrack. Speeds are tweaked for kid racers, so you needn't worry about accidents.

For food, the **HyperDrive Cafe** does burgers, pancakes and fries, while **Blu Kouzina** *(blukouzina.co)* serves Greek platters. **Palawan food trucks** dish out fresh sizzling treats served from a pastel set of trailers; the crate-made seating and fairy lights add a convivial air.

While **+Twelve** is the enclave's adults-only beach club, families have their own slice of fun with **Splash Tribe** *(thepalawansentosa.com/splash-tribe)*. The child-friendly beachside restaurant includes a water-play park, so the kids can frolic on slides as the adults chow down on hot pizza and frothy beer.

Awaken Your Senses

Stroll the Sentosa Sensoryscape

Strolling the 350m-long **garden walkway** *(sensoryscape.sentosa.com.sg; free)* that stretches between Resorts World Sentosa and Sentosa's beaches feels that much shorter thanks to the captivating installations along the route. Decked in lights and set on two levels, each of the pavilion-like displays offers a different sensory escape.

Start with the **Lookout Loop** at Imbiah Station for a scenic overview of what's to come. Framed by trees and foliage, and with peeks of the coast down south, the vantage makes this a great photo stop. Before you proceed, download the Imagi-Nite mobile app to reveal the sixth sense, 'imagination'. As you meander through the points, follow the app's instructions

BEST FREE ACTIVITIES

Beaches: Pack a picnic and spend a day lounging on the white sands of Sentosa's three beaches.

Fort Siloso: Walk through history at Singapore's last preserved coastal fort, taking in the view at Siloso Skywalk.

Sensoryscape: Frequent light and sound projections bring the beautifully planned walkway to life every evening.

Nature trails: Choose the Imbiah Nature Trail (p192) for a forested walk and the Coastal Trail for views of the ships and sea.

Photo walk: Snap impressive backdrops ranging from heritage military buildings to the Universal Globe and biophilic WEAVE mall.

DRINKING IN SENTOSA: BEST SUNSET SPOTS

Tanjong Beach Club: For coffee or cocktails, these snazzy beach day beds are some of the best on the island. *11am-10pm Mon-Fri, from 9am Sat & Sun*

Coastes: Offers relaxed seaside vibes as you toast frozen margaritas after a session of water sports at sea. *hours vary*

+Twelve: Part of the Palawan lifestyle enclave, this beach club has a swim-up bar and private cabanas with attached pools. *11am-9pm Mon-Thu, 9.30am-10.30pm Fri-Sun*

WHAT'S AT SENTOSA COVE?

Swanky **Sentosa Cove**, in the east of the island, is mostly home to some very expensive property but also has some great dining options if central Sentosa is too crowded. The designer **W Singapore** *(w-hotels.marriott.com)* is the one of the only hotels in this part of the island. Guests exclusively enjoy the expansive pool, but nonguests can feast on steaks at its renowned SKIRT Restaurant or have a tipple at WOOBAR. Nearby **Quayside Isle** has a fine selection of restaurants and cafes, along with a view of sleek yachts and a pier for strolling. Sentosa Cove is 10 minutes away from Beach Station via Sentosa shuttle bus B (free) or 10 minutes from VivoCity by taxi (around S$8 minus entry).

at each site to discover cinematic effects over the structures, from fluttering clouds of butterflies to hypnotic marine animals gliding through space. The flight of Senseri – a mystical superbeing – can be seen on the upper decks. The other 'spheres' offer something for each sense. **Tactile Trellis** has plants with textured surfaces to touch, **Scented Sphere** focuses on naturally fragrant herbs and flowers to perfume the space and the sound of trickling water makes you linger at **Symphony Streams**. The final light installation, **Glow Garden**, is more an archway of bowing flowers. Come during the night to see them at their most magnificent, especially when nearby attraction **Wings of Time Fireworks Symphony** *(mountfaberleisure.com; seats from S$19.80)* sets off its nightly fireworks (7.40pm and 8.40pm). Retracing your steps after dark is highly recommended if you have the time, as mesmerising light effects convey a whole new mood to the experience.

Thrills & Spills

Get your adrenaline pumping

If Universal Studios' roller-coasters and rides aren't exciting enough, Sentosa has plenty of other ways to satisfy adrenaline junkies. **Mega Adventure** *(sg.megaadventure.com; from S$18)* features a climbing course and trampolines atop Mt Imbiah, reachable via the Imbiah Nature Trail (p192). If you hear screams overhead, don't be alarmed. That's the activity highlight, the MegaZip – a 450m-long zip line over the treetops that goes directly across Siloso Beach, ending on an islet. Other blood-curdling yells can be heard at nearby **Skypark Sentosa by AJ Hackett** *(skyparksentosa.com; from S$59)*, this time thanks to its heart-stopping 50m-high bungee jump

SENTOSA DEVELOPMENT CORPORATION

Symphony Streams, Sensoryscape

and giant swing right over the sands. If you're too nervous, strap a friend alongside and attempt them together.

At **Skyline Luge Singapore** *(sentosa.skylineluge.com; from S$27)*, take the Skyride chairlift to the top of Mt Imbiah (yet again) and then hurtle down four winding slope tracks on a luge. It has just crossed over 100 million rides, so you know you won't be disappointed. There's also a night luge experience. The difference? Colourful lights and music beats make this a groovy downhill ride. After you're done, it's just a short walk to **AltitudeX** *(altitudex.com; from S$69)*, where you can free-fall in one of the world's largest indoor wind tunnels (as high as six storeys). The worst thing you can do is tense up here, so relax and follow the instructions, and soon you'll be doing backflips in the air...or maybe not. Calm yourself down afterwards at the **SkyHelix Sentosa** *(mountfaber leisure.com; adult/child from S$18/15.30)*. The seated slow ascension is hardly action-packed, but look up and you'll see it's the panoramic views that thrill.

BEST VIEWPOINTS

Siloso Skywalk: See Siloso Beach and Keppel Harbour from the 11-storey-high bridge connecting to Fort Siloso.

SkyHelix Sentosa: Dangle your feet on this 79m-tall open-air gondola ride from Mt Imbiah with 360-degree views.

Sentosa Cable Car Line: Sail over the treetops from Imbiah Lookout to Siloso Point, taking in views of the distant islands.

1-Altitude Coast: Catch the sunset or fireworks from the island's tallest bar. Dipping in the pool makes it even cooler.

Southernmost Point of Continental Asia: The tower at this landmark is popular with those eager to observe a slow sunset.

Walk Through Sentosa's History

Glimpse the island's past at Fort Siloso

Fort Siloso *(sentosa.com.sg; free)*, on the western tip of Sentosa, is Singapore's last well-preserved coastal fort and well worth a visit for those who love history or military relics. Bus A and the 'beach tram' drop you off at **Siloso Point**, where you'll start your walk with panoramic views from the 11-storey-tall **Siloso Skywalk** *(free)*. Take your time here as the views are some of the best on the island, but

SURRENDERING THE ISLAND

See the location where the British surrendered to the Japanese during WWII at the **Former Ford Factory** (p151) along Upper Bukit Timah Rd. The site is now a museum and memorial of Singapore's time as Syonan-to.

SEE SENTOSA FROM THE AIR

There's no more scenic way to enter and leave Sentosa than the cable car. Back in the day, it was the first sky-cable system to span a harbour. Today, it's still making waves with the **SkyOrb Cabin**, the world's first chrome-finished spherical cable-car cabin. Technical achievement aside, the dangling gondola is coveted for its glass-floor feature, which allows passengers to have a bird's-eye view of the channel as they pass. Two separate lines operate, with one shuttling between Singapore's Mt Faber and Sentosa Island, and the other an internal route. Bought separately, the ticket would cost S$50 for an adult, so the no-brainer here is to buy the bundle at S$35. For the SkyOrb Cabin, you'll need to top up an additional S$15.

NOEMIESCRIBANO/ALAMY

Imbiah Nature Trail

shades and umbrellas might be necessary to shield from the harsh sun. At the end, you'll walk to the start of the **Heritage Trail**. The bunkers and the old barracks and tunnels have been transformed into galleries that recreate moments from Singapore's history under British rule with dioramas and audio clips, so leave a good hour to explore slowly. The **Surrender Chambers**, with a waxed-figure recreation of the historical handover, are particularly poignant.

Another military remnant sits on Mt Imbiah. If you follow the Imbiah Nature Trail to the Mega Adventure (p190) hilltop site, there's a small side road on the left just before you reach the actual compound. Follow it and you'll see the remains of the **Imbiah Battery**. The guns may be gone but the supporting structures give a rough picture of what it must have been like.

Many of the colonial-era buildings that were once military barracks and quarters have been repurposed. Look for the iconic black-and-white buildings that now house hotels – many of these lodgings offer exclusive guest-only tours, so ask around if you're staying in one of them.

Time to Go Wild

Hike the Imbiah Nature Trail

For all of its landscaped nature, Sentosa does have some nice little nature trails for a serene walk. The forested **Imbiah Nature Trail** offers a chance for flora and fauna spotting, and has some mini waterfalls and even a few 'dragon bones' to excite the little ones.

Our preferred route starts at Imbiah Station. Head up a series of long escalators to reach the Madame Tussauds museum. Walk next past SkyHelix Sentosa and you'll notice signs pointing to the Sentosa Nature Discovery. From the small museum, you'll be linked to the treetop canopy walk. This lovely stretch is actually built over the former monorail tracks, which you'll see go off into the distance when you make a right at the end. You'll soon come to an official Mt Imbiah greeting billboard detailing the route and some natural highlights to spot along the way. The loop itself is under 1km. While it's possible to go in either direction, choose the left path for its flow. Look out for signs spotlighting local insects like cicadas and calls from the oriental magpie-robin. You'll quickly come to the first of three cascades, which are underwhelming. Continue on and pass small resting pavilions and some mega-sized 'dragon ribcages' before reaching the large waterfall. It's a great spot to rest and refresh with a drink, and reapply some insect repellent. Trudge on and you'll finally arrive at a life-sized dragon's head, the fountain sculpture pouring with water from its mouth. After this, you could continue on in the same direction to circle back to the start, or turn around and head up the small path to the hilltop attraction and battery. Either way, at a steady pace, the mountainside trail shouldn't take you more than an hour to complete and is a great way to experience a different side of Sentosa.

UNTOUCHABLE RESIDENTS

Never failing to stop visitors in their tracks, Sentosa's resident peacocks have become something of a mascot, trailing their iridescent tails over lawns across the island since the 1980s. The abundance of greenery has nurtured their numbers to over 60 today, with variations of Indian peafowls (blue) and Javan peafowls (green) in the mix. Once confined to certain plots and hotels, they now roam the entire island freely, thanks to their ultra-VIP status. But they're not exactly the brightest bulb in the bunch. During mating season (March to July), they call out with shrill crows and, embarrassingly, mistake reflective surfaces as fellow competing peacocks. While they seem friendly, resist the urge to touch or feed them. If you spot one, consider it your brush with Sentosa royalty.

An Orchid-Scented Journey

Make your own perfume at Scentopia

Step into the redolent space at **Scentopia** *(scentopia-singapore.com; from S$95)* and there's no mistaking what's coming up – you're making some perfume. Located across from Siloso Beach Resort, this local-helmed business takes you on a journey of matching your personality to notes before having you blend your own personal fragrance.

After answering a few questions on a tablet, you'll be given your report. It distributes your result into five categories: Citrus, Floral, Fresh, Woody and Oriental. You'll likely be in three categories or more. The staff explain what you have to do as you move through five rooms, smelling the wall scent tubes from your prescribed notes and stamping their oils on a provided card. After you've narrowed it down to six scents (for the 30mL version; the 50mL and 100mL may pick 10 oils), you bring the card to the assistant who curls your card into a cone and you take greedy whiffs to see if you enjoy the final result. If not, you're welcome to have another go picking from the rooms – even going out of your prescribed notes. When you're satisfied with the formula, you pump out the chosen oils into the perfume bottle and the assistant shakes and securely packs it.

It's an immersive way to craft a customised fragrance to call your own, given how vividly the rooms are decorated with relevant props. If you notice that quite a few scents are similar, it's because the main oils are based on orchids. For the fragrance enthusiast – especially if you like florals – it's an unexpectedly thoughtful experience that beautifully lingers.

Day Trips from Singapore

Researched by Jaclynn Seah

Singapore's location allows for budget-friendly quick getaways to offshore islands and neighbouring countries steeped in lush nature and cultural heritage.

Places

Singapore's offshore islands are mostly uninhabited pockets of greenery, a hint of what the land was like before it was overtaken by modernisation and concrete buildings. Only a handful of these islands can be visited, mostly by boat – the perfect quick escape from the city. For those looking to venture further, Singapore is connected by land to Johor Bahru in Malaysia and by sea to Indonesia's Riau islands of Batam and Bintan. These places share cultural and historical ties with Singapore, but each has its own charm worth further exploration. Costs of food, transport and shopping are generally lower in Malaysia and Indonesia, ideal for those on a tight budget wanting to stretch their dollar.

Pulau Ubin

TIME FROM CHANGI POINT FERRY TERMINAL: **10MIN** 

TOP TIP

Avoid commuting to Malaysia and Indonesia during long weekends and school holidays – customs queues and traffic jams can steal hours.

See the wild side of Singapore

Keep a sharp eye out when critter-watching on Pulau Ubin: some of the plants and animals you might spot can no longer be found on the mainland. The 100-hectare **Chek Jawa Wetlands** *(nparks.gov.sg/pulau-ubin; free)* on the island's east coast is particularly notable, with six distinct ecosystems in a single location. It's a favourite place for spotting migratory birds and intertidal exploration. The **mangrove and coastal boardwalks** take you up close to the flora and fauna, and the 21m-tall **Jejawi Tower** offers a bird's-eye view. Explore with care, as you may encounter wild boars and macaques along the way.

EATING & DRINKING ON PULAU UBIN: OUR PICKS

Cheong Lian Yuen: Small place in Pulau Ubin village serving home-style *zi char* (sharing) and seafood dishes. *noon-5pm Fri-Tue, to 6pm Sat & Sun* $

Ah Ma Drink Stall: Just before Jelutong Bridge; cool down by the mangroves with a fresh coconut juice. *hours vary* $

Melah Cafe: Quaint weekend-only place serving halal Malay dishes such as *lontong* (coconut-curry vegetable stew). *6.30am-3pm Sat & Sun* $

Season Live Seafood: Fresh seafood dishes near Pulau Ubin village with a sea view. *10am-6pm Wed-Mon, to 6.30pm Sat & Sun* $$

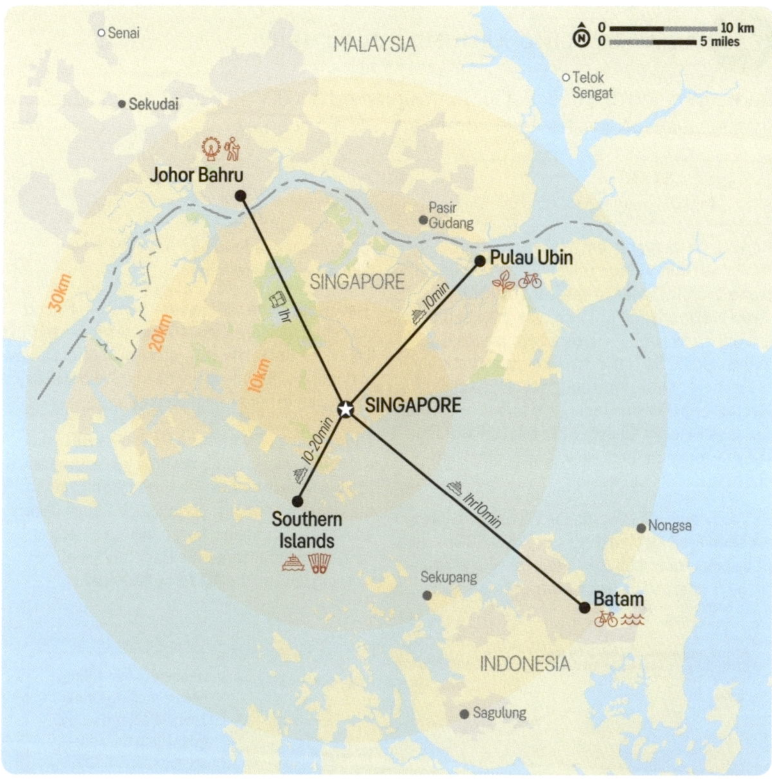

Go camping

Typically only residents with a Singpass account can book and pay for the required camping permit (Temporary Occupation Licence) if they want to camp outdoors in Singapore, but Pulau Ubin makes an exception for foreigners who want to stay in any of the three **campsites** *(pulau-ubin.nparks.gov.sg/camping; free)* on the island. **Jelutong** is the most convenient within walking distance to the Pulau Ubin Jetty, while **Endut Senin** is a 30-minute walk westwards near Ubin Quarry. **Mamam Beach** is the quietest campsite but requires a 40-minute walk north to reach.

Pedal or paddle

Pick your favourite way to explore Pulau Ubin. At only 10 sq km, the island is easy enough to hike, but cycling saves you time and energy – it takes just 20 minutes to cycle (versus 45 minutes of walking) to the furthest points east and west of **Pulau Ubin Village**, where there are plenty of rental shops and bicycle-hire options.

Serious mountain bikers can also test their skills on the trails of **Ketam Mountain Bike Park**, beside an abandoned granite quarry on the western side of the island. The park

GETTING TO PULAU UBIN

Take a public bus or a taxi to **Changi Point Ferry Terminal**, from which many small bumboats (motorised sampans) travel to Pulau Ubin in 10 minutes. Each bumboat takes up to 12 people; boats leave only when they're full. A one-way ride is S$4, and it is an extra S$2 per bicycle. Have exact change to pay in cash directly to the boater. Boats run from 6am to 6pm; aim to leave well before 6pm as there is no other way to get off the island.

A DAY CYCLING AROUND PULAU UBIN

Rent a bike and discover Pulau Ubin's untamed beauty on two wheels. Cycle through lush forests, heritage homes and scenic quarries.

START	END	LENGTH
Pulau Ubin Village	Pulau Ubin Ferry Terminal	14km; 4-6hr

Hop off the ferry and rent a bicycle from ❶ **Pulau Ubin Village** (p195). Cycle 20 minutes east along Jln Durian towards the ❷ **Chek Jawa Wetlands** (p194). Leave your bike at the entrance and stroll towards ❸ **House No 1**, a conserved 1930s Tudor-style mansion that's also the visitors centre. Walk the coastal boardwalk through beaches and mangrove forest, and climb the seven-storey ❹ **Jejawi Tower** (p194) along the way for panoramic views and coastal bird-spotting opportunities.

As you head back towards the village, pop into ❺ **Ubin Fruit Orchard**, home to over 30 species of tropical fruit trees. See a typical village house at the conserved ❻ **Teck Seng's Place**, then follow the meandering ❼ **Sensory Trail** to glimpse old plantations.

Grab a bite in the village, then head west along Jln Jelutong. More than 140 species of butterfly live on ❽ **Butterfly Hill**, which also offers a view of floating wetlands at the nearby Pekan Quarry, now home to heron-nesting platforms.

Keep cycling till you reach ❾ **Puaka Hill**, where a short but steep climb rewards you with a view of Ubin Quarry below. The furthest point along the west path for casual cyclists is Ketam Quarry. Seasoned mountain bikers can hit the trails at ❿ **Ketam Mountain Bike Park** (p195) before heading back to the ⓫ **ferry terminal**.

Check the tide tables before visiting **Chek Jawa Wetlands**. Low tide, when the shores are exposed, is the best time to visit.

The **German Girl Shrine** honours an unidentified 18-year-old German girl who tragically died escaping British internment during WWI.

From the viewing jetty behind House No 1, look for a small islet called **Pulau Sekudu** (Frog Island) with a frog-shaped rock on it.

Chek Jawa Wetlands boardwalk (p194), Pulau Ubin

is unstaffed, and not recommended for beginners as even the easy paths have some steep sections with poor traction.

If you prefer to use a paddle, book a kayaking tour with **Adventures by Asian Detours** *(adventures.network; from S$106)* or **Kayakasia** *(kayakasia.org; adult/child S$135/85)* to explore the island's coastline and the waterways that cut through its many mangrove forests.

Eat seafood on a floating restaurant

Kelongs (floating fish farms) were a common sight along the coasts of early Singapore. **Smith Marine Floating Restaurant** *(smithmarine.com.sg),* just off Pulau Ubin's southern tip, is one of the country's last remaining *kelongs*. Here you can enjoy a sea-to-table meal in the middle of the water. Bookings are a must, and there's an additional fee for the chartered bumboat (motorised sampan) that will take you there from Changi Point Ferry Terminal.

Southern Islands

TIME FROM MARINA SOUTH FERRY TERMINAL: **10-20MIN**

Cruise around the southern islands

Spend a day cruising around Singapore's southern coast. Only a handful of Singapore's uninhabited offshore southern islands can be visited as they're mostly home to heavy industries.

The easiest way to explore is by public ferry that leaves from **Marina South Ferry Terminal**. Regular daily services from **Singapore Island Cruise** *(islandcruise.com.sg)* and **Marina South Ferries** *(marinasouthferries.com)* take you to St John's Island, Kusu Island and Big Sister's Island. One-day island-hopping tickets cost S$15, with services starting at 9am and the last boats leaving the islands at about 6pm.

For those on Sentosa Island, **YachtCruiseSG** *(yachtcruisesg.com; S$25)* has a round-trip speedboat transfer from Sentosa

GRANITE ISLAND

A biodiversity treasure trove, Singapore's second-largest island is a throwback to early village life. Pulau Ubin translates as 'Granite Island', and granite was one of the primary reasons people came to live here back in the day.

Today's Pulau Ubin is a reminder of Singapore in the time before its tropical forests became a concrete jungle. While early quarrying destroyed much of the primary vegetation, time and conservation efforts have turned the island green again – over a thousand species of animal, insect and plant are found here, along with almost all of Singapore's known mangrove species. It's also one of the last places to witness the old *kampong* (village) lifestyle.

Visit on weekdays to avoid the crowds, though some shops and eateries may be closed. Bring cash, as there are no ATMs.

TALES OF THE SOUTHERN ISLANDS

Singapore's idyllic southern islands hold fascinating histories and legends.

St John's Island has the most colourful history – it's where the British first arrived in 1819, a day before reaching the mainland. It later served as a quarantine station, opium-rehabilitation centre, refugee camp for Vietnamese boat people and holding centre for political detainees.

Lazarus Island, with its beautiful white-sand beach, was historically a burial ground for those who died on neighbouring St John's Island. **Kusu Island** celebrates interracial harmony stemming from a tale of friendship between a Malay and Chinese shipwrecked on the island. The **Sisters' Islands** were apparently named for a tragic tale of two sisters who drowned while fleeing pirates.

SAMI PELTOKANGAS/SHUTTERSTOCK

Lazarus Island

Jetty@Cove to **Seringat Jetty** on **Lazarus Island** with two departure times from Sentosa, at 10.40am and 3pm. Marina South Ferries and YachtCruiseSG also offer sunset dinner cruises and private water-taxi services for the southern islands.

Private charters are ideal for large groups or if you want flexibility with itineraries and times. These can range from simple water-taxi transfers to luxurious private-yacht charters that run the gamut of gourmet dining and water-sports equipment rental.

Kusu Island pilgrimage

Kusu Island translates as 'Tortoise Island' – the name is based on a legend about a giant tortoise that transformed into an island to save some drowning sailors. Normally a tranquil destination, tiny Kusu gets particularly busy during the ninth lunar month (around September or October), when throngs of worshippers make their annual pilgrimage to pray at the **Da Bo Gong Temple** and the three **Malay keramats** (shrines) on the hillock behind the temple.

Dive the underwater trails

While Singapore's murky waters are a far cry from the crystal-clear seas of its neighbours, muck-diving enthusiasts may find some surprises with the help of a good torch. Scuba-diving sites around the islands of **Pulau Hantu** and **Pulau Jong** are home to crustaceans, cuttlefish and even some unusual nudibranchs.

Local operators including **Cuddlefish Divers** *(cuddlefish divers.com; from S$135)* and **Marlin Divers** *(marlindivers.com.sg; from S$125)* organise regular dive trips to Pulau Hantu, typically weekend half-day sessions consisting of two boat dives. Pay extra for gear rental and a dive guide.

A DAY-LONG SOUTHERN ISLANDS CRUISE

Spend a day island-hopping by ferry to uncover hidden beaches, tranquil trails and historical surprises.

START	END	LENGTH
Marina South Ferry Terminal	Marina South Ferry Terminal	33km; 6hr

Board the ferry from 1 **Marina South Ferry Terminal** (p197) to 2 **Big Sister's Island** (p200). Head north to the 3 **observation tower** (p200) for scenic views. Exit the forest trail in the south and follow the 4 **floating boardwalk** (p200) lined with corals back to the jetty.

Next, alight at 5 **Kusu Island**. Turn right after the pier towards the 6 **Da Bo Gong Temple**, dedicated to the local god of prosperity. Further on, climb the hill to see three 7 **Malay keramats** (shrines) where devotees pray for wealth and health. Look out for the 8 **tortoise sanctuary**, home to hundreds of tortoises.

Catch the next boat to 9 **St John's Island** (p200), then saunter across the causeway to 10 **Lazarus Island** and frolic on the beautiful white sand at 11 **Lazarus Island Beach**. Enjoy the view of mainland Singapore from the northern end, which used to be the separate island of 12 **Pulau Kias**.

Back on St John's Island, walk westwards to the 13 **Old Governor's House** overlooking St John's Island Beach, perfect for picnics and intertidal exploration. Head inland to see the remnants of the old village, which also housed a quarantine centre. Stop by the 14 **Marine Park Outreach & Education Centre** (p200) on the east side to learn about the local marine life before catching the ferry back to the mainland.

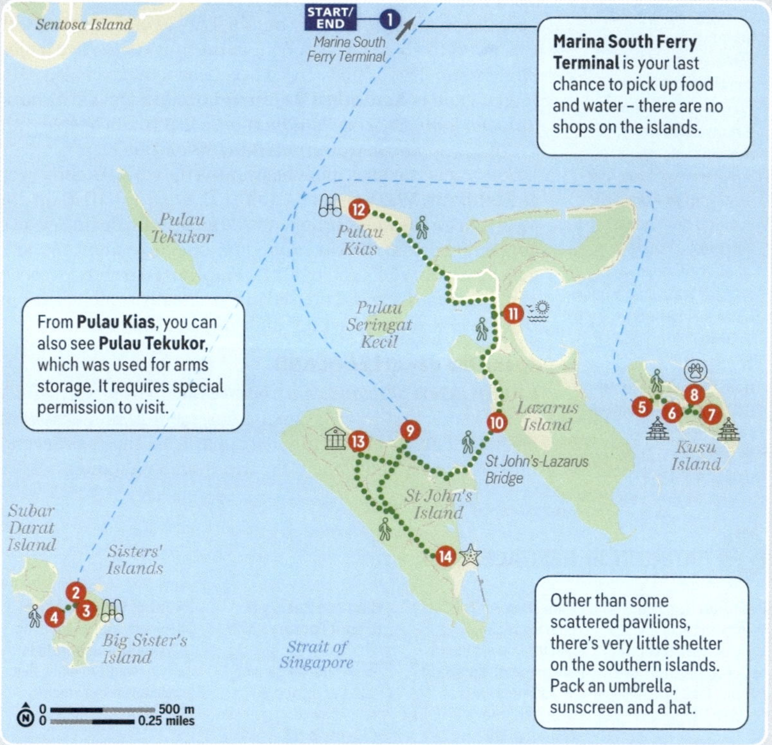

Marina South Ferry Terminal is your last chance to pick up food and water – there are no shops on the islands.

From **Pulau Kias**, you can also see **Pulau Tekukor**, which was used for arms storage. It requires special permission to visit.

Other than some scattered pavilions, there's very little shelter on the southern islands. Pack an umbrella, sunscreen and a hat.

GETTING TO JOHOR BAHRU

Woodlands Checkpoint, Immigration & Quarantine (CIQ) sees the bulk of cross-border traffic, while the **Tuas Second Link** is for those headed to LEGOLAND or Kukup Fishing Village.

Public buses are cheap and convenient. **Causeway Link** *(causewaylink.com.my)*, **SBS** *(sbstransit.com.sg)*, **SMRT** *(smrt.com.sg)* and **Transtar** *(transtar.travel)* buses make the journey, with multiple routes and pickup points in Singapore and JB Sentral.

Going across the causeway by car at Woodlands or Tuas is convenient for groups – you don't have to disembark for immigration – but best avoided during school and public holidays, when traffic can swell waiting times to hours.

The **KTM Shuttle Tebrau** *(shuttleonline.ktmb.com.my; RM5)* train from Woodlands CIQ to JB Sentral takes five minutes; book tickets way in advance in peak periods.

Learn about marine conservation

A visit to the southern islands is a good way to learn about Singapore's conservation plans.

Sisters' Islands were relaunched in 2024 as Singapore's first park protecting coral and marine life. While **Small Sister's Island (Pulau Subar Darat)** is strictly for conservation, you can visit **Big Sister's Island (Pulau Subar Laut)** by public ferry. There's a **floating boardwalk** on the west of the island, with a lagoon tidal pool and coral nursery. Cut through the centre of the island to the top of a small hill where there's an **observation tower** perfect for birdwatching.

On **St John's Island**, head to the Public Gallery at the **Marine Park Outreach & Education Centre** *(nparks.gov.sg; free)*, which has interactive displays showcasing the rich biodiversity found in Singapore's waters.

Johor Bahru (Malaysia)

TIME FROM SINGAPORE: **1HR**

Stroll around JB Heritage District

Less than 10 minutes' walk from the immigration checkpoint at JB Sentral along Jln Wong Ah Fook, Jln Tan Hiok Nee and Jln Dhoby is the **Johor Bahru Heritage District** – just look for the landmark Red House.

Beyond the many heritage eateries with long histories, check out the city's cultural sites. **Johor Ancient Temple** *(facebook.com/Johor.Ancient.Temple)* on Jln Trus is one of the oldest structures in JB and a testament to the unity of the five major Chinese sub-groups that settled here. Down the road along Jln Ungku Puan is **Arulmigu Rajamariamman Devasthanam** *(rajamariammandevasthanam.com)*, a 1911 Hindu temple with a striking *gopuram* (tower) marking its entrance.

The streets becomes more bustling as the sun sets. Stop over at **Meldrum Walk Street Food** *(1-11.30pm Fri-Wed)* on Jln Meldrum for the many little roadside food stalls, or Jln Segget's happening **Pasar Karat** *(6pm-2am Tue-Sun)* night market, which hawks snacks and trinkets. **Hookah District** *(facebook.com/hookahdistrictjb)*, housed in hip containers along Jln Tan Hiok Nee, is good for supper and smoking sheesha.

Spend the day at LEGOLAND

LEGOLAND *(legoland.com.my; adult/child from RM199/169)* is Malaysia's first international amusement park. Located in Iskandar Puteri, just 30 minutes by car from the Tuas Second Link, it's a very convenient day trip from Singapore.

EATING IN JB: HERITAGE FOOD

Restoran Hua Mui: Traditional Hainanese-style coffeeshop, one of the oldest in JB and famous for its Hainanese Chicken Chop. *8am-5pm* **$$**

Kam Long Ah Zai Curry Fish Head: Enjoy your fish three ways (head, tail or meat), drenched in clay-pot bowls of delectable savoury curry. *8am-4pm* **$$**

Hiap Joo Bakery & Biscuit Factory: With over 100 years of history, no wonder its banana cakes and coconut buns draw long queues. *7.30am-5pm* **$**

A Jabar Sup Kambing: Of the many stellar *kambing sup* (mutton soup) stalls along Meldrum Walk, this one stands out. *noon-10.30pm Fri-Wed* **$**

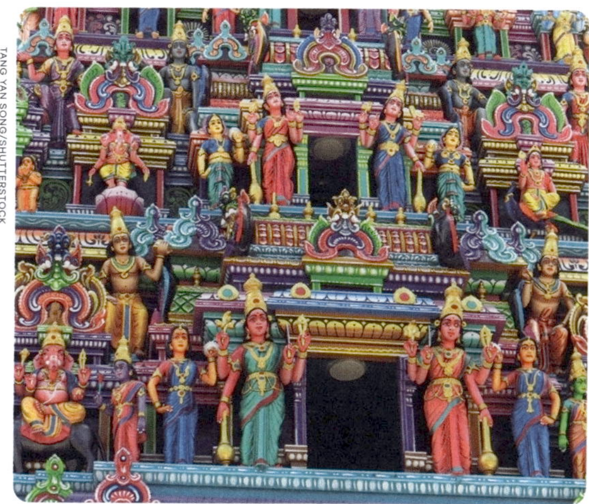

TANG YAN SONG/SHUTTERSTOCK

Arulmigu Rajamariamman Devasthanam, Johor Bahru

The **LEGOLAND Theme Park** *(closed Wed)* has more than 40 attractions including roller-coasters, fun rides and lots of LEGO sculptures – ride **The Dragon** for thrills, or admire the intricate recreations of world monuments from LEGO bricks at **Miniland**. Right next door is **LEGOLAND Water Park** *(closed Tue)*, which has water rides, a wave pool and a lazy river. Neighbouring **SEA LIFE Aquarium** is home to more than 13,000 creatures across 11 habitat zones.

WTS Travel *(wtstravel.com.sg)* and **EU Holidays** *(euholidays.com.sg)* offer day-trip packages from Singapore that include two-way direct coach transfers and entrance tickets to the various parks.

Hiking in Gunung Pulai

For higher peaks to hike than in Singapore, head north to **Gunung Pulai**. At 654m, it's about four times higher than Bukit Timah Hill. Reaching the summit takes about two to three hours of hiking from the trailhead on the western slope. There's a small waterfall 20 minutes' walk from the car park.

There are other trails from **Kangkar Pulai** on the eastern slope. Of note is the trail to **Tasik Biru**, a strikingly blue quarry lake; the trailheads start at **Dewa Fu Lai Temple** and **Taman Awam BBKP** park.

JOHOR NEIGHBOURHOODS

Mount Austin: Bursting with trendy cafes and boutiques. Family fun at Austin Heights Water & Adventure Park and escape rooms at Eco Palladium.

Bukit Indah: Adventure recreation at Sireh Park, 18-hole golf at Bukit Indah Recreation Club and relaxing massages at Eminent Reflexology.

Kulai: Quirky sights at Hakka Putuo Village and Purple Bamboo Valley, or shopping at Johor Premium Outlets. Scale the slopes of Gunung Pulai.

Desaru Coast: Beaches for lounging and water sports including surfing. Visit mangroves with Lebam River Cruise or feast on fruits at Desaru Fruit Farm.

Kota Tinggi: Encounter dazzling fireflies on an evening cruise along Johor River at Kota Tinggi Firefly Park, or zipline over the canopy at RAF Point.

EATING IN JB HERITAGE DISTRICT: OUR PICKS

Seek out the hidden cat lounge inside the restaurant!

Palates & Bagels by TAM: Industrial-chic cafe specialising in savoury and sweet bagels stacked with a huge variety of fusion ingredients. *8am-10pm* $$

Bev C Cafe: Sip on handcrafted coffee in this hipster cafe, artfully decorated with knick-knacks above a vintage clothing store. *10am-6pm* $$

Merah Kitchen & Bar: Behind its vending-machine door is a retro-inspired eatery with inventive cocktails and Malaysian cuisine. *5pm-1am Tue-Sun* $$

Flowers in the Window: Cosy garden-themed decor and an exterior draped with greenery, plus tasty vegan-friendly food. *9am-4pm Wed-Mon* $$

BATAM: GETTING THERE & AROUND

Board a ferry from **Singapore Cruise Centre** *(singaporecruise.com.sg)* at **HarbourFront** or **Tanah Merah**. Various operators offer schedules departing Singapore as early as 7.40am and from Batam by 8.30pm. The journey takes about 70 minutes, with one-way ticket prices from S$38 to S$44.

Renting a car at the **Batam Centre Ferry Terminal** is possible, but driving in Batam can be hectic if you're unfamiliar with the roads. Consider hiring a car with driver instead – it's usually cheaper and certainly more convenient than taking taxis. Most drivers use WhatsApp to communicate with customers.

Rideshare apps such as Grab and Gojek can also be used, but tensions with the local taxi industry mean there are limited pickup points within the city area.

AKHMAD DODY FIRMANSYAH/SHUTTERSTOCK

Stand at Asia's southernmost point

Tanjung Piai National Park *(johornationalparks.gov.my/tanjung-piai; adult/child RM20/10)* touts itself as the southernmost point of continental Asia, covering 926 hectares of lush mangrove forest and intertidal mudflats. Enjoy views of Singapore and Indonesia from the coastal boardwalks. It's a favourite for birdwatchers, particularly during migration season from March to September.

A 15-minute drive up the coast takes you to rustic **Kukup Fishing Village** with its stilt houses over the water. Feast on fresh seafood at cosy **WohBee Canteen** *(wohbeecanteen.com; bookings essential)* or **New Kukup Seafood Restaurant** before returning to Singapore.

Private transport is needed to get to the park; it's about 40 minutes' drive from Singapore's Tuas Second Link.

Batam (Indonesia)

TIME FROM SINGAPORE: **70MIN** 

Cycle across the Barelang Bridge

There aren't any true must-see sights on Batam, but the **Barelang Bridge** can be considered one of its icons. It's actually made up of six bridges and is named for the three largest islands that it connects: Batam, Rempang and Galang. Avid cyclists can traverse its 50km-plus route that ends at a **beach** on the southern tip of **Galang Baru Island**. Book a guided cycling

EATING IN BATAM: BEST FOODIE AREAS

Nagoya Food Court: With 60-plus stalls, this open-air food court is one of the best places to sample Batam's delights. *6.30am-1am Sun-Fri, to 2am Sat* $

Pasar Penuin Wet Market: Local wet market to buy fresh produce, with several long-time food stalls; it's especially popular for breakfast. *5am-1pm* $

Pasat Pasir Putih: Close to Batam Centre, this busy food court is popular with both locals and foreigners. *8am-1pm Mon-Fri, 7.30am-2pm Sat & Sun* $

A2 Food Court: One of Batam's larger and most established food courts, it's most crowded in the evening for alfresco dining. *6am-1am* $

Barelang Bridge, Batam

tour for easy bicycle rental and safety, as the areas around the ferry and bridge get jammed with traffic when it's busy. Also, this route is quite hilly throughout – especially challenging in Batam's tropical humidity – so you may want to opt for a van transfer back. **Jacqtours** *(jacqtours.com)* and **JA Travel** *(ja-travel.com)* offer bespoke cycling tours from Singapore.

End your adventure in style by eating seafood in a *kelong* on stilts near the bridge; check out **Barelang Seafood Restaurant** *(barelangseafood.com)* or **Kopak Jaya 007** *(kopakjaya.com)*.

Adventurous activities and family fun

Batam is a haven for water sports on a budget. Popular spots include **Harris Resort Barelang** *(discoverasr.com/harris)* and **Batam View Beach Resort** *(batamview.com)* for Jet Skis, banana boating and parasailing, while **Batam WakePark** *(instagram.com/batamwakepark)* is for cable-tow wakeboarding.

If you prefer to stay dry, head to **Golden City Go-Kart** *(instagram.com/golden_gokart)* in Bengkong for go-karting, tackle a high-elements adventure course and paintball at **Belalang Adventure** *(belalangadventure.co.id)*, or do some trekking at **Panbil Nature Reserve** *(panbilhospitality.com/panbil-nature-reserve; hiking from 185,000Rp)*. For something more sedate, chill out on **Nongsa Beach** or **Melayu Beach**, or tee off at one of Batam's many golf courses.

WHY SINGAPOREANS LOVE BATAM

Batam is one of the most popular day-trip and weekend-getaway spots for Singaporeans. Just an hour's ferry ride away, it offers duty-free shopping, fresh seafood, relaxing massages and a refreshing change of pace, all without blowing your travel budget.

Despite representing separate countries today, historically Singapore, Batam and the nearby Riau Islands were all part of the ancient Malay sultanates that ruled this region. Today's Batam is the largest city in the Riau archipelago and a major industrial and commercial hub.

A reminder when travelling between the two areas to check your clocks: despite its proximity to Singapore, Batam follows Western Indonesian Time (WIB) and is one hour ahead of Singapore.

EATING IN BATAM: TOP CAFES

Volla Social House: This modern and photogenic cafe serves Indonesian and European cuisine. *10am-midnight Mon-Fri, to 1am Sat & Sun* **$$**

Anchor Cafe & Roastery: Perfect for serious coffee aficionados; pick your brewing method and bean type alongside yummy pastries. *8am-8pm* **$$**

Tatido Coffee Roasters: Speciality coffee roaster with single-estate coffee beans from around the world. *7am-8pm Mon-Fri, to 9pm Sat & Sun* **$$**

Jill's Cafe: Cafe, bakery and co-working studio; yummy sandwiches and desserts as well as stellar handcrafted drinks. *10am-10pm Wed-Mon* **$$**

Where to Stay

Staying in Singapore is expensive, especially in the CBD and around Orchard Rd. More modest and budget-friendly digs are available in Little India and Chinatown. Options range from simple backpacker dorms to some of the most luxurious lodgings in Asia.

Where to Stay If You Love...

Architecture, history & knockout vistas

Downtown & Marina Bay (p42) Flush with museums and a mix of historic and cutting-edge architecture, it's pricey but worth it for the views.

Hip restaurants, cocktail dens & buzzing markets

Chinatown, Tanjong Pagar & the CBD (p68) Packed with markets, hawker centres, temples and trendy nightspots. Options vary from swanky hotels to hip hostels.

Street art, boutiques & religious shrines

Little India & Kampong Glam (p86) Central location with plenty of cheap accommodation and some higher-end boutique and modern hotels.

Designer stores & mega malls

Orchard Road (p102) Singapore's famous shopping strip littered with high-end hotels and a smattering of trendy slumber pads.

Superlative gardens & trendy enclaves

Holland Village, Botanic Gardens & Dempsey Hill (p114) Due to the proximity of Orchard Rd, options are limited, with a few good ones in Holland Village.

Peranakan culture, cool cafes & village vibes

Eastern Singapore (p126) Joo Chiat is the best base, and the new MRT line allows easy access to the city. Convenient to East Coast Park and the airport.

Wildlife wonders & jungle trails

Northern & Central Singapore (p144) Vast area with a mix of distinctive stays, from boutique options to convenient business hotels around Novena.

Museums, nature & offbeat attractions

West & Southwest Singapore (p162) A variety of overnight stays, from playful slumber pads to luxurious villas among nature reserves.

Adrenaline thrills & beachside chills

Sentosa Island (p178) Resort-style hotels and easy access to kid-friendly attractions and beaches. Getting off the island can be a slight hassle.

Downtown & Marina Bay

HERITAGE HOTELS

21 Carpenter $$
MAP P57
Once a prominent remittance house, this boutique hotel in Clarke Quay has a mix of heritage and modern-design rooms, and a rooftop infinity pool with a CBD skyline view.

Warehouse Hotel $$$
MAP P57
Industrial-chic hotel restored from an 1895 warehouse in Robertson Quay, featuring 37 stylish rooms and lofts along with two excellent restaurants.

Mett Singapore $$$
MAP P62
Colonial-style hotel overhauled with 85 luxurious modern rooms. Perched along the slopes of Fort Canning, it was part of the British Far East Command military complex.

Fullerton Hotel $$$
MAP P45
The former General Post Office, a gazetted national monument, is a 400-room hotel with Singapore River panoramas on one side and Marina Bay views on the other. The newer, smaller Fullerton Bay Hotel is also nearby.

Raffles Singapore $$$
MAP P62
Established in 1887, this heritage hotel with 115 timelessly elegant suites and impeccable butler service is a favourite with visiting dignitaries and superstars.

STUNNING VIEWS

Heritage Collection on Boat Quay $$
MAP P57
Boutique hotel in former shophouse units along Boat Quay, featuring modern rooms with nostalgic touches. Splurge on the river-facing loft rooms.

Marina Bay Sands $$$
MAP P45
Over 2000 luxurious rooms spread across three towers. Guests enjoy panoramic views of either Marina Bay or Gardens by the Bay, and access to the famous infinity pool.

Ritz Carlton Millenia Singapore $$$
MAP P45
Uber-luxe hotel decked out with art pieces along Marina Bay. Spacious suites with floor-to-ceiling windows provide stunning views of Marina Bay and the Singapore Flyer.

Fullerton Bay Hotel $$$
MAP P45
Sleek, modern 100-room hotel on the waterfront between the historical Customs House and Clifford Pier – a more intimate alternative to the older Fullerton Hotel.

ON A BUDGET

KINN Habitat $
MAP P57
Minimalistic, sparkling-clean hotel with snug rooms and capsule beds in Boat Quay. More capsules in sister property KINN Capsule nearby.

LYF Funan $
MAP P53
Colourful motifs dominate at this social hotel connected to Funan Shopping Centre. Small rooms have access to a communal gym, kitchen, laundry and co-working lounge.

ST Signature Bugis Middle $
MAP P62
Marked by a striking mural of a Chinese opera performer on its facade, this co-living hotel with 38 rooms in Bras Basah has a shared kitchen and balcony spaces.

HOW MUCH FOR A NIGHT IN A...

Luxury abode
from S$600 per night

Midrange hotel
from S$300 per night

Hostel
from S$30 for a dorm room

Chinatown, Tanjong Pagar & the CBD

HERITAGE SHOPHOUSES

Amoy Hotel $$
MAP P70
Tucked-away boutique property with 37 rooms. A temple turned museum welcomes guests into stylish rooms in conserved shophouses with heritage touches.

Ann Siang House $$
MAP P70
Rooms here lean into a bygone era, yet it surprises with bold flourishes including lime plexiglass panels in the lobby and sleek designer seating in the rooms.

HOSTELS

Wink @ Upper Cross Street $
MAP P70
This hostel outlet is a crowd favourite thanks to the numerous room types and large public yard for meals and socialising.

Jyu Capsule Hotel $
MAP P70
Delightfully clean and organised, with helpful staff, this hostel has spacious capsules with their own TVs and even options for two guests.

SPLURGE

Clan Hotel $$$
MAP P70
With touches of Chinatown history and a modern design, this plush hotel provides curated walking tours, a ceremonial tea welcome and impeccable service.

Mondrian Singapore Duxton $$$
MAP P70
The property is riddled with art and luxurious in its fittings. Take a picture with the gigantic Kaws figurine or scan your room's artwork to see it come alive.

CONTEMPORARY

Claude Hotel $
MAP P70
Compact but elegant, rooms are designed to maximise functionality, with subdued neutrals and clean lines providing restful comfort.

Kinn Studios $$
MAP P70
Spa-like boutique hotel with a wellness slant. Perk up with the lobby coffee kiosk or head out to foodie enclave Keong Siak.

Mercure ICON Singapore City Centre $$
MAP P70
Opened in 2024, rooms are bathed in sunlight courtesy of the floor-to-ceiling windows. Upgrade to the balcony rooms for soaring views.

Little India & Kampong Glam

COSY

Dream Chaser $
MAP P97
Boutique capsule hotel in Kampong Glam offering jewel-coloured shared pods and private rooms.

Coliwoo Hotel Kampong Glam $
MAP P97
Clean, space-efficient rooms with their own washer-dryer and microwaves? Yes, please. Ask for rooms away from the street if you like your quiet.

lyf Bugis $$
MAP P97
Fun vibes all round; the co-living design includes communal pantry stations, a well-stocked kitchen, laundrette and snazzy gym.

MIDRANGE

Wanderlust $$
MAP P88
A peaceful respite in Little India, this converted 1920s schoolhouse features sharp, modern rooms and lofts, with kitchens and washers in some.

Serangoon House $$
MAP P88
The delightfully ornate rooms have canopy beds that hide a second tier for another guest. Wake up to plated breakfasts at the basement restaurant.

Ibis Singapore on Bencoolen $$
MAP P97
Recently refurbished, with watercolour murals and botanical drawings – along with

JINEE CHEN/SHUTTERSTOCK

Wanderlust, Little India

a window bay seat with plump cushions – that turn the no-frills brand fancy.

SPLURGE

Andaz Singapore $$$
MAP P97
Located in a futuristic twin-towered complex, the high-level suites have a restful air and overlook the bay. The rooftop bar with tepee seating is a vibe at sunset.

Parkroyal on Beach Road $$$
MAP P97
A colourful lobby leads into spacious rooms with understated luxury interiors in a gold-toned palette. The bar is a gem and the twinkling pool is magical at night.

Vagabond Club $$$
MAP P88
With touches of Parisian charm, this hotel is swathed in red velvet and art. Rooms are modestly sized but richly appointed, and you'll love the jazz bar.

Orchard Road

LUXURY ABODES

Pan Pacific Orchard $$$
MAP P104
This urban escape brings jungle cool to Orchard Rd with stacked sky gardens, chic interiors and service so sharp it feels almost telepathic.

St Regis $$$
MAP P104
Swanky hotel blending modern sophistication with classic charm. Rooms are huge, with lavish textiles, tasteful art and 24-hour butler service.

Shangri-La Hotel $$$
MAP P104
If you're travelling with little ones in tow, it's hard to beat the sprawling tropical garden, resort-style pool, amazing kids' club and exclusive family floors.

SKY-HIGH PRICES

Hotel rates skyrocket during big concerts and the F1, rooms vanish fast and even budget stays cost a premium. Prices are also high during school holidays (June and December) and Chinese New Year.

Goodwood Park Hotel $$$
MAP P104
This hilltop heritage hotel blends colonial-era architecture with luxury amenities and gracious service.

SO HIP, SO COOL

Standard $$
MAP P104
It's dramatic and bold, with mid-century modern interiors. Rooms are compact yet perfectly formed – if you need extra space, the suites will do the trick.

Singapore EDITION $$$
MAP P104
The hip brand's Asian debut redefines luxury on the shopping strip with a modern edge. Sleek interiors, curated greenery and flawless service.

BANG FOR YOUR BUCK

Lloyd's Inn $$
MAP P104
A minimalist 34-room haven steps from Orchard Rd, featuring a nature-integrated design with light-filled spaces, rooftop terrace and dipping pool.

voco Orchard $$
MAP P104
A great mix of sustainability, stylish comfort and warm hospitality. The rooftop pool with a bar adds a touch of fun.

JEN Singapore Orchardgateway $$
MAP P104
Smack bang in the heart of Orchard Rd, this sophisticated hotel connects directly to 313@somerset mall. Enjoy epic city views from the rooftop pool.

Holland Village, Botanic Gardens & Dempsey Hill

CONVENIENT CRASH PADS

Park Avenue Rochester $
OFF MAP P116
Designed for business travellers but ideal for leisure guests seeking a peaceful and convenient retreat just outside the city for a few days' stay.

Citadines Connect Rochester Singapore $$
OFF MAP P116
Sleek aparthotel with lovely views. The self-service amenity machine is a great touch, and robot butler ARIA can deliver items to your room.

FOR A LONGER STAY

Quincy House Singapore $$
MAP P116
Stylish serviced residence in Holland Village with studios and apartments, co-working space, laundrette and a rooftop pool. Minimum six-night stay.

Eastern Singapore

BUDGET

Betel Box $
MAP P130
Affordable and well-maintained hostel in the middle of Joo Chiat. Be sure to book one of its neighbourhood tours for candid local lore.

Venue Hotel $
MAP P130
The nicer sibling of the two along Joo Chiat Rd with added design elements; you're just steps away from the vibrant Koon Seng shophouses.

STORIES Joo Chiat, a Hotel by Cove $
MAP P130
A sparkling new addition to the area, it offers aesthetic flair in rooms and the lobby paired with impressive value.

ISA Hotel $
MAP P130
Apartment-like setup, tastefully designed with green emerald swatches as the theme, though rooms can be on the smaller side.

MIDRANGE

Santa Grand Hotel East Coast $$
MAP P130
Modern renovated rooms feature comfortable anti-dust-mite mattresses and a touch of Peranakan flair.

Grand Mercure Roxy $$
MAP P130
Massive rooms that you won't want to leave, except maybe to visit the hotel's all-day restaurant serving a buffet of local delights like laksa.

Village Hotel Katong $$
MAP P130
Some rooms come across as a little dated, but the comfort is still top-notch at this longstanding property.

Holiday Inn Express Katong $$
MAP P130
Breakfast is included here, along with squeaky-clean facilities, giving you some of the best views of the neighbourhood.

FANCY

Hotel Indigo $$$
MAP P130
Character-rich Peranakan-inspired hotel bursting with nostalgic memorabilia. There's an awesome rooftop infinity pool with its own small bar.

Northern & Central Singapore

UNIQUE GETAWAYS

Orchid Country Club $$
MAP P146
Spacious rooms with views of the golf course or the Lower Seletar Reservoir. A rare hotel in the Yishun district and the only place in Singapore for night golf.

Mandai Rainforest Resort by Banyan Tree $$$
MAP P146
Next door to the wildlife parks, this luxury eco-resort with a stunning rooftop pool blends the rainforest into its biophillic design and wellness activities.

Colugo Camp $$$
MAP P146
Permanent campsite with 20 luxury tents. All-inclusive glamping includes dining, access and guided tours to Singapore Zoo, Bird Paradise and River Wonders.

Swiss Club Guesthouse $$$
MAP P146
Refurbished in 2025, 13 comfortable contemporary rooms in a three-storey building are surrounded by tropical greenery, a 10-minute drive to the Rail Corridor.

PLUS PLUS!
Top hotels often add a ++ to quoted rates – ignore at your peril! Those pluses mean service charge and GST, a combined 19% that inflates your bill far beyond the price you first saw.

BUSINESS-FRIENDLY

Oasia Hotel Novena $$
MAP P146
Sitting atop Novena MRT station, two stops away from the Orchard Rd shopping belt. Complimentary activities include forest walks and art workshops.

Aloft Singapore Novena $$
MAP P146
On Balestier Rd, rooms are split across two buildings on either side of Zhongshan Park. Cosy modern rooms for the midrange traveller.

Courtyard Singapore Novena $$$
MAP P146
This swanky hotel not only has an excellent location, its rooms provide stunning city views and the infinity pool on level 33 could rival Marina Bay Sands.

West & Southwest Singapore

CONCEPT HOTELS

Shipping Container Hotel @ Haw Par Villa $
MAP P164
Cargo containers converted into modern cabins with kitchenettes, bathrooms, patios and air-con. Convenient to the Haw Par Villa MRT station.

Train Pod @ one-north $
MAP P164
For a fun stay, book one of eight capsule pods inside a decommissioned MRT train, complete with 24/7 vending cafe and outdoor dining for community vibes.

Labrador Villa $$$
MAP P164
Housed in beautifully restored 1920s British officers' quarters, these luxurious rooms provide the perfect city escape, set within a serene nature reserve.

GARY SEE/SHUTTERSTOCK

Village Hotel Sentosa, Sentosa Island

MIDRANGE

Genting Hotel Jurong $$
MAP P170
Conveniently close to the Jurong East shopping hub and MRT station, this modern hotel has a rooftop pool with sweeping views and shuttle service to Sentosa.

Momentus Hotel Alexandra $$
MAP P164
Chic contemporary hotel on the edge of Redhill and Queenstown estates, with a rooftop sky bar offering city views.

Hotel Faber Park Singapore – Handwritten Collection $$
MAP P164
Moments from the city buzz, this funky, greenery-drenched hotel is a tranquil retreat snuggled in Mt Faber's foothills.

Sentosa Island

GREAT FOR FAMILIES

Village Hotel Sentosa $$
MAP P180
Families will love the playful details for kids in the stylish 'beach shack' rooms, and the stunning Pamukkale pool.

Siloso Beach Resort $$
MAP P180
A rustic sanctuary unto itself, this resort is designed with lots of ecofriendly touches. It's a beachside hideaway with Madagascan vibes.

HERITAGE

Amara Sanctuary $$
MAP P180
Bathed in neutrals and clean lines, this serene retreat runs a heritage tour to its air-raid shelter. The pool provides peeks of the nightly fireworks at Wings of Time.

Barracks Hotel $$$
MAP P180
Old-world charm has been updated at this handsome spot inspired by the golden age of travel. Learn about the property's military heritage with free audio guides.

CONTEMPORARY

Hotel Ora $$$
MAP P180
Lively designer details shaped around sustainable values and a sophisticated palette in the lofty rooms.

Outpost Hotel $$$
MAP P180
Monochromatic property with thoughtful touches like customised minibars and an adults-only pool club for golden-hour cocktails and witching-hour parties.

Equarius Villas $$$
MAP P180
Splurge on a room at the Equarius Ocean Suites for a chance to fall asleep to a view of fish and rays swimming by your window.

THE VERY BEST

Capella $$$
MAP P180
Rooms mix contemporary luxury with curated detail, and the corridors act like meditative trails. The forest hugging the stacked pools provides a jungle feel.

Raffles Sentosa $$$
MAP P180
The all-villa concept reveals itself in taupe, with hand-painted botanical panels and open-plan elegance. This is quiet tropical glamour perfected.

TOOLKIT

The chapters in this section cover the most important topics you'll need to know about in Singapore. They're full of nuts-and-bolts information and valuable insights to help you understand and navigate Singapore and get the most out of your trip.

Buddha Tooth Relic Temple (p72), Chinatown

OLEH_SLOBODENIUK/GETTY IMAGES

Money

CURRENCY: SINGAPORE DOLLAR (S$)

Cash or Card

Major credit cards are widely accepted, including digital payments. Some smaller shops and hawker stalls remain cash only, so carry some small notes with you.

ATMs & Money-Changers

ATMs are easily located in malls, MRT stations and commercial areas. Banks can change money, but rates are better at the money-changers in shopping malls.

GST & Service Charges

Singapore applies a 9% goods and services tax (GST) to goods and services. Most prices in shops and food outlets have GST included; the symbol ++ shows that GST and service charge (10%) are not included and will be added to the bill. This is common in hotels, restaurants and luxury spas.

Tourist Refund Scheme

Tourists can claim a refund on the 9% GST paid on their purchases if they spend more than S$100 at participating shops – look for the 'Tax-Free Shopping' logo and have your passport ready to show. Claim your refund at eTRS kiosks at the airport or cruise terminal.

HOW MUCH FOR A...

Museum ticket
S$8–40

Walking tour
S$40–60

Local theatre show
S$30–80

Beach-club sunlounger
S$50–100

HOW TO... Save Some Dollars

Student cards will get you a slight discount at attractions and museums, and bundle tickets will definitely yield savings. Free walking tours are offered by numerous providers (tips welcome) – book in advance for our pick **Monster Day Tours** *(monsterdaytours.com)*. For cheap, yummy eats, head to hawker centres or mall food courts. Public transport is inexpensive and will connect you with most areas quickly and in air-conditioned comfort.

TO BARGAIN OR TIP?

In Singapore, tipping is not common practice. Instead, most restaurants include a 10% service charge in the bill, and tipping is not expected at hawker centres. When taking taxis, it's considered polite to round up the fare or let the driver keep the change. Generally, prices are fixed, except in certain touristy markets and shops, where bargaining may be acceptable. If you choose to haggle, remember to do so in a friendly manner and not be too pushy, which will cause everyone to lose face.

LOCAL TIP

Always carry some small coins when visiting hawker centres and wet markets, as some charge 10 to 20 cents to use the bathroom facilities.

Family Travel

Travelling around Singapore with kids is a breeze – the city is safe, clean and efficient, with short distances and stroller-friendly, air-conditioned public transport. Children are welcomed everywhere, and family zones, nursing rooms, playgrounds, kid-friendly menus and clean public restrooms make outings easy. Plus, shady parks and splash areas help everyone cool off on hot days.

Getting Around

Children below 90cm tall travel free on trains and buses with a fare-paying adult. All MRT stations are equipped with lifts – stroller users should look for the blue Priority Use signs, which help to navigate the safest and easiest route. Strollers are accepted on buses, and there's a designated space with stroller-restraint systems. Rideshare service Grab offers family options with car restraints; book via the app.

Facilities

Malls and many restaurants are equipped with changing facilities, parent rooms and child-sized toilets. Breastfeeding in public is not common, as Singapore is a conservative society, but it's becoming more prevalent with changing attitudes and education. Pavements are in tip-top condition, so prams roll smoothly. Most hotels have cots available, but it's best to reserve in advance.

Cooling Down

Many outdoor parks, attractions and malls, including the Singapore Zoo, Gardens by the Bay and Jurong Lake Gardens, have free water-play areas for children, so pack your kids' swimming gear along with their hat and sun protection.

Discounted Tickets

Small children enjoy discounted tickets for, or free admission to, many of Singapore's museums and attractions. Student ID cards are valid for discounted entry at many places as well.

KID-FRIENDLY PICKS

Mandai Wildlife Reserve (p154)
Features four action-packed wildlife parks: Bird Paradise, Singapore Zoo, Night Safari and River Wonders.

Gardens by the Bay (p46)
Futuristic botanical marvel that includes a dedicated Children's Garden with a splash park, adventure trail and playground.

ArtScience Museum (p49)
Fun and educational exhibitions that will captivate and entertain kids of all ages.

Singapore DUCKTours (p55)
Kids will love touring Marina Bay (land and water) aboard one of these brightly coloured amphibious vehicles.

SENTOSA: ISLAND OF FUN

Sentosa is Singapore's carefully planned beachside playground, and it makes for a perfect day out for the young and young-at-heart. Here you'll find palm-fringed stretches of sand replete with restaurants, beach clubs and thrill-seekers' entertainment – floating aqua park or beach bungee, anyone? Moments from the beach, the rest of the island heaves with theme parks and amusements, evening spectaculars, luxe resorts and a swanky harbour dotted with million-dollar yachts. Little history buffs will love discovering Fort Siloso, Singapore's only preserved British coastal fort. Entry via the 11-storey, 181m-long Skywalk is only half the fun!

CLOCKWISE FROM TOP LEFT: JED RT/SHUTTERSTOCK, AVN PHOTO LAB/SHUTTERSTOCK, M2IPERFECT/SHUTTERSTOCK

Food, Drink & Nightlife

When to Eat

Breakfast The traditional Singaporean breakfast set features *kaya* (coconut and egg jam) toast, soft-boiled eggs and *kopi* (coffee).

Lunch Usually served 11.30am to 2.30pm. Hawker centres will be heaving. Good-value set menus at restaurants.

Happy hour Most bars offer drink deals, anytime between noon and 9pm.

Dinner Restaurants usually open at 6pm and are ready for closing at 11pm.

Where to Eat

Hawker centre Open-air collection of food stalls selling a number of different local cuisines with a community vibe.

Food court Located in shopping malls, usually in the basement. Basically air-conditioned hawker centres with marginally higher prices.

Buffet restaurant Usually found in large, swanky chain hotels. The decadent Sunday (and sometimes Saturday) free-flow champagne brunches are legendary.

Restaurant Take your pick from local hot spots, trendy cafes and celebrity-chef-created fine dining. There's plenty to satisfy all tastes and budgets.

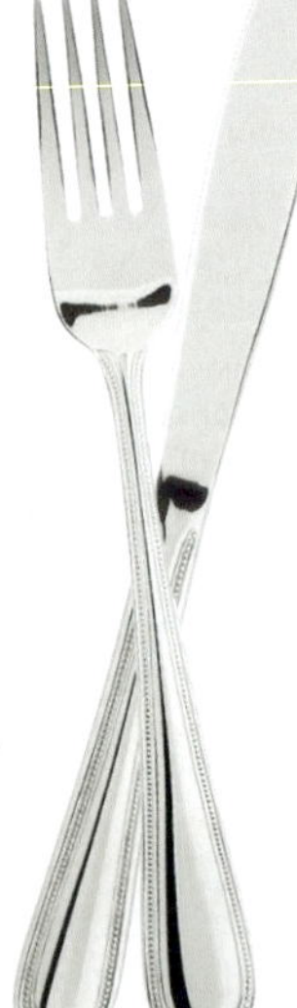

MENU DECODER

Dabao takeaway

Market price check price for item and whole meal before ordering

Zi char to cook and fry; describes dishes influenced by home-cooked Chinese food meant for sharing

Makan eat

Ayam chicken

Congee rice porridge

Bee hoon rice vermicelli noodles

Ho fun thick rice noodles

Mian hand-pulled wheat noodles

Mee yellow wheat noodles

Won ton Chinese dumpling

Murtabak Indian stuffed pancake

Roti prata South Indian flatbread

Char stir-fried

Laksa coconut-based noodle soup

Popiah spring roll with soft, paper-like skin

Nasi padang steamed rice with a selection of dishes; originated in Indonesia's Padang city

Rojak vegetable and fruit salad

Kueh bite-sized snack or dessert typically made from rice flour or glutinous rice

Ice kachang shaved ice, red-bean, jelly and sweet-syrup dessert

HOW TO... Hawker Like a Pro

Hawker centres can get quite crowded, so securing a seat first is advisable. Even if someone from your group sits at a table, it's common practice to *chope* (save) the number of seats you need by placing a packet of tissues at each. Sharing tables with strangers is customary. Hawkers typically don't provide serviettes (napkins), but you can find sellers near the entrance if you need to buy some. If there's a table number, note it, as the hawkers use it for food delivery. If the stall has a 'self-service' sign, you'll have to carry the food to the table yourself; otherwise, the hawker will bring your order to you. It's now required by law to return your tray to a designated tray station when you're done, although there are a few roaming cleaners who'll take your empties.

For more on hawker centres, read our essay (p234).

HOW MUCH FOR A...

Kopi
S$1.10

Hawker meal
S$4–7

Beer at a hawker stall
750mL bottle S$8

Glass of wine at a bar
S$18–25

Cocktail at a bar
S$25–35

Meal at a restaurant
S$25–35

Fine-dining dinner
S$150–500

HOW TO... Order a Coffee the Singaporean Way

Despite Singapore's British colonial history and predominately Asian population, the national drink is not tea but coffee – *kopi,* to be precise.

This thick brew is traditionally crafted using robusta beans, known for their high caffeine content. The beans are roasted with butter, margarine or lard, and occasionally with sugar, until they're beautifully caramelised. The beans are then ground, brewed inside a long flannel bag, and poured from a long-necked kettle to create a thick cuppa.

Kopi is traditionally served in a china cup and saucer, but it can also come in a tall glass mug. A typical Singaporean downs four to six cups a day.

Kopi Black coffee with condensed milk
Kopi-O Black coffee with sugar
Kopi O kosong Black coffee without sugar
Kopi C Black coffee with sugar and evaporated milk
Kopi C kosong Black coffee with evaporated milk
Kopi gah dai Black coffee with extra condensed milk
Kopi siew dai Black coffee with less condensed milk
Kopi pok Weaker coffee with condensed milk
Kopi gau Strong coffee with condensed milk
Kopi peng Iced coffee with condensed milk

Tea lovers can order a cup by switching out *kopi* for *teh.*

A Buttery Brew

Singaporeans have been indulging in the health trend of bulletproof coffee for decades now. Called *kopi gu you*, it's a robust brew with butter added. Head to Heap Seng Leong in Kampong Glam to try a cup.

A NIGHT OUT ON THE LITTLE RED DOT

A typical night out in Singapore kicks off with after-work drinks at a local bar, where happy-hour prices beckon the crowds. As the sun sets, the city's spirited inhabitants gravitate towards the water or to rooftop bars, either flocking to the captivating Marina Bay or sauntering along the quays. Prime spots go in a flash, so reservations are often necessary.

Once the night takes over, the culinary journey begins. Patrons set out to satiate their appetites, dining on mouth-watering delights at local hawker centres or settling in at the trendiest restaurants. The well-heeled slip into the latest degustation temples, embracing the prime 8pm seating like connoisseurs of indulgence, and hidden bars quietly unlock their doors, welcoming cocktail aficionados to savour the artistry of Singapore's top mixologists.

As the clock strikes 11pm, the atmosphere shifts. Some gracefully retreat home, while the night owls emerge, ready to ignite the dance floors of the pulsating clubs in Clarke Quay and Marina Bay. Gamblers are drawn to the flashy underground casinos, where no one knows whether it's day or night.

But wait, the gastronomic journey continues! Amid the night's festivities, a number of late-night dim-sum stops are ready and waiting to fill partygoers' tummies with dumplings and noodles.

Despite all the excitement, be sure to keep in mind that the night has its own rules. The sale of alcohol is prohibited between 10.30pm and 7am at supermarkets, convenience stores, petrol stations and similar establishments, and the city's streets are an alcohol-free zone.

LGBTIQ+ Travellers

Singapore is a conservative society. It took until 2022 for the government to repeal the controversial 377A law, inherited from British rule, which banned sex between two men. Local attitudes are changing, and there's increasing support for LGBTIQ+ rights, but there are still no anti-discrimination laws to protect the LGBTIQ+ community nor any laws recognising gay relationships.

Paint the Town Pink

The **PinkDot SG** *(pinkdot.sg)* festival is held each June to coincide with global Pride Month. It's a celebration designed to bring LGBTIQ+ Singaporeans closer to their family and friends. Due to regulations, only Singaporean citizens and permanent residents can attend, but fringe **Pink Fest** *(pinkfest.sg)* holds events for diverse audiences in the lead-up, and everyone is welcome. The use of pink comes from the colour of Singapore's identity cards and is also a mix of red and white, the colours of the national flag.

A WALK TO INCLUSIVITY

Meander down tiny lanes and through public spaces as tour guide Isaac Tng walks you through Singapore's journey towards an inclusive nation. The tour, peppered with historical and personal stories, details the oppression the LGBTIQ+ community has faced and also celebrates the rights they have gained. Your tour concludes with a perfect Pink Sling cocktail. Check *pridecommunity.co* for dates.

BAR-HOPPING

The bulk of Singapore's LGBTIQ+ bars are clustered in Chinatown, including stalwarts like **Tantric** (p84) and Backstage Bar on Neil Rd. Other hot spots worth checking out are cocktail bar **Slippery Slope** (p84) and nightclub **Rabbit's Hole** (p84). For raucous parties, follow **Hypertainment** *(hyper.com.sg)*, known for throwing some of the best events in Asia.

Queer Connections

Looking to get in touch with fellow members of the LGBTIQ+ community? Look no further than **Prout**, a safe virtual space for the Singapore LGBTIQ+ crew to connect, find out about queer events, access resources and get support. Join the team's Telegram channel (The Qurrent) for news and events.

SHOW YOUR PRIDE

If you want a super-cute memento of your time in Singapore, check out local advocacy-focused brand **Heckin' Unicorn** *(heckinunicorn.com)* – by queer people for queer people. It makes everything from trendy backpacks to crazy socks, but the hero product is the cute, unique Pride pins for LGBTIQ+ people and allies. Buy online; there's even a quiz so you can find your perfect design.

Scan to buy Pride pins

A Safe Stay

There is no specific LGBTIQ+ accommodation in Singapore, but because the country's tourism and business sectors are very internationally focused, most hotels are LGBTIQ+ friendly. Several higher-end hostels offer private rooms or pods as well.

CLOCKWISE FROM TOP LEFT: NITO/SHUTTERSTOCK, SURADECH PRAPAIRAT/SHUTTERSTOCK

Health & Safe Travel

HEAT EXHAUSTION

Singapore is hot and humid all year round. If you're not used to high temperatures, limit your time outside during the middle of the day and always wear a hat and sunscreen. Hydration is also important: drink water regularly throughout the day and carry a portable fan if you tend to sweat a lot.

Dengue Fever

Singapore has suffered a sharp rise in cases of this mosquito-borne disease in recent years. Peak biting periods are dawn and dusk, though it's best to apply insect repellent regularly throughout the day and wear long-sleeved tops and long pants when you're outdoors in nature. Symptoms include high fever, severe headache, body aches and rash.

Wildlife

Singapore has abundant wildlife. Most creatures are harmless, but there are a few to watch out for. Monkeys and wild boars are found in forested areas and are best given a wide berth – in any case, feeding wildlife will incur a hefty fine. The country's otter population is booming, having more than doubled since 2017. Again, observe from afar.

TAP WATER

The tap water in Singapore is safe to drink.

Scan to check the current conditions

HAZE INDEX

Good (green)
0–50:
Normal activities

Moderate (blue)
51–100:
Normal activities

Unhealthy (yellow)
101–200:
Reduce prolonged or strenuous outdoor physical exertion

Very Unhealthy (orange)
201–300:
Avoid prolonged or strenuous outdoor physical exertion

Hazardous (red)
>300:
Minimise outdoor activities

Health Care

Singapore has a world-class health-care system. Emergency rooms are found in private and public hospitals, wait times are generally short, and costs are reasonable in the public system. Needless to say, travel insurance is advisable, as not only does it cover medical costs but theft, loss and cancellations too.

CRIME

Singapore has one of the world's lowest crime rates due to strict laws, harsh punishments, a swift justice system and a comprehensive CCTV network monitoring practically every centimetre of the island. Therefore, you're unlikely to be attacked, robbed, fleeced or even touted. Pickpocketing is something of a concern, however, so remain vigilant in crowded spaces.

Responsible Travel

Climate Change & Travel

It's impossible to ignore the impact we have when travelling; Lonely Planet urges all travellers to engage with their travel carbon footprint, which will mainly come from air travel. While there often isn't an alternative, travellers can look to minimise the number of flights they take, opt for newer aircrafts and use cleaner ground transport, such as trains. One proposed solution – purchasing carbon offsets – unfortunately does not cancel out the impact of individual flights. While most destinations will depend on air travel for the foreseeable future, for now, pursuing ground-based travel where possible is the best course of action.

The **UN Carbon Offset Calculator** shows how flying impacts a household's emissions.

The **ICAO's carbon emissions calculator** allows visitors to analyse the CO_2 generated by point-to-point journeys.

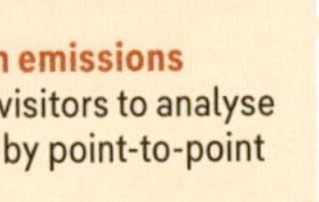

The Singapore Green Plan 2030 seeks to advance Singapore's national agenda on sustainable development. It aims to strengthen the country's commitments under the UN's 2030 Sustainable Development Agenda and Paris Agreement.

Singapore's 'green buildings' exemplify sustainability, incorporating recycled materials and ecofriendly technologies. Foliage-covered structures such as the Oasia Hotel Downtown (pictured above) showcase the city's commitment to a greener future.

Shop Mindfully

The Social Space *(thesocialspace.co)* is a socially conscious multi-concept store featuring a cafe, fair-trade shopping and a nail salon. It promotes greater awareness of sustainability and more accessible conscious living.

Cook Local Dishes

Join a cooking class at **Food Playground** *(foodplayground.com.sg)*, where stay-at-home mothers and active seniors share heritage recipes while gaining flexi-work employment opportunities, all in a friendly, hands-on environment that celebrates Singapore's culinary traditions and community spirit.

DINE IN THE DARK

NOX *(noxdineinthedark.com)* employs blind and vision-impaired hosts to guide you through a unique dining experience. Eat in total darkness, then test your senses by guessing each dish before the menu is revealed.

SWIM SUSTAINABLY

Sandbar Swimwear *(wearesandbar.com)* produces eco-gear for the whole family made from recycled plastic bottles. There's no plastic in its supply chain, and each piece of swimwear purchased funds the removal of 1kg of ocean plastic.

Escape to Lazarus Island

Stay in an ecofriendly tiny house *(escapeatlazarus.com)* constructed with sustainable composite building materials that are primarily powered by solar energy. Food waste is composted on-site, and guests use biodegradable shampoo and body products.

Grab a Green Grab

Rideshare app Grab allows riders to prioritise cleaner-energy vehicles for their booking and reduce their carbon footprint by donating 10 cents for each ride to the Green Programme, which funds forest-protection and solar-energy initiatives.

Eat for a Good Cause

Breakthrough Cafe *(breakthroughmissions.org.sg)*, which serves delicious French cuisine in Changi Village, offers former drug offenders employment, allowing them to hone their skills and make a fresh start.

Have a Meaningful Massage

Seeking a revitalising reflexology session or massage? Visit **My Foot Reflexology** *(myfoot.com.sg)* in Great Word City, where behind its ordinary shopfront lies a heartfelt mission: employing people with disabilities and older workers.

Learn Singapore's Sustainability Story

Explore the interactive **Sustainable Singapore Gallery** *(pub.gov.sg)* at Marina Barrage, which offers insights into the city's sustainable development plans: climate targets aligned with the Paris Agreement, greening initiatives and the vision for a car-lite Singapore.

The Islandwide Cycling Network aims to lengthen Singapore's cycling paths to 1300km by 2030.

From 2030, all new cars registered must be cleaner-energy models – electric, hybrid or hydrogen vehicles.

Four-Pillar Sustainability

Singapore has been certified as a sustainable destination based on the Global Sustainable Tourism Council's Destination Criteria, which assess performance in four pillars: sustainable management, socio-economic sustainability, cultural sustainability and environmental sustainability.

RESOURCES

nparks.gov.sg
Singapore's National Parks Board (NParks)

greenplan.gov.sg
Singapore Green Plan 2030

bca.gov.sg
Information on the BCA Green Mark 2021, an internationally recognised green building certification scheme

CLOCKWISE FROM TOP LEFT: YASEMIN OZDEMIR/SHUTTERSTOCK, MICHAEL DECHEV/SHUTTERSTOCK, KRAVTZOV/SHUTTERSTOCK

Accessible Travel

Singapore aims to create products and environments accessible to as many people as possible, following Universal Design principles that emphasise a space's equitability and flexibility. With its world-class public transport, and easy-to-access attractions and infrastructure, it's undoubtedly one of the most accessible cities in the world.

Wheelchairs for Hire

Most main attractions offer free wheelchairs on a first come, first served basis. **AGIS Medical** *(agis.com.sg)* has mobility scooters and wheelchairs for daily hire, with delivery and collection available.

Airport

Changi Airport *(changiairport.com)* supports travellers with reduced mobility, visual or hearing impairments and invisible disabilities. Its website details services including special assistance (request 48 hours ahead), mobility-equipment hire, accessible amenities and a navigation guide.

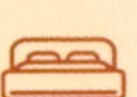

Accommodation

Many larger modern hotels in Singapore are equipped with facilities such as accessible rooms and bathrooms, but older-style shophouse and hostel accommodation often is not. Call ahead to discuss your requirements.

MRT

All stations have priority lifts, tactile wayfinding, easy-to-follow signage, visual and audible indicators in lifts and on platforms, and wheelchair-accessible toilets. Staff and service ambassadors are there to help; approach the Passenger Service Centres.

Buses

All public buses are wheelchair-accessible and almost all stops are barrier-free. The rear-door ramp will be deployed and the bus captain will assist you in boarding. Designated spaces are marked; engage brakes once in a rear-facing position.

NATIONAL MUSEUM OF SINGAPORE

The museum building and all galleries are wheelchair-accessible, and free wheelchairs are available. Find information about Quiet Mornings, Quiet Corners, a designated Quiet Room, and the availability of sensory bags and visual schedules at *nhb.gov.sg/nationalmuseum.*

RESOURCES

Visit Singapore *(visitsingapore.com)* provides information about navigating Singapore's modes of transport and built environment with ease.

HWA *(hwa.org.sg)* can provide information on accessibility in Singapore and also offers transport services.

MyTransport.SG app in the Google Play and Apple stores allows you to check for lift outages at the stops on your route.

Serenity Seekers *(serenityseekers.sg)* aims to provide inclusive experiences and accessible journeys for travellers with disabilities.

Taxis

There's no taxi surcharge for wheelchairs, but usually only smaller, foldable ones can fit in the boot. Rideshare app Grab has wheelchair-accessible vehicles ranging from ramp-equipped cars to those with ample storage for assistive devices.

Nuts & Bolts

OPENING HOURS

Hours are consistent year-round, but hawker stalls will close once they've sold out.

Banks 8.30am to 4.30pm Monday to Friday, 9.30am to noon Saturday

Restaurants Noon to 2.30pm and 6pm to 11pm

Hawker centres, food courts and coffeeshops 7am to 10pm

Bars 3pm to 1am

Clubs 10pm to 3am or 6am

Malls 10am to 9pm

Smoking

Prohibited practically everywhere in Singapore, including parks, beaches and bus stops, except at designated smoking points. E-cigarettes and vapes are illegal.

Chewing Gum

Import, sale and manufacture of chewing gum is banned. Gum with health benefits can be sold, but you'll need identification.

Toilets

Free public toilets are plentiful and usually of the sit-down variety. A small fee may apply in hawker centres.

GOOD TO KNOW

Time zone
GMT/UTC + 8

Country code
65

Emergency number
995

Population
6.04 million

Electricity

230V/50Hz

Type G
230V/50Hz

PUBLIC HOLIDAYS

Most malls, shops, attractions, museums and restaurants remain open on public holidays, except for the two-day holiday for Chinese New Year, when virtually all shops close. The Istana, the official residence and office of the president of Singapore, opens its grounds on numerous public holidays across the year; see *istana.gov.sg*.

New Year's Day 1 January

Chinese New Year Two days in January/February

Hari Raya Puasa (Eid al-Fitr) February/March

Good Friday March/April

Labour Day 1 May

Vesak Day May

Hari Raya Haji (Eid al-Adha) April/May

National Day 9 August

Deepavali October/November

Christmas Day 25 December

THE SINGAPORE

STORYBOOK

Our writers delve deep into different aspects of Singaporean life.

Sultan Mosque (p96), Kampong Glam

RONNIE CHUA/SHUTTERSTOCK

A HISTORY OF SINGAPORE IN 15 PLACES

Singapore. Singapura. Temasek. Pulau Ujong. From its earliest reference in 3rd-century CE historical records through to today, the Lion City has always been the star of an inspiring story: a thriving port city with a diverse migrant population that's making waves on the world map thanks to its strategic location.
By Jaclynn Seah

WHILE THERE ARE few historical records documenting Singapore's early days, the many names the island has held give clues to its past. The earliest reference comes from a Chinese account in the 3rd century that named the island Pulau Ujong (The Island at the End of the Peninsula).

Later navigational maps charted courses to Temasek, a 'sea town' in the midst of the flourishing Srivijaya Kingdom that stretched from Sumatra to Malaya.

At the turn of the 14th century, Singapore gained a defining new name. Legend tells that Srivijayan prince Sang Nila Utama saw the island in the distance, and for good luck named it after the majestic *singah* (lion) that he saw on it, which is how Singapura (The Lion City) came about.

Singapore's economy and population boomed after 1819, when the British set up a key trading post that attracted the early Chinese, Bugis, Arab, Indian and European settlers who would form the base of Singapore's population.

Singapore was Syonan-to for three painful years during WWII's Japanese occupation, and it was briefly part of Malaysia in a year-long merger following the departure of the British in the 1960s. It became the independent sovereign nation of Singapore in 1965.

1. Fullerton Hotel

HISTORICAL SITE AT THE RIVER MOUTH

The magnificent Palladian-style Fullerton Hotel was Singapore's first General Post Office in 1928, government offices during the British administration and a refuge for Allied soldiers during WWII. More importantly, it was built on a site once called Rocky Point, where the country's oldest artefact, the Singapore Stone, was unearthed. This massive slab of sandstone covered in undeciphered Kawi script dates back as far as the 10th century. Unfortunately, it was blown up in 1843 to build Fort Fullerton, the predecessor to the current building. Only three small fragments of the stone remain – they're on display at the National Museum of Singapore.

For more on Fullerton Hotel, see p205.

2. Labrador Nature Reserve

GRANITE GATEWAY TO SINGAPORE

Early maps of Singapore indicate that it was a thriving port town before the arrival of the British. Twin rock markers jutting out of the water off Singapore's southern tip – one called Batu Berlayar or Lot's Wife on the main island of Singapore, and another on offshore Sentosa Island – were key navigational tools guiding sailors through the narrow channel. Sometimes called Long Ya Men (Dragon's Teeth Gate), these iconic rocks were blown up by a British surveyor to widen the channel for larger ships in 1848. A replica of Batu Berlayar is in Labrador Nature Reserve at Berlayer Point.

For more on Labrador Nature Reserve, see p168.

3. Singapore River

WHERE SINGAPORE'S COMMERCIAL LIFE BEGAN

The British transformed the swampy river banks at the mouth of the Singapore River with the country's very first land reclamation to even out the banks, creating the government district on the north bank and Commercial Sq in the south. For over 150 years, warehouse trade along the river was the lifeline of Singapore's development. Later, mechanisation would shift business elsewhere. These days the once-polluted river has been cleaned up, the former warehouses of Boat Quay, Clarke Quay and Robertson Quay are thriving nightlife spots, and the many small bumboats that trawled the river have become river taxis.

For more on the riverside quays, see p56.

4. Kampong Glam

MALAY QUARTER AND ROYAL SEAT

A legacy of British colonial times is the 1822 Jackson town plan, where early settlers in Singapore were divided according to their race and allocated areas to live in. The seafaring Bugis and Arabs settled near the coast around the Rochor River, near the palace that belonged to then-ruler Sultan Hussein Shah. Commissioned by the sultan and built by the British in the Palladian style, the Istana survives today as the Malay Heritage Centre, archiving the history of the Malays in Singapore. In 1824, the sultan was also responsible for building the focal point of the neighbourhood: the majestic Sultan Mosque.

For more on Kampong Glam, see p96.

Clarke Quay (p58), Singapore River

RICHIE CHAN/SHUTTERSTOCK

5. Telok Ayer Street

MULTI-RELIGIOUS FORMER WATERFRONT

Telok Ayer translates as 'bay water', an odd name for a street seemingly far inland, but this stretch of Chinatown used to be the waterfront where new immigrants would first set foot in Singapore. Later, various land-reclamation efforts pushed the shoreline much further out. The street's formerly coastal location is also the reason for the diverse religious buildings that exist side by side, as the first thing most new arrivals wanted to do after enduring a long, arduous and often perilous boat journey to get to Singapore was give thanks to their god of choice for safely reaching land.

For more on Telok Ayer St, see p77.

6. Sri Mariamman Temple

SINGAPORE'S OLDEST HINDU TEMPLE

Originally slated to be constructed along Telok Ayer St, this beautiful South Indian-style temple was moved to its current location along South Bridge Rd because of a lack of fresh water for Hindu rituals. Dedicated to the goddess Mariamman, who is believed to cure diseases, the temple was built in 1823 and features a magnificent colourful *gopuram* (pagoda tower) above the main entrance that is covered with detailed carvings of various Hindu deities. Construction was funded by Naraina Pillai, a pioneer of the Indian community who came to Singapore with the British and became the island's first building contractor.

For more on Sri Mariamman Temple, see p75.

7. Tiong Bahru

SINGAPORE'S FIRST PUBLIC HOUSING ESTATE

Tiong Bahru is Singapore's oldest public housing estate, built on top of a former cemetery and swamp to provide accommodation and address the sanitation issues prevalent in the old villages and slums. The very first block of prewar flats (Block 55) was completed in 1936, and its unique art deco and international-style architecture can still be admired today. Many of the road names here commemorate prominent Chinese businesspeople and philanthropists. The district has experienced a revival in recent years, with trendy eateries and shops moving in amid the traditional businesses. It's now considered a hip hangout.

For more on Tiong Bahru, see p82.

8. Fort Canning

FORMER WAR COMMAND CENTRE

Malay kings ruled from the top of 48m-tall Bukit Larangan (Forbidden Hill) in the 14th century, and during WWII the site was transformed into a British artillery fort and army barracks. In the tunnels of what is now called the Battlebox lie the headquarters of the Far East Command Centre. This is where the British made the pivotal decision to surrender Singapore to invading Japanese forces on 15 February 1942. You can visit the bomb-proof bunker, set nearly 9m underground. Above, the open green spaces on the hill now see invasions only by picnickers and concert-goers during outdoor productions and events.

For more on Fort Canning, see p64.

9. Kent Ridge Park

HISTORIC WWII BATTLE SITE

It's hard to believe today, but this serene green park along the Southern Ridges walk was where one of the last and fiercest WWII battles in Singapore was fought over two days in 1942. A commemorative plaque near car park B marks the site of this historic battle where a 1400-strong Malay regiment courageously fought to the death against Japanese forces with almost 10 times more men. More of the regiment's story is told in Reflections at Bukit Chandu, a small museum housed in a colonial-style bungalow near where the men made their last stand.

For more on Kent Ridge Park, see p176.

10. Padang

FIELD OF DREAMS

What looks like an unassuming green field in front of the National Gallery of Singapore is actually a significant site in the city's modern history. The Padang has hosted many of Singapore's key events, from the victory parade by returning British forces at the end of WWII in 1945 to Singapore's very first National Day Parade in 1966 to mark a year of the country's independence. The field is one of the oldest public recreation spots in Singapore, and it's been a popular place for sports such as cricket and rugby from the earliest years after the British arrival.

For more on the Padang, see p54.

11. Arts House

THE CITY'S OLDEST SURVIVING COLONIAL STRUCTURE

Singapore's Civic District and former government quarter is chock-full of prominent conserved architecture, but the building currently known as the Arts House is the oldest colonial structure left standing in Singapore. Originally a neo-Palladian-style building that housed government offices, it has been renovated several times, most notably into a neoclassical building where parliament sessions were held after Singapore became independent. While parliament shifted to a new location at the turn of the millennium, the parliament chamber was retained and the building reopened as an arts venue, playing host to concerts and exhibitions, in 2004.

Lorong Buangkok (p160)

Bandstand, Singapore Botanic Gardens (p118)

12. Lorong Buangkok

SINGAPORE'S LAST MAIN-ISLAND VILLAGE

Amid the high-rise residences and skyscrapers in the Singapore of today, a last remaining *kampong* (village) is tucked quietly into a northeastern corner of the city. At its peak, 40 Chinese and Malay families lived here, but now just over half of them remain. The humble plot has (so far) managed to escape redevelopment, and its zinc roofs, wooden walls, lush greenery and wandering poultry provide a rare chance for visitors to see what Singapore would have looked like in the days before the now ubiquitous public housing blocks were built across the island.

For more on Lorong Buangkok, see p160.

13. Singapore Botanic Gardens

THE ONLY TROPICAL UNESCO BOTANIC GARDENS

The Singapore Botanic Gardens are the oldest gardens on the island. Modern Singapore's founder, Sir Stamford Raffles, first mooted the idea of a garden to research tropical botany and experiment with the cultivation of cash crops. The current site in Tanglin was built by the local agri-horticultural society in 1859, and after independence the gardens were a key driver of the massive tree-planting programme that realised the 'Garden City' vision for Singapore. Today the gardens span 82 hectares and house the National Orchid Garden, home to Asia's largest collection of orchids. The site achieved UNESCO World Heritage status in 2015.

For more on the Singapore Botanic Gardens, see p118.

14. Changi Airport

WORLD-CLASS GATEWAY TO SINGAPORE

Singapore's first international airport was constructed in 1959 and located in Paya Lebar, but in just 20 years it had begun to outgrow its premises. The airport was shifted away from the residential area to the eastern coast of Singapore and the current Changi Airport was built on reclaimed land, officially opening its doors in 1981 and going on to win multiple Best Airport awards in the following years. There are currently four terminals, two runways and the Jewel retail complex with the world's tallest indoor waterfall; a fifth terminal and third runway are in the works for the near future.

For more on Changi Airport, see p140.

15. Marina Bay

ICONIC SKYLINE OF SINGAPORE TODAY

It's hard to believe that the representative Singapore skyline shot of Marina Bay only took shape as recently as the 2000s. For 30 years beforehand, this area was empty land that had been left to sit fallow after an ambitious land-reclamation project had filled in what was once Singapore's main waterfront. Take a stroll around the bay and snap shots of the notable landmarks here: the distinct three towers of Marina Bay Sands, the swirling lines of the Helix Bridge that connects to the spiky twin domes of the Esplanade, and (right next to it) the spouting half-lion, half-fish Merlion statue.

For more on Marina Bay, see p44.

MEET THE SINGAPOREANS

Singapore is an exciting salad bowl of cultures, characterised by the unique colloquial Singlish language. Nellie Huang introduces her people.

SINGAPORE'S ETHNIC DIVERSITY is an eclectic fusion of cultures – it's often compared to a local dish, the *rojak* (a salad with fermented prawn-paste sauce). Since Sir Stamford Raffles set up a free trading port on the island in 1819, the Little Red Dot has been defined by its wave of migrants, from early Chinese workers to today's modern expats seeking their corporate fortunes. With no fewer than four official languages, it's a place where Chinese dim-sum restaurants sit next to street-side Malay satay stands and mosques sidle up to Hindu and Taoist temples.

Some 75% of Singapore's six-million-strong population is ethnically Chinese, the descendants of workers who came from China to seek their fortunes from 1821. Malays – the island's original inhabitants – account for 13.5% of Singapore's headcount. Most Malays are practising Sunni Muslims, as seen from the popularity of the *tudung* (head scarf) and *baju kurung* (long-sleeved tunic worn over a sarong) among Malay-Singaporean women. At 9% of the population, Indians might constitute a relatively small group in Singapore, but their rich culture and tradition shine through on the streets of Little India.

Since independence, modern Singapore's founding father, Prime Minister Lee Kuan Yew, emphasised equality and forged racial harmony through a plethora of policies in education, housing, national service and the sharing of national economic wealth. English became the main language of communication in Singapore, even though Singaporeans also learned the language of their ethnic group as a mother tongue. People came together but held onto their respective religions, traditions and languages.

While Singapore ranks third-best in the world for English proficiency, Singaporeans love speaking their own unique take on English. Singlish is a colourful local vernacular spiked with borrowed words from Hokkien, Tamil and Malay – a direct product of the island's multilingual history. A typical conversation between Singaporeans might sound like this: 'Eh, this Sunday you free *anot?* No *ah?* Why like that? Don't be so boring *lah*!' The particle *'lah'* is often added to the end of sentences for emphasis, as in 'No good *lah*'. Long stress is placed on the first syllable of phrases, so that the standard English 'government' becomes *'gahh-men'*.

While often seen as broken English spoken in a singsong manner, Singlish has become a cultural marker for Singaporeans. Most Singaporeans are absolutely capable of writing and speaking formal English; Singlish is simply a language that we identify with. Pick up some popular Singlish phrases, such as *shiok* (very good), *dabao* (takeaway food) or *chope* (reserve a table), and Singaporeans will surely warm up to you immediately. So *don't pray pray ah* (a popular Singlish slang phrase that means 'don't mess around with us')! For more on Singlish, see p230.

Towards the Future

When Singapore became independent in 1965, it was relatively poor, with low literacy rates. By implementing a universal education system, low taxes and liberal immigration policies, the island nation quickly thrived: its GDP per capita is now around US$94,000, higher than the US or the UK.

CLOCKWISE FROM TOP LEFT: FILIPE.LOPES/SHUTTERSTOCK, 1000 WORDS/SHUTTERSTOCK, CARLINA TETERIS/GETTY IMAGES, ALEN THIEN/SHUTTERSTOCK

WHO ARE THE SINGAPOREANS?

I was born in Singapore, and like the majority of Singaporeans I am of Chinese descent. My ancestors came from mainland China almost 100 years ago, when the British declared that they would develop Singapore into a free-trade port. Immigrants also flooded in from nearby India, Indonesia and Malaysia to seek their fortunes, and they too put down roots and settled in various communities. Today, Singapore remains an ethnic mosaic, with even greater diversity in recent decades that has been driven by waves of foreign workers. Almost half of Singapore's residents these days are non-Singaporeans. A huge number are low-paid construction and service-industry workers from China and South Asia, but there are just as many highly skilled professionals working in finance, biomedical science and IT. This open-to-foreigners policy is one of the reasons Singapore has developed at lightning speed and evolved into an international, cosmopolitan city rivalling Dubai and New York.

MENTATDGT/SHUTTERSTOCK

THE POLITICS & POETRY OF SINGLISH

Tiny Singlish particles reveal the humour, history and identity shaping Singapore's distinctive national voice. By Dawn Wong

SINGAPORE IS FAMOUS for many things: the zealously efficient Changi Airport, hawker centres galore, urban-planning feng shui and relentless humidity. But for the traveller listening hard enough on the MRT, a more intriguing national treasure emerges – Singlish, the city-state's unofficial linguistic emblem. It's the true national anthem, a language whose finest lyricism happens in particles no longer than a heartbeat.

For the uninitiated, Singlish seems like English after a long, sweaty day out. Slightly dishevelled, pleasantly direct and maybe a bit rough around the edges. But don't be fooled – beneath its casual gait lies a remarkably intricate system of tones, rhythms and emotional micro-signals. A Singaporean can negotiate business deals, express moral judgment and flirt, all by simply adjusting pitch and intent.

The Particle Pantheon

Distorted, cheeky, charming – Singlish is a linguistic funhouse mirror that reveals emotional truths no other tongue can quite express. Nowhere else in the world can a single syllable carry an entire sentence and convey the weight of centuries of migration. Few linguistic systems are as compact yet emotionally loaded as the famous particles of Singlish: *lah, lor, leh, meh,* and their lesser-sung but equally spirited cousins *sia, hor, ah*. They are the punctuation marks of the Singaporean psyche.

Let's begin with the ubiquitous *lah,* the Beyoncé of particles. Omnipresent and versatile, it's a particle that functions as sentence seasoning. Sprinkle it on, and you instantly sound friendlier and more colloquial. 'Don't like that *lah*' softens a reprimand; 'Can *lah*' signals confidence; 'Come *lah*' is both an invitation and gentle coax. Beyond a word, *lah* is a mood itself.

Then comes *lor,* arguably the most philosophical of the particles, the particle of resignation. 'Like that *lor*' is what Singaporeans say when faced with unpredictable public transport breakdowns, micromanaging bosses and exorbitant Electronic Road Pricing (ERP) hikes. It's an acceptance of cosmic futility, wrapped in three letters. *Bo pian lor* ('No choice *lor*') is the Singaporean existential motto, a surrender to bureaucracy, humidity or fate. If *lah* is enthusiasm, *lor* is stoicism.

Leh is the gentle diplomat, a particle of persuasion or a softener used when suggesting alternatives. 'Up to you *leh*' means 'I have an opinion, but this is not the hill I will die on'. It's the Singaporean way of negotiating without confrontation.

Meh is the raised eyebrow of the lexicon. 'Really *meh?*' carries equal parts scepticism, teasing and incredulity. It's a particle that allows Singaporeans to question the world without sounding rude though the sarcasm, if intended, is unmistakable.

And beyond these celebrities lie the essential supporting cast, the lesser-known yet essential particles: *hor* (warning disguised as chit-chat), *ah* (seeking agreement) and *sia* (the flamboyant garnish for moments of heightened emotion).

These particles function like social grease. They (could) smooth conflicts, create solidarity and encode emotions that English, in its grammatical correctness, cannot quite accommodate. To the untrained ear, they blur together. To a Singaporean, they are emotional Morse code.

The Great Singlish Identity Crisis

In Singapore, the politics of Singlish is a national soap opera. Besides eating, perhaps the most national of pastimes is debating whether Singlish is cultural treasure or linguistic tragedy. For decades, official discourse treated it like a recalcitrant child. It was loveable to some extent but ultimately needing correction. Campaigns like 'Speak Good English' advocated crisp consonants and globally comprehensible grammar. Still, Singlish persisted with the stubborn resilience of durian trees sprouting from compost.

Beneath that polished veneer, Singlish has steadily grown into a symbol of authenticity. For many, it's a badge of belonging. It expresses what formal English often cannot: intimacy across class and ethnicity; humour that thrives on shared cultural cues; and above all, creative subversion of rigid expectations. It's the language of the wet market, the taxi driver, the school canteen, the late-night *prata* supper.

This tension between embarrassment and pride mirrors a deeper anxiety about Singaporean identity. Are we globalised cosmopolitans or heartland traditionalists – the everyday Singaporeans rooted in humble Housing & Development Board (HDB) estates, neighbourhood *kopitiams* (coffeeshops) and communal routines?

Singlish outside a cafe in Pulau Ubin (p194)

MICHAEL ELLERAY/WIKIMEDIA COMMONS

Subversion Behind the Syllables

Singapore is a nation that values order. We have efficient queues and neatly painted HDB blocks, and even the car breakdowns on the Pan Island Expressway follow a kind of unspoken schedule. In such a setting, Singlish is a small but mighty act of cultural defiance. It operates in the cracks, celebrating imperfection.

Unconfrontational yet quietly subversive, Singlish resists homogenisation. It assures us that identity need not be curated and expression need not be polished. When a Singaporean chooses to speak Singlish over BBC-worthy English, they're not being sloppy – they're choosing to sound like themselves. It's the linguistic equivalent of wearing worn slippers to the *kopitiam* in the most proudly unpretentious manner even though you own a pair of Italian loafers.

From Kopitiam to Canon

Singlish made its way onto screens long before it was launched into academic journals. Phua Chu Kang – the legendary contractor from a wildly popular 1990s sitcom in Singapore, with his yellow boots, curly hair and that unforgettable mole – catapulted the vernacular into living rooms and across borders. His catchphrases like 'Use your brain *lah!*' distilled the nation's humour into one unforgettable, gloriously nasal line.

Today, the language thrives everywhere, from the sharp satire of SGAG (Singapore's largest homegrown social-media comedy platform) to the manic energy of TikTok creators. Even Singaporean poets like Gwee Li Sui and, occasionally, Edwin Thumboo have folded Singlish into literary expression, unveiling its lyrical potential. When placed in poetry, Singlish particles acquire surprising depth – *lah* becomes a lamention, *leh* transforms into longing. What began as street vernacular now carries the weight of artistic expression and has even occupied an elevated position in the realm of literature.

The Language That Says 'We'

Singlish is a reminder that language doesn't need a permit to exist. It grows where people live, in the irreverent everyday. In a nation often described as hyper-regulated, Singlish flourishes precisely because it is unregulated. It's the linguistic soundtrack of Singapore's everyday life.

Its particles are miniature rebellions, blending English to local rhythms, asserting that identity is not something dictated from above but forged everywhere beneath – at the bus stop, at the wet market, in the open-air communal spaces beneath public housing blocks where neighbours mingle in the humid breeze.

TO SPEAK SINGLISH IS TO BELONG; TO UNDERSTAND ITS PARTICLES INTUITIVELY IS TO BE INSIDE A CULTURAL CIRCLE OF TRUST.

Singlish signals membership. It collapses social distance. To speak Singlish is to belong; to understand its particles intuitively is to be inside a cultural circle of trust. It allows a banker and a *kopi* uncle to communicate as equals.

Little Words, Huge Weight

In the end, Singlish particles are more than linguistic oddities. They are Singapore's fingerprints – distinct and instantly recognisable. These particles map the complicated terrain of Singaporean identity, one shaped by migration, modernity, multiculturalism and the constant balancing act between global aspirations and local roots.

Call it patois, call it pride or problematic, but it's clear that Singlish endures. So the next time someone sighs '*Aiyah* why like that *lor*', listen closely. There are centuries of history in that, a whole worldview and philosophy – tiny words powerful enough to unite an entire country. No doubt, in the smallest syllables, Singapore finds its biggest voice.

Lau Pa Sat (p81), Downtown
TANG YAN SONG/SHUTTERSTOCK

TRAY-RETURN NATION

Beneath fluorescent lights and rising steam, Singapore's most democratic dining room collapses class divides, preserves heritage and captures the nation's soul. By Dawn Wong

IN A CITY that prides itself on efficiency, order and the occasional government intervention, the venerable hawker centre is a curiously democratic oasis. Singapore's unofficial temples of equality are fluorescent-lit, fan-cooled, slightly sticky shrines to the idea that everyone, regardless of wealth or pedigree, must still *chope* (reserve) a seat using a packet of tissues. Here, amid the rhythmic percussion of wok against flame and the haze of sizzling garlic, Singapore's stratified social structure experiences a momentary, almost magical collapse. Bankers, taxi drivers, students, retirees, celebrities, ministers – everyone converges here with an empty stomach and a dubious respect for the unspoken queueing code. The tycoon in Gucci loafers stands behind the taxi uncle in weathered slippers, both waiting for the same plate of *char kway teow* (broad noodles, clams and eggs fried in chilli and black-bean sauce). Singapore's great leveller is a rare arena in which privilege dissolves not by ideology, but simply because absolutely no one, not even the well-heeled, can skip the queue.

Singapore's Most Competitive Sport

The rules of the hawker centre are delightfully egalitarian. Prestige wins you zero reservations. Everyone brandishes the iconic packet of tissue paper, each a miniature symbol of territorial claim in the lunchtime battlefield – a humble, almost farcical emblem of Singaporean dining etiquette. There's no exclusive private area, no maitre d' with a discreet guest list. Instead, everyone commits to the same national sport. You scout the perimeter like a hawk for a table, scanning the horizon for diners displaying the telltale signs of imminent departure, performing the universally understood act of polite predation. Once seated, strangers share tables, because in hawker centres personal space is a negotiable concept. For a society characterised as meticulously stratified, this is where hierarchy dissolves into the steam rising from claypot rice.

Hawker Centres as Cultural Identity

To speak of hawker centres is to speak, inevitably, of national identity. Their inscription on the UNESCO Intangible Cultural Heritage list in 2020 was not so much an accolade as a formal acknowledgment that hawker food is Singapore's cultural lingua franca. Chicken rice, nasi lemak (coconut rice) and *roti prata* (Indian flatbread) coexist not merely in shared spaces, but in shared heritage. A single meal accomplishes what months of diplomatic summits often strive for. Multiculturalism has rarely been so casually enacted or delicious.

Tradition Meets Modernity

Yet, like all cultural institutions, hawker centres sit uneasily at the crossroads of tradition and modernity. The archetypal silhouette of the stoic elderly hawker is now met by an emerging generation of trendy Gen Z and Millennial hawkers armed with innovative branding strategies and TikTok accounts. These Promethean pioneers have inherited not only recipes, but the

existential burden of preserving a culture that was never designed to be curated.

Meanwhile, some older stalls are closing due to a lack of heirs willing to trade the comfort of air-conditioning for a roaring wok burner. With each closure comes the gradual erosion of collective memory. A disappearing bowl of prawn mee (noodles) is not just a missing option at lunch, but a chapter torn from Singapore's living archive.

The Bureaucratisation of Chaos

Unsurprisingly, the state has intervened through grants, incubators and regulatory frameworks that aggressively orbit the hawker universe. One could argue that what began as a humble culture has become swaddled in administrative silk. The question is a poignant one: can a culture born out of improvisation, chaos and community truly thrive under the weight of bureaucracy? Or must it remain something gloriously, stubbornly lived?

Hawker centres are not museums – they are theatres of daily life. Political debates simmer over *kopi* (coffee) and *kaya* (coconut and egg jam) toast. Migrant workers find respite in familiar flavours at the end of gruelling shifts. Students exchange salacious secrets over steaming bowls of *ban mian* (egg-noodle dish). Countless friendships, heartbreaks and business ideas have been powered by cheap *kopi* refills. The hawker centre is, at its core, a social glue like no other.

Chicken rice, Maxwell Food Centre (p72), Chinatown

Responsibility, Mandated

And then there's the matter of trays. In Singapore, diners are now required to return their trays after eating or risk warnings and fines. The infamous tray-return campaign has become a fascinating barometer of national temperament. What started as a gentle appeal to civic grace has gradually ossified into a behavioural expectation, then a formalised mandate, and finally a litmus test for one's moral fibre. Some hail it as the pinnacle of Singaporean responsibility, proof that we can, indeed, become the 'tray-return nation' the authorities dream of. Others interpret it as an ominous sign that even the unassuming hawker centre isn't exempt from Singapore's unwavering commitment to structured living. Regardless, the debate encapsulates a deep Singaporean tension: how do we balance personal convenience with the collective good when our hands, quite literally, are full?

Singapore's Sustainability Puzzle

Sustainability lingers at the edges of this conversation too. Styrofoam boxes and plastic bags rest awkwardly beside green national ambitions, like relics from a former era reluctant to retire. Achieving change in this area demands more than stringent top-down policies – it requires a recalibration of habit, which could prove to be the most difficult ingredient to adjust.

Equality in a Bowl

Despite these frictions, the hawker centre endures. It's where strangers share tables without fuss, where cultures coexist in the form of recipes, where wealth doesn't liberate you from a queue. And it's here, amid the clatter of chopsticks and the hiss of hot woks, that old Singapore meets the ambitions of the new. So if you wish to understand this country intimately, start with a plate of chicken rice, eaten with everyone else beneath a rattling fan. It's there, in the democratic glow of fluorescent lights, that you'll find the real Singapore – occasionally contradictory but irresistibly alive.

A LABORATORY FOR TOMORROW'S CITIES

Why Singapore's compact size, strong governance and openness to technology make it an ideal testing ground for smart-city technologies. By Pei Shyuan Yeo

SINGAPORE IS KNOWN for being futuristic. Visitors arriving at Changi Airport are treated to a biophilic architecture complex with the world's tallest indoor waterfall. The expressway to the city is tree-lined, with little to no traffic. Constantly innovating not merely to survive but to thrive, Singapore is the world's most sophisticated urban laboratory, uniquely positioned to prototype innovations that much larger cities around the globe are looking to adopt.

Necessity is the Mother of Invention

Two significant factors make Singapore an ideal testing ground for urban innovation. First, consider the city's constraints. Singapore's total land area is approximately 736 sq km, around the size of New York City. Unlike NYC, however, it's not just a city but also a country – and that means that every square metre counts. Therefore, urban planning is important to make the most out of the limited land space.

Second, the government sets out multiple plans that are constantly being revised. The city's physical development is guided by the Long-Term Plan, which contains broad guidelines for the next 40 to 50 years. These long-term visions (reviewed every 10 years) are then translated into detailed implementation plans (known as Master Plans), which are themselves reviewed every five years. This forward-thinking approach creates an environment where innovations can be tested and refined.

Car-Lite, Car-Free

Have you ever felt like you've spent countless hours in a bad traffic jam? In some cities you literally do, but maybe less so in Singapore. There are two main reasons, the first being the prohibitive cost of vehicle ownership. In Singapore, a heavy vehicle tax is imposed (starting at 100% and going all the way up to 320%). Second, the city-state utlises a congestion reduction scheme where vehicles pay to enter certain zones of the city.

Pioneering road-congestion pricing, Singapore's first iteration was the Area Licensing Scheme (ALS), where drivers entering the city had to pay for a paper licence. ALS was replaced by Electronic Road Pricing (ERP), an electronic toll system that charges vehicles based on time and congestion levels.

The success of congestion pricing spread globally, with London rolling out a similar congestion charge in 2003 and, more recently, New York City in 2024. ERP 2.0 will be even more advanced, utilising distance-based technology powered by the Global Navigation Satellite System (GNSS), thereby eliminating the need for physical gantries.

Going further towards making Singapore car-lite, the country is in trials to

PARKROYAL

deploy self-driving vehicles in the next few years to strengthen last-mile connectivity within the public transport network.

Greening the City

It may come as a surprise that Singapore is one of the greenest cities in the world, with almost half of the city covered in green spaces. This laudable achievement is the result of sustained efforts over the last few decades.

Even in the early years of industrialisation, the government was determined not to turn the island into a concrete jungle, differentiating itself from other developing countries. Besides improving the quality of life for the residents, greening the city served another purpose: showcasing a well-organised Singapore to the world for tourism and investment.

Edible community garden

HELLOITSME_SR/SHUTTERSTOCK

SINGAPORE IS ONE OF THE GREENEST CITIES IN THE WORLD, WITH ALMOST HALF OF THE CITY COVERED IN GREEN SPACES.

Greenery is not confined to nature trails and public parks – it also extends vertically. In the last 10 years or so, the government has introduced new policies that have incentivised green architecture. As a result, the city is filled with buildings designed with sustainable principles in mind. This is exemplified by architectural gems like PARKROYAL COLLECTION Pickering and Oasia Hotel Downtown where lush vegetation has become part of the building, transforming urban structures into vertical ecosystems. This concept has also cross-pollinated into public developments integrating vertical greenery, community farming spaces and rooftop gardens to create third spaces for the community.

Rethinking Food Security

In 2019, Singapore announced the bold goal of locally producing 30% of its nutritional needs by 2030.

However, persistent challenges such as rising energy costs, labour shortages and the mirage of tech farming have forced a recalibration. Recently, this policy was revised to a more realistic goal of 20% fibres and 30% protein by 2035. New models have been proposed to lower the start-up costs for local farms by providing infrastructure and shared utilities.

The refreshed strategy builds on four pillars – growing local, diversifying imports, stockpiling and global partnerships. The real opportunity lies not just in thinking about yield and output, but in producing food in a restorative way. Across the city, there's been an increase in the popularity of edible community gardens and allotment plots. These spaces, leased out by the government for gardeners to grow edibles, not only produce food but also foster social connection among the city's residents, young and old.

Going Underground

Is going up and out the only way for a city to grow? With limited land, an alternative option is to go underground. The Jurong Rock Caverns, Southeast Asia's first underground oil-storage facility, is an engineering masterpiece. As tall as the Great Pyramids of Giza, it's the country's deepest public-works project.

And it's not just storage that goes underground. In Singapore, the first underground service reservoir was built beneath a park, eliminating the need to use precious above-ground land.

It's this unique trilogy of compact size, strong governance and openness to harnessing technology that has made Singapore an ideal testing ground for smart-city solutions. These current innovations will become blueprints to take the city to the next 50 years and beyond.

PARKROYAL COLLECTION Pickering
PAER SVENSSON/SHUTTERSTOCK

INDEX

Map Pages **000**

Map Pages **000**

Map Pages **000**